■ United States Holocaust M_
Center for Advanced Holocaust Studies

Documenting Life and Destruction

Holocaust Sources in Context

SERIES EDITOR

Jürgen Matthäus

CONTRIBUTING EDITOR

Jan Lambertz

DOCUMENTING LIFE AND DESTRUCTION

HOLOCAUST SOURCES IN CONTEXT

This groundbreaking series provides a new perspective on history using first-hand accounts of the lives of those who suffered through the Holocaust, those who perpetrated it, and those who witnessed it as bystanders. The United States Holocaust Memorial Museum's Center for Advanced Holocaust Studies presents a wide range of documents from different archival holdings, expanding knowledge about the lives and fates of Holocaust victims and making these resources broadly available to the general public and scholarly communities for the first time.

BOOKS IN THE SERIES

1. *Jewish Responses to Persecution, Volume I, 1933–1938*, Jürgen Matthäus and Mark Roseman (2010)
2. *Children during the Holocaust*, Patricia Heberer (2011)
3. *Jewish Responses to Persecution, Volume II, 1938–1940*, Alexandra Garbarini with Emil Kerenji, Jan Lambertz, and Avinoam Patt (2011)
4. *The Diary of Samuel Golfard and the Holocaust in Galicia*, Wendy Lower (2011)
5. *Jewish Responses to Persecution, Volume III, 1941–1942*, Jürgen Matthäus with Emil Kerenji, Jan Lambertz, and Leah Wolfson (2013)
6. *The Holocaust in Hungary: Evolution of a Genocide*, Zoltan Vagi, Laszlo Csősz, and Gabor Kadar (2013)
7. *War, Pacification, and Mass Murder, 1939: The Einsatzgruppen in Poland*, Jürgen Matthäus, Jochen Böhler, and Klaus-Michael Mallman (2014)

This publication has been made possible by
support from

Claims Conference ועידת התביעות
The Conference on Jewish Material Claims Against Germany

The William S. and Ina Levine Foundation

and

The Blum Family Foundation

Documenting Life and Destruction
Holocaust Sources in Context

WAR, PACIFICATION, AND MASS MURDER, 1939
The Einsatzgruppen in Poland

Jürgen Matthäus, Jochen Böhler,
and Klaus-Michael Mallmann

Edited by the Center for Advanced Holocaust Studies,
the Deutsches Historisches Institut Warschau, and the
Forschungsstelle Ludwigsburg der Universität Stuttgart

Rowman & Littlefield
in association with the United States Holocaust Memorial Museum
2014

For USHMM:
Project Manager: Mel Hecker
Translators: Kathleen Luft, Yedida Kanfer, Stephen Scala, Stephen Pallavicini
Research Assistants: Holly Robertson, Chris Henson, Kathryn Cornelius

Published by Rowman & Littlefield
4501 Forbes Boulevard, Suite 200, Lanham, Maryland 20706
www.rowman.com

Estover Road, Plymouth PL6 7PY, United Kingdom

Front cover: (top row, left to right) USHMMPA WS# 15872, courtesy of the Institute of
National Remembrance; USHMMA RG 11.001M (RGVA 500-1-431), courtesy of the
Russian State Military Archives; USHMMPA WS# 50646, courtesy of the Institute of
National Remembrance; (bottom row, left to right) USHMMPA WS# 18542 courtesy
of Yad Vashem; Map 1: The Routes of the Einsatzgruppen in Poland, 1939, p. ix;
USHMMPA WS# 15752, courtesy of Gertrude Adams.

British Library Cataloguing in Publication Information Available
Library of Congress Cataloging-in-Publication Data
Matthäus, Jürgen, 1959-
  War, pacification, and mass murder, 1939 : the Einsatzgruppen in Poland / Jürgen Mat-
thäus, Jochen Böhler and Klaus-Michael Mallmann.
     pages cm. — (Holocaust sources in context)
  Includes bibliographical references and index.
  ISBN 978-1-4422-3141-2 (cloth : alk. paper) — ISBN 978-1-4422-3142-9 (electronic :
alk. paper) 1. Nationalsozialistische Deutsche Arbeiter-Partei. Einsatzgruppen des
Sicherheitsdienstes und der Sicherheitspolizei. 2. World War, 1939-1945—Atrocities—
Poland. 3. World War, 1939-1945—Atrocities—Poland—Sources. 4. Holocaust,
Jewish (1939-1945)—Poland. 5. Holocaust, Jewish (1939-1945)—Poland—Sources.
6. Mass murder—Poland—History—20th century. 7. Mass murder—Poland—History—
20th century—Sources. I. Böhler, Jochen, 1969- II. Mallmann, Klaus-Michael. III. Title.
  D804.3.M374 2014
  940.53⟩1809438—dc23   2013046871

  ISBN 978-0-8108-9555-3 (pbk : alk. paper)

♾™ The paper used in this publication meets the minimum requirements of American
National Standard for Information Sciences—Permanence of Paper for Printed Library
Materials, ANSI/NISO Z39.48-1992.
Printed in the United States of America

Contents

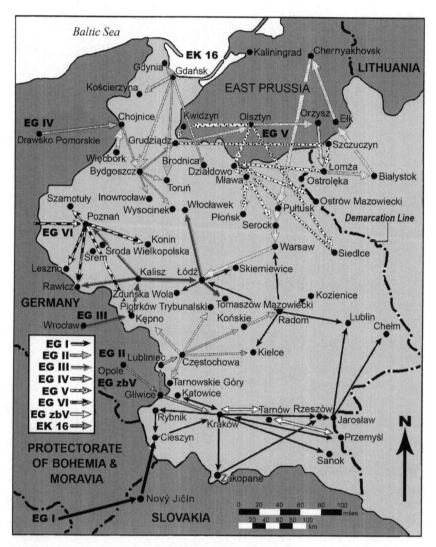

Map 1: The Routes of the Einsatzgruppen in Poland, 1939.

Map 2: Poland, 1940.

ABBREVIATIONS

APK	State Archive Katowice (Archiwum Państwowe Katowice)
APŁ	State Archive Łódź (Archiwum Państwowe Łódź)
APP	State Archive Poznań (Archiwum Państwowe Poznań)
APW	State Archive Warsaw (Archiwum Państwowe Warszawa)
BAB	German Federal Archive (Bundesarchiv), Berlin
BAL	German Federal Archive, Ludwigsburg Branch (Bundesarchiv Aussenstelle Ludwigsburg)
BA-MA	German Federal Archive–Military Archive (Bundesarchiv-Militärarchiv), Freiburg
BDC	Berlin Document Center
BdO	Commander of the Order Police (Befehlshaber der Ordnungspolizei)
BdS	Commander of the Sipo and SD (Befehlshaber der Sicherheitspolizei und des SD)
BGK	*Biuletyn Głównej Komisji Badania Zbrodni Hitlerowskich w Polsce*
BIPN	*Biuletyn Instytut Pamięci Narodowej*
BOK-Ł	*Biuletyn Okręgowej Komisji Badania Zbrodni Hitlerowskich w Łodzi*

BOK-P	*Biuletyn Okręgowej Komisji Badania Zbrodni Hitlerowskich w Polsce*
BŻIH	*Biuletyn Żydowskiego Instytutu Historycznego*
CAW	Central Military Archive (Centralne Archiwum Wojskowe)
CdO	Chief of the Order Police (Chef der Ordnungspolizei)
CdS	Chief of the Sipo and SD (Chef der Sicherheitspolizei und des SD)
CdZ	Chiefs of Civil Administration (Chefs der Zivilverwaltung)
EG	Einsatzgruppe of the Sipo and SD
EK	Subunit(s) of an Einsatzgruppe (Einsatzkommando)
Gestapo	Secret State Police (Geheime Staatspolizei)
GPU	Soviet State Political Main Administration (Glavnoe političeskoe upravlenie)
GSR	*German Studies Review*
HGS	*Holocaust and Genocide Studies*
HSSPF	Higher SS and Police Leader (Höherer SS- und Polizeiführer)
IdS	Inspector of the Sipo and SD (Inspekteur der Sicherheitspolizei und des SD)
IfZ	Institute for Contemporary History (Institut für Zeitgeschichte), Munich
IMT	Trial of the Major War Criminals before the International Military Tribunal, Nuremberg
IPN	Institute of National Remembrance (Instytut Pamięci Narodowej)
IPNW	Institute of National Memory (Instytut Pamięci Narodowej), Warsaw
IZ	West Institute (Instytut Zachodni), Poznań
KdO	Commanding Officer of the Order Police (Kommandeur der Ordnungspolizei)
KdS	Commanding Officer of the Sipo and SD (Kommandeur der Sicherheitspolizei und des SD)
Kripo	Criminal Police (Kriminalpolizei)

NARA	National Archives and Records Administration, College Park, Maryland
NSDAP	Nazi Party (Nationalsozialistische Deutsche Arbeiterpartei)
OB	Army Commander (Oberbefehlshaber)
ObdH	Army High Commander (Oberbefehlshaber des Heeres)
OKH	Army High Command (Oberkommando des Heeres)
OKW	Wehrmacht High Command (Oberkommando der Wehrmacht)
Orpo	Order Police (Ordnungspolizei)
RGVA	Russian State Military Archive (Rossiiskii Gosudarstvennyi Voennyi Arkhiv), Moscow
RSHA	Reich Security Main Office (Reichssicherheitshauptamt)
SA	Nazi storm troopers (Sturmabteilung)
SD	"Intelligence service" of the Nazi Party (Sicherheitsdienst)
SDHA	SD Main Office (SD-Hauptamt)
Sipo	Security Police, comprising Gestapo and Kripo (Sicherheitspolizei)
SS	Nazi security squad (Schutzstaffel)
TK	Subunit(s) of an Einsatzkommando (*Teilkommando*)
USHMM	United States Holocaust Memorial Museum, Washington, DC
USHMMA	United States Holocaust Memorial Museum Archives
USHMMPA	United States Holocaust Memorial Museum Photo Archives
VfZ	*Vierteljahrshefte für Zeitgeschichte*
YVA	Yad Vashem Archive, Jerusalem
YVS	*Yad Vashem Studies*
z.b.V.	"For special use" ("*zur besonderen Verwendung*")
ŻIH	Jewish Historical Institute (Żydowski Instytut Historyczny), Warsaw

Editors' Note

THIS VOLUME is the result of a cooperative project between the United States Holocaust Memorial Museum's Center for Advanced Holocaust Studies (CAHS), the Research Institute of the University of Stuttgart (Forschungsstelle Ludwigsburg der Universität Stuttgart) in Germany, and the German Historical Institute in Warsaw, Poland. The authors would like to express sincere gratitude to our colleagues at these institutions for their help in preparing this volume, particularly Heidrun Baur and Stephan Lehnstaedt. This book offers a revised English-language version of previously published German and Polish editions[1] and includes additional source material. Significantly restructured to provide more contextual information on both the topic and the featured documents, it is tailored for classroom use. We have reduced the number of footnotes in this edition; readers interested in further biographical information on persons mentioned here and in additional source leads and foreign-language publications should consult the German and Polish editions. Part I, our introduction, not only complements the documents featured in

---

1. Klaus-Michael Mallmann, Jochen Böhler, and Jürgen Matthäus, *Einsatzgruppen in Polen: Darstellung und Dokumentation* (Darmstadt: WBG, 2008); Klaus-Michael Mallmann, Jochen Böhler, and Jürgen Matthäus, *Einsatzgruppen w Polsce* (Warsaw: Bellona, 2009). Testimonies by Polish witnesses that formed part of West German postwar judicial investigations and are now housed at the Bundesarchiv Ludwigsburg (BAL) have been translated from German as many of the Polish originals could not be located.

part II but also lays out the importance of this early, yet crucial, chapter in the history of World War II and the Holocaust.

Stephan Lehnstaedt and Jochen Böhler have recently, under the auspices of the German Historical Institute in Warsaw, published a German-language print edition of all reports issued by the Einsatzgruppen and their subunits in Poland, *Die Berichte der Einsatzgruppen aus Polen 1939*. In contrast to their publication, which is comprised of the full text of the Einsatzgruppen reports only, this book focuses on one specific aspect of these units' activities: the persecution of Polish civilians, both Jews and non-Jews. In addition to relevant Einsatzgruppen reports or selections from them, we have included documents from other sources, especially eyewitness accounts by victims or onlookers where available. Such accounts provide an alternative, often much more realistic perspective on the nature and consequences of the actions referenced in documentation generated by perpetrators.

Maps and other explanatory tools included in this volume offer further background information on the Einsatzgruppen and the context in which they operated. We have used Polish place names, according to post-1945 borders, throughout this volume, except where German place names formed part of a unit's name or appeared in the original documents themselves. Readers will find concordances between geographical designations as well as between German military, police, and SS ranks on p. 171. Abbreviated references to Einsatzgruppen subunits (Einsatzkommandos, EK) include a unit number, followed by an Einsatzgruppen designation; for instance, EK3/V refers to Einsatzkommando 3 of Einsatzgruppe V.

Note that the photograhic documents included in this book are also available at rowman.com/isbn/9781442231412 for better viewing.

This volume would not have been possible without the help of a greater number of people in the three participating institutions than we can acknowledge here. We are immensely grateful to the Conference on Jewish Material Claims against Germany, the William S. and Ina Levine Foundation, the Blum Family Foundation, and Dr. Alfred Munzer and Mr. Joel Wind for their generous support. Peter Klein alerted us to two crucial documents from the Russian State Military Archive, Gabriel Bielek provided the first transcriptions from the Einsatzgruppen reports, and Daniel Brewing recreated a draft of the Einsatzgruppen itinerary. For crucial help with scholarly advice at different stages in the project, we are indebted to Jürgen Hensel, Emil Kerenji, Alina Skibinska, and Roza Zielnik.

Many USHMM colleagues have participated in the project in one way or another. We thank the staff of the Museum's Library, Archives, Photo Archives, Art and Artifacts Section, and Center for Advanced Holocaust Studies. Our translators Yedida Kanfer (Yiddish), Stephen Scala (Polish), Kathleen Luft, and Stephen Pallavicini (German) played a key role in the project, as did our research assistants at CAHS, Holly Robertson, Kathryn Cornelius, and Chris Henson. The contributing editor, Jan Lambertz, played a decisive role in facilitating the publication of another volume in the *Documenting Life and Destruction* source series; we could not have reached this goal without her. At AltaMira Press we would like to thank Susan McEachern and Elaine McGarraugh for their dedication to the project. Special thanks go to the members of the United States Holocaust Memorial Museum's Academic Committee for their ongoing support and to Jacob Chadwick for the creation of the maps.

Jürgen Matthäus, Jochen Böhler, and Klaus-Michael Mallmann
January 2014

PART I

INTRODUCTION

THE EINSATZGRUPPEN AND THE SOURCES
DOCUMENTING THEIR ACTIONS

AMONG THE German units notorious for their murderous role in the Holocaust, the Einsatzgruppen stand out. Beginning with the German attack on the Soviet Union on June 22, 1941, these relatively small squads of German SS and policemen contributed massively to Nazi anti-Jewish policy as it passed the threshold from persecution to annihilation. By the end of 1941, the Einsatzgruppen, together with Wehrmacht units and local auxiliaries, had killed more than half a million Jewish men, women, and children in the occupied Soviet Union. The murderous activities of the Einsatzgruppen in Soviet territory attracted the attention of postwar state prosecutors and historians early on and can be regarded as fairly well researched.[1] However, we cannot say the same about Einsatzgruppen involvement in the brief yet intense campaign

---

1. The first deployment of Einsatzgruppen dates back to the German annexation of Austria in March 1938 and the western part of Czechoslovakia in early 1939; see Helmut Krausnick, *Die Truppe des Weltanschauungskrieges. Die Einsatzgruppen der Sicherheitspolizei und des SD 1938–1942* (Stuttgart: Deutsche Verlags-Anstalt, 1981), 19–31. On the function of Einsatzgruppen in the war against the Soviet Union, see Christopher R. Browning, with contributions by Jürgen Matthäus, *The Origins of the Final Solution: The Evolution of Nazi Jewish Policy, September 1939–March 1942* (Lincoln and Jerusalem: University of Nebraska Press and Yad Vashem, 2004), 224–34.

against Poland, code-named "Operation Tannenberg," that started on September 1, 1939.

Within a period of roughly five weeks, from September 1 to early October 1939, Germany won the military campaign in Poland by massively and indiscriminately applying overwhelming force. To quash any real or imagined Polish resistance, the invading Wehrmacht armies received assistance from Heinrich Himmler's police and SS units deployed behind the front line.[2] Based on a German-Soviet nonaggression pact concluded on August 23, 1939, the Red Army joined in the third week of the campaign by taking control of Poland's eastern territories. By the end of the year, the country had vanished from the political map of Europe, its German-dominated regions either annexed to the Reich or included in a semicolonial fiefdom in the form of the Generalgouvernement.[3] "Despite its brevity," historian Alexander Rossino writes in his pathbreaking study of Wehrmacht atrocities during this war, "the historical importance of the Polish campaign cannot be overestimated."[4] Indeed, it set the stage for the systematic targeting of civilians that would define the Third Reich's subsequent warfare in southeastern and eastern Europe.

During the Polish campaign, the Einsatzgruppen and their subunits, the Einsatzkommandos (EK), consisted of a force of roughly two thousand members of the German security police (Sicherheitspolizei, Sipo)—a combination of the Criminal Police (Kriminalpolizei, Kripo) and the secret state police (the notorious Geheime Staatspolizei, Gestapo) under the command of Reinhard Heydrich—and the Nazi Party's (NSDAP) intelligence service (Sicherheitsdienst, or SD, also headed by Heydrich). These Sipo/SD units, subordinated since late September 1939 to the newly created Reich Security Main Office (Reichssicherheitshauptamt, RSHA) with Heydrich at the helm, were established in the

---

2. Hitler appointed Heinrich Himmler (1900–1945), active in Nazi circles from the early 1920s, leader of the SS in 1929. After 1933 Himmler advanced rapidly from his power base in Bavaria to become head of the Gestapo in Prussia and chief of the entire German police by mid-1936. During the war Himmler expanded his SS and police powers further and played a key role in implementing the genocide of Europe's Jews. See Peter Longerich, *Heinrich Himmler* (Oxford: Oxford University Press, 2012); Richard Breitman, *The Architect of Genocide: Himmler and the Final Solution* (New York: Alfred A. Knopf, 1991).

3. See Map 2, p. ix, showing Poland 1940.

4. Alexander B. Rossino, *Hitler Strikes Poland: Blitzkrieg, Ideology, and Atrocity* (Lawrence: University Press of Kansas, 2003), xiii.

planning phase of the war to cooperate closely with the German military in the goal of "pacifying" the occupied Polish territories.[5]

Almost immediately they became a deadly tool in the repertoire of Nazi subjugation policies, targeting thousands of real or imagined "enemies of the Reich" ("*Reichsfeinde*") and enforcing the "Germanization" of vast parts of Poland. According to estimates, ten thousand civilians were executed during the fighting. Up to the end of October, the German military, SS, and police units shot an additional sixteen thousand Polish noncombatants, among them an unknown number of Jews.[6] For the Polish regions annexed by Germany, the number of Polish civilians killed up through the end of 1939 is estimated at more than sixty thousand people.[7] In the Generalgouvernement, Nazi administrators were determined to relegate the Polish and Jewish population to the status of serfs or "undesirables" with no future in a German-dominated "living space" ("*Lebensraum*").

This volume includes documentation from a variety of sources showing that, in contrast to long-held beliefs, the Third Reich established a murderous occupation regime in Poland right from the start of the war and illustrating the role the Einsatzgruppen played in this development. The sources available allow only a partial reconstruction of how that mass murder unfolded. During the campaign, the Einsatzgruppen and their subunits compiled regular written reports but did not comprehensively record executions and the other violent measures they took against the civilian population in Poland.[8] Relatively few extant survivor accounts attest to the Einsatzgruppen's actions and their consequences for the victims. And the proliferation of uniformed Germans in the

---

5. Involved with radical right-wing circles since the early 1920s, Reinhard Heydrich (1904–1942) received a commission from SS chief Heinrich Himmler in mid-1932 to create the SD, which he headed until his death. In the autumn of 1939, Heydrich merged the SD with the Security Police to form the RSHA, the most important agency overseeing Nazi anti-Jewish policies in Germany and the occupied territories. He later served as the acting Reich protector of Bohemia and Moravia and orchestrated the 1942 Wannsee Conference to discuss and coordinate implementation of the "Final Solution." He died after an attack by partisans in Prague. See Mark Roseman, *The Wannsee Conference and the Final Solution: A Reconsideration* (New York: Metropolitan Books, 2002); Robert Gerwarth, *Hitler's Hangman: The Life of Heydrich* (New Haven, CT: Yale University Press, 2011).

6. Jochen Böhler, *Auftakt zum Vernichtungskrieg. Die Wehrmacht in Polen 1939* (Frankfurt am Main: Fischer Taschenbuch Verlag, 2006), 241–42.

7. See Richard J. Evans, *The Third Reich at War, 1939–1945* (London: Allen Lane, 2008), 9–15.

8. See Stephan Lehnstaedt and Jochen Böhler, eds., *Die Berichte der Einsatzgruppen aus Polen 1939* (Berlin: Metropol, 2013).

ranks of the Wehrmacht, Order Police (Ordnungspolizei), Sipo/SD, and SS, in combination with the violence inflicted by ethnic German (*Volksdeutsche*) collaborators, made it difficult for survivors to identify those responsible for their misery and the murder of their families and friends. Postwar investigations by Polish and German authorities helped untangle the web of early violence; yet later, and in many instances even more violent, war experiences often overshadow eyewitness recollections of the Polish campaign.[9]

The overwhelming majority of the accessible sources on the Einsatzgruppen in 1939 have been neither comprehensively assembled nor fully researched. The deployment of Sipo and SD units provided the first operational test for Heydrich's RSHA.[10] In fact, the mobile Einsatzgruppen resembled in miniature the stationary RSHA at the Reich's center: an organization structured to integrate different security police agencies for the purpose of ensuring peace and order, Nazi style, in the newly conquered territories. Einsatzgruppen files, located in the German Federal Archives in Berlin (Bundesarchiv Berlin, BAB), allow the reconstruction of their origins in 1939 but tell us little about many aspects of these units' deployment. Although they regularly telegraphed reports to a specially created section in Heydrich's Berlin head office—the Sonderreferat Tannenberg—the reality of the "Blitzkrieg" lagged behind its planning. Beyond this, Einsatzgruppen reports contain numerous errors, particularly regarding unit locations, as well as serious omissions.

Historians may search in vain in the RSHA files for any mention of, for example, the mass shootings undertaken by the Einsatzgruppe labeled "for special use" ("*zur besonderen Verwendung*," z.b.V.) in Przemyśl and its environs as part of its assignment to assist the Wehrmacht with "the suppression and disarmament of Polish bands, executions, arrests" in the region of East Upper Silesia.[11] A laconic reference by the Berlin head office simply states, "Einsatzgruppe

9. See Rossino, *Hitler Strikes Poland*; Martin Cüppers, *Wegbereiter der Shoah. Die Waffen-SS, der Kommandostab Reichsführer-SS und die Judenvernichtung 1939–1945* (Darmstadt: WBG, 2005), 33–60; Klaus-Michael Mallmann, "'. . .Missgeburten, die nicht auf diese Welt gehören.' Die Ordnungspolizei im besetzten Polen 1939–1941," in *Genesis des Genozids. Polen 1939–1941*, ed. Klaus-Michael Mallmann and Bogdan Musial (Darmstadt: WBG, 2004), 71–89.

10. See Michael Wildt, *An Uncompromising Generation: The Nazi Leadership of the Reich Security Main Office* (Madison: University of Wisconsin Press, 2009), an abridged translation of Michael Wildt, *Generation des Unbedingten: Das Führungskorps des Reichssicherheitshauptamtes* (Hamburg: Hamburger Edition, 2003).

11. Special Order No. 14 by Commander 14th Army/Quartermaster General, September 12, 1939, BA-MA, RH 20-14/129. See also document 46.

z.b.V.: No reports."[12] Instead, the "Tannenberg reports" consciously attempted to hide the actual nature of the Einsatzgruppen's tasks and actions. Facts and figures that many a commando leader in the field had clearly reported were edited out in Berlin before summary reports were distributed. For example, Einsatzkommando 16 in Bromberg (Polish: Bydgoszcz) informed the regional Sipo/SD leader on September 30, 1939, that there had been "a considerable number of more or less illegal shootings or executions of hostages" in the city, but this detail is missing from the RSHA's summary report for the same day; instead, it only refers to the unit's "search measures."[13]

Other sources help shed light on what happened during the Polish campaign. Document collections in the state archives in Łódź, Poznań, and Katowice, in the Poznań West Institute (Instytut Zachodni, IZ), and in the archive of the Warsaw Department of the Institute of National Remembrance (Instytut Pamięci Narodowej, IPN) contain valuable textual and photographic information on individual units and what they actually did in Poland in 1939. Eyewitness reports on Einsatzgruppen massacres offer some corrective to documentation created by the agents of mass murder but are scattered throughout the collections of the IPN, IZ, and Jewish Historical Institute (Żydowski Instytut Historyczny, ŻIH) in Warsaw. In addition, a trove of material can be found in the Ludwigsburg branch office of the German Federal Archives (Bundesarchiv Aussenstelle Ludwigsburg, BAL).[14] Although the voices of victims are largely missing from the judicial record, there are abundant accounts in West German prosecutorial files by former Einsatzgruppen members, who for the purpose of escaping justice had an interest in falsifying the historical record. These still provide us—mostly unwittingly, hesitantly, or indirectly—with valuable background information on the deployment of the Einsatzgruppen in the field. The Berlin Document Center collection held at the Bundesarchiv and, in the form of microfilm copies, at the U.S. National Archives and Records Administration (NARA) in College Park, Maryland, contains Sipo/SD personnel records. In addition, wartime documentation on the Einsatzgruppen

---

12. CdS daily reports "Operation Tannenberg" for September 15–19, 1939, USHMMA RG 15.007M (BAB, R 58/7001), reel 2, file 1:84–122.

13. EK 16 to IdS Northeast, September 30, 1939, IPNW, NTN 196/179; CdS daily report, September 30, 1939, USHMMA RG 15.007M (BAB, R 58/7002), reel 2, file 2:56–62.

14. Due to German archival data protection regulations, our footnote references have anonymized the names of some persons interrogated in the course of West German judicial investigations. The USHMMA is in the process of acquiring copies of the BAL case files; accretions to this collection are made available to researchers on an ongoing basis.

survives in the archives of the former Soviet Union as well as the United States Holocaust Memorial Museum (USHMM) in Washington, DC.

These document collections, either opened to researchers after World War II ended or made available since then, form the foundation for part II of this volume. In our introductions and annotations to the documents, we will address some of the problems raised by or inherent in individual sources.[15] Drawing on accounts from as many perspectives as possible, this volume represents the first comprehensive English-language edition documenting and annotating Einsatzgruppen activities against the background of war and Nazi racial policy in Poland in 1939. We hope that it will serve as a basis for further study of this chapter in the history of World War II as well as for research into other forms of Nazi mass violence equally fatal to those who were victimized.

PREPARING FOR THE WAR ON POLAND

From 1938 Hitler and the Wehrmacht leadership had actively pursued different scenarios for a massive German expansion through military aggression. At the start of the war on September 1, 1939, the roughly 2 million German soldiers and the members of the twenty-one Order Police battalions involved in the invasion of Poland constituted a force much more likely to leave scars on the communities in the occupied regions than the Einsatzgruppen, with their initial two thousand men. The Wehrmacht's military aggression in Poland, in conjunction with the Nazi leadership's radical policies, established a context of violence within which the Einsatzgruppen developed their brutal measures.[16]

As early as March 25, 1939, Hitler lectured the commander in chief of the army (*Oberbefehlshaber des Heeres*, ObdH), Generaloberst Walther von Brauchitsch, on how he intended to resolve the "Polish question" that had existed in the minds of German nationalists since the end of World War I: "Poland would have to be so thoroughly beaten down that, during the next few decades, she need not be taken into account as a political factor."[17] On August 14, Hitler informed Brauchitsch and his chief of staff (*Generalstabschef*), Generaloberst Franz Halder, that he was striving for more than a military defeat

---

15. For information on the source collections used, see also the editor's note above.

16. See Gerhard Weinberg, *A World at Arms: A Global History of World War II* (New York: Cambridge University Press, 1994), 28–34; Nicholas Bethell, *The War Hitler Won: September 1939* (London: Penguin, 1972).

17. "Directive from the Führer to the Commander in Chief of the Army on March 25, 1939," in *Documents on German Foreign Policy, 1918–1945*, ed. HMSO (London: HMSO, 1956), 6:117. Cf. Geoffrey P. Megargee, *Inside Hitler's High Command* (Lawrence: University Press of Kansas, 2000), 67–86.

of Poland and intended to "annihilate Poland" ("*Vernichtung Polens*").[18] Hitler elaborated on August 22, speaking to the leaders of the army groups and the commanders of each of the three branches of the Wehrmacht at his Alpine retreat on the Obersalzberg. "Destruction of Poland in the foreground. Aim is to remove living forces and not reaching a certain line," he explained, according to abbreviated notes, demanding, "Hearts closed to empathy. Brutal action. 80 million [Germans] must have their rights. Their existence must be secured. The stronger is right. Extreme severity."[19]

With this injunction, the Wehrmacht leadership knew that their supreme commander wanted the coming military conflict to differ from a conventional campaign. Poland was to be obliterated, not only as a state but as a nation; reaching well beyond geopolitical goals, the attack was to bring about a racial and demographic redrawing of the map. The generals understood this, for Hitler's ideas were not alien to the military. Within and far outside German conservative circles, the Polish state had been regarded as an illegitimate aberration created by the Versailles peace treaty, which had forced Germany to cede large chunks of territory.[20] German demands for territorial revisions of the treaty targeted primarily the borders in the east. Military officers found the very notion of the "Polish corridor" geographically disconnecting East Prussia from the Reich as offensive as the concept of Gdańsk (German: Danzig) as a "free city" under a mandate of the League of Nations. Halder had already in the spring of 1939 explicitly referred to "annihilation" in reference to the imminent attack on Poland, adding that "the occupation of the country will to a large extent be undertaken by paramilitary units of the Party," an allusion to the role of the SD and other Nazi agencies.[21]

---

18. Franz Halder, *Kriegstagebuch. Tägliche Aufzeichnungen des Chefs des Generalstabes des Heeres 1939–1942*, ed. Hans-Adolf Jacobsen (Stuttgart: W. Kohlhammer Verlag, 1962), 1:25; see also Jörg Hillmann, ed., *Der "Fall Weiss." Der Weg in das Jahr 1939* (Bochum: Winkler, 2001).

19. Translated from *Akten zur deutschen Auswärtigen Politik*, series D, 7:171–72 (IMT 1014-PS). For different text versions of the Hitler speech, see also Halder, *Kriegstagebuch*, 1:25–26, and Winfried Baumgart, "Zur Ansprache Hitlers vor den Führern der Wehrmacht am 22. August 1939. Eine quellenkritische Untersuchung," *VfZ* 16 (1968): 120–49.

20. For the German perception of Poland at the time, see Tomasz Szarota, "Poland and Poles in German Eyes during World War II," *Polish Western Affairs* 19 (1978): 229–54; Carsten Roschke, *Der umworbene "Urfeind." Polen in der nationalsozialistischen Propaganda 1934–1939* (Marburg: Tectum, 2000); Martin Broszat, *Zweihundert Jahre deutsche Polenpolitik* (Frankfurt am Main: Suhrkamp, 1972), 129–253.

21. Christian Hartmann and Sergej Slutsch, "Franz Halder und die Kriegsvorbereitungen im Frühjahr 1939: Eine Ansprache des Generalstabschefs des Heeres," *VfZ* 45 (1997): 483, 493.

Recent research has shown that the atrocities committed by German soldiers in the first few months of the war resulted from a combination of indoctrination that bred contempt for the Polish population, violence correlated with combat action, and a widespread phobia of partisans.[22] Brauchitsch provided a code of conduct in an instruction leaflet issued to the troops after the beginning of the attack: "The German soldier in the occupied territories is a representative of the German Reich and its power. He should think and act as such. [. . .] Each insult and each attack on the German Wehrmacht and the German people should be dealt with through the harshest means." When he stated, "It is not necessary to mention how the soldiers are to behave toward the Jews,"[23] it was clear what he expected from his men.

Similarly, the Sipo and SD murders in Poland resulted to a large degree from factors on the ground as well as from an institutional culture already established by Himmler before the war began. Security police and SD chief Heydrich had been making preparations for the war in Poland since May 1939. On July 5 he discussed "essential questions" on the forthcoming invasion with his top officers, among them SS-Brigadeführer Dr. Werner Best and SS-Oberführer Heinrich Müller, the latter heading the Gestapo. The "questions" included the creation of what were to become four Einsatzgruppen comprising two thousand men subdivided equally into Einsatzkommandos for deployment in conjunction with the Wehrmacht army groups. "Sonderreferat Tannenberg," under Best in the SD Main Office (SD-Hauptamt, SDHA), was to serve as the central hub for all information and to receive the reports sent from the field twice daily.[24] On August 18, 1939, Best noted in his diary, "Instruction from the Führer of a large-scale action for the Security Police."[25] That same day, Himmler and Heydrich outlined assignments in general terms at a conference in Berlin, with all future leaders of the Einsatzgruppen and Einsatzkommandos in attendance.[26]

Three days before the attack, Heydrich and Best discussed the planned Sipo/SD deployment in the area of military operations with Wehrmacht

---

22. Böhler, *Auftakt*, 54–75.

23. ObdH, guidelines for German soldiers in occupied Poland, September 19, 1939, BA-MA, RH 20-8/32; see also Böhler, *Auftakt*, 33–35; Alexander B. Rossino, "Destructive Impulses: German Soldiers and the Conquest of Poland," *HGS* 7 (1997): 351–65.

24. Note SDHA II 12, July 8, 1939, BAB, R 58/7154; SDHA I 11 to SDHA III 2, July 22, 1939, USHMMA RG 11.001M (RGVA 500-1-20), reel 1.

25. Indictment Prosecutors Office Berlin (Staatsanwalt beim Kammergericht Berlin), February 10, 1972, BAL, B 162/5689.

26. See document 2.

Oberst Eduard Wagner, the quartermaster general. Wagner noted in his diary how he found both men "inscrutable types, Heydrich especially disagreeable." Nevertheless, the parties "quickly came to an agreement."[27] They signed off on "Guidelines for the Foreign Deployment of the Security Police and SD," which charged the Einsatzkommandos with "the fight against all elements hostile to the Reich and Germans to the rear of the fighting troops."[28] As it turned out, this sweeping yet imprecise assignment empowered local commanders to define the concrete meaning of "hostile elements" and their treatment. Speaking to the relationship between Einsatzgruppen field units and the Wehrmacht, the guidelines called for a "permanent connection" and "smooth communication" without providing clear-cut directives. For the Wehrmacht, it was self-evident that "all police forces" would accept the military's prerogative. Yet, with the exception of directing that Einsatzgruppen leaders would answer to the commanding generals, the guidelines spelled out no direct subordination of Sipo/SD personnel to the Wehrmacht.[29]

At the end of August, five Einsatzgruppen gathered in cities south, west, and north of the border in order to march into Poland in a semicircle formation. The largest of them was based in Vienna, with four commandos consisting of ninety men each, heading for western Galicia through eastern Slovakia; beginning on September 4, it was designated as Einsatzgruppe I under the command of SS-Brigadeführer Bruno Streckenbach.[30] The members of what was later known as Einsatzgruppe II under SS-Obersturmbannführer Dr. Emanuel Schäfer[31] assembled in Opole with two commandos. The future

27. Elisabeth Wagner, ed., *Der Generalquartiermeister: Briefe und Tagebuchaufzeichnungen des Generalquartiermeisters des Heeres General der Artillerie Eduard Wagner* (Munich: G. Olzog, 1963), 103.

28. See document 1.

29. Special regulations OKH regarding provisions, August 9, 1939, BA-MA, RH 19 I/91; see Hans Umbreit, "Die Verantwortlichkeit der Wehrmacht als Okkupationsarmee," in *Die Wehrmacht: Mythos und Realität*, ed. Rolf-Dieter Müller and Hans-Erich Volkmann (Munich: Oldenbourg, 1999), 743–53.

30. Bruno Streckenbach (1902–1977) had been a member of a Freikorps since 1919 and of the Nazi Party since 1930 before his appointment as Gestapo chief in Hamburg. Following his assignment as head of Einsatzgruppe I, he became BdS Kraków and, in mid-1940, head of RSHA Office I. Arrested in 1945, he was in Soviet custody until 1955; an investigation opened against him in Hamburg was closed in 1974.

31. Emanuel Schäfer (1900–1974) had been, prior to the war, Gestapo chief in Wrocław and Opole. The head of Einsatzgruppe II became Gestapo chief in Katowice, since October 1940 in Cologne. In January 1942 he took over as BdS in Serbia; after the war he was imprisoned in Yugoslavia from 1953 to 1956.

Einsatzgruppe III, commanded by SS-Obersturmbannführer Dr. Hans Fischer[32] and assembled in Wrocław (German: Breslau), comprised three hundred men. Drawsko Pomorskie (German: Dramburg) in Pomerania served as the gathering point for the staff and two commandos of Einsatzgruppe IV, with 200 to 250 men under SS-Brigadeführer Lothar Beutel.[33] Einsatzgruppe V, with SS-Standartenführer Ernst Damzog[34] as its commander, was stationed in the East Prussian city of Olsztyn (German: Allenstein) and also had two commandos with 250 men when it was put together. These five groups and their twelve commandos crossed the border shortly after September 1, forming the first wave of Sipo/SD personnel deployed in Poland.[35]

Obsessive German security concerns made anyone who carried a weapon or could pose a threat behind the front line appear to be a partisan.[36] Because the Wehrmacht's quick advance left pockets of isolated Polish troops in the rear areas, the fragmented battlegrounds blurred the distinction between regular and irregular warfare, thus feeding the Germans' paranoia about partisans. Colonel Wagner noted on September 3, "Everywhere in Upper Silesia there is heavy fighting with guerrilla bands, which can only be broken with draconian measures,"[37] and Generaloberst Halder observed that same day, "14th Army needs police for the rear army area."[38] Himmler drew two conclusions from the military's call for help. First, on September 3, he ordered the formation of the additional Einsatzgruppe z.b.V. in order to "radically destroy with all available

---

32. Hans Fischer (1906–?) had been a Nazi Party member since 1932 and Gestapo chief in several German cities before his appointment as head of Einsatzgruppe III. After a tour of duty as Sipo/SD chief in Vienna, Stuttgart, and Strasbourg, he became IdS in Berlin. Fischer disappeared at the end of the war; he was never prosecuted.

33. Lothar Beutel (1902–1986), trained pharmacist and Nazi Party member since 1930, served in several Sipo/SD posts before the war. In October 1939, he was removed from his post as head of Einsatzgruppe IV due to corruption. Drafted into the Waffen-SS in 1944, he was imprisoned in the Soviet Union until 1955.

34. Prior to his appointment as head of Einsatzgruppe V, Ernst Damzog (1882–1945), a career policeman, had served in a number of Sipo/SD offices in the Reich. In November 1939, he became IdS in Poznań and led the regional Resettlement Office (Umwandererzentralstelle).

35. See interrogation of Bruno Streckenbach, November 2, 1961, BAL, B 162/3622, Bl. 126ff.; interrogation of Hellmut R., November 10, 1970, BAL, B 162/16662; interrogation of Erich M., November 30, 1964, BAL, B 162/Vorl. AR-Z 13/63, vol. 1, pp. 113ff.; interrogation of Walter T., September 5, 1962, BAL, B 162/Vorl. AR-Z 12/62, vol. 3, pp. 598ff.

36. Böhler, *Auftakt*, 57ff.

37. Wagner, *Der Generalquartiermeister*, 123.

38. Halder, *Kriegstagebuch*, 1:57; see also Christian Hartmann, *Halder. Generalstabschef Hitlers 1938–1942* (Paderborn: F. Schöningh, 1991).

means the Polish uprisings flaring up in the newly occupied territories in Upper Silesia." Einsatzgruppe z.b.V. consisted of four battalions of the Order Police and a Security Police special commando, with 350 men under the command of SS-Obergruppenführer Udo von Woyrsch.[39] It assembled on September 6 in Gliwice (German: Gleiwitz), initially attached to the 8th Army Corps and later the 14th Army.[40] Second, Himmler decided to dispatch more Order Police battalions. Halder rejoiced at the "police steamrollers behind the armies."[41] At the end of September, in addition to his Sipo/SD units, Himmler had twenty-one Order Police battalions and two mounted units in action in Poland.[42]

Other reinforcements were meant to intensify the German police presence in the occupied territories. On September 9, a new Einsatzgruppe VI led by SS-Oberführer Erich Naumann with two commandos was assembled in Frankfurt an der Oder "to occupy the province of Posen."[43] Three days later Einsatzkom-

---

39. World War I veteran and Freikorpsmember Udo von Woyrsch (1895–1982) joined the Nazi Party in 1929 and from 1930 helped build the SS organization in Silesia. A friend of Himmler, in 1940 he became HSSPF until early 1944, when he was removed from office for incompetence. In 1948, West German courts sentenced Woyrsch to twenty years for his role in the SS murders in 1934 (the so-called Röhm Putsch); though released in 1952, he was sentenced to an additional ten years in 1957.

40. RFSS to von Woyrsch, September 3, 1939, BA-MA, RH 24-8/97; Alexander B. Rossino, "Nazi Anti-Jewish Policy during the Polish Campaign: The Case of the Einsatzgruppe von Woyrsch," *GSR* 24, no. 1 (February 2001): 35–53.

41. Halder, *Kriegstagebuch*, 1:62. On the German military's responsibility for the escalation of violence behind the front line, see Czesław Madajczyk, "Die Verantwortung der Wehrmacht für die Verbrechen während des Krieges mit Polen," in *Kriegsverbrechen im 20. Jahrhundert*, ed. Wolfram Wette and Gerd R. Ueberschär (Darmstadt: Primus, 2001), 113–22; Jochen Böhler, "Intention oder Situation? Soldaten der Wehrmacht und die Anfänge des Vernichtungskrieges in Polen," in *Krieg und Verbrechen. Situation und Intention: Fallbeispiele*, ed. Timm C. Richter (Munich: Martin Meidenbauer, 2006), 165–72; Jochen Böhler, ed., *"Grösste Härte . . ." Verbrechen der Wehrmacht in Polen September/Oktober 1939* (Warsaw: Friedrich-Ebert-Stiftung, Historisches Forschungszentrum, 2005).

42. See Edward B. Westermann, "Friend and Helper: German Uniformed Police Operations in Poland and the General Government, 1939–1941," *Journal of Military History* 58 (1994): 643–61; Edward B. Westermann, *Hitler's Police Battalions: Enforcing Racial War in the East* (Lawrence: University Press of Kansas, 2005), 127ff.; Mallmann, ". . . Missgeburten," 72.

43. CdS daily report, September 9, 1939, USHMMA RG 15.007M (BAB, R 58/7001), reel 2, file 1:33; decree CdS on formation of new Einsatzgruppe, September 12, 1939, USHMMA RG 14.016M (BAB, R 58/241), fiche 4:179. Erich Naumann (1905–1951) had commanded several SD districts before the war and in October 1939 was appointed IdS in Berlin. Between November 1941 and March 1943, as commander of Einsatzgruppe B, he orchestrated the destruction of the Jews in Belorussia. He subsequently returned to Berlin and took over several leading Sipo/SD posts. Naumann was sentenced to death in the 1948 Nuremberg Einsatzgruppen Trial for his role as commander of Einsatzgruppe B and hanged.

mando 16 was set up in Gdańsk, initially with one hundred men, "for the area of the Military Commander West Prussia" under SS-Obersturmbannführer Dr. Rudolf Tröger.[44] In addition, on September 13, a newly formed Einsatzkommando 3 of Einsatzgruppe V headed toward North Mazovia, then on October 3 back to Olsztyn.[45] This organizational structure, agreed to by the Wehrmacht, formed the basis for Sipo/SD deployment during the invasion of Poland. Over the course of September, the altogether sixteen Einsatzkommandos totaling roughly twenty-seven hundred men traversed the territory occupied by Germany; scarcely any of the large Polish towns lay outside of their operational areas. More than one Einsatzgruppe was deployed in East Upper Silesia, western Galicia, the Poznań region, and Danzig–West Prussia, sometimes two or more simultaneously, sometimes in succession.[46] As a result, in the autumn of 1939 these areas saw the largest number of civilian deaths.

PERSONNEL AND TASKS

Despite the lack of comprehensive sources on Einsatzgruppen personnel, it is evident that most unit members had previously manned Sipo and SD posts in eastern Germany. It was left to unit commanders to fill the ranks, whereas the central office in Berlin determined mid-ranking and senior officers, with Heydrich or Himmler reserving the decision about whom to appoint as commanders of the Einsatzgruppen and Einsatzkommandos.[47] The fact that twenty-one unit commanders came from leadership positions in the sixty-four Gestapo bases in the Reich and the Protectorate of Bohemia and Moravia (the German-annexed part of former Czechoslovakia) attests to the importance of "Operation Tannenberg" in the minds of their Berlin

---

44. Rudolf Tröger (1908–1940) was a lawyer who had joined the NSDAP in 1933. In August 1937 he worked at the Gestapo and later took command of the Stapo office in Chemnitz. In November 1939, he became IdS in Gdańsk. He was killed during the German campaign against France in June 1940.

45. CdS daily reports, September 12 and 26, October 3, 1939, USHMMA RG 15.007M (BAL R 58/7001 and 7002), reel 2, file 1:41–45, 50–56, and file 2:67. On the personnel composition of the Einsatzgruppen, see Rossino, *Hitler Strikes Poland*, 11.

46. See Map 1, p. viii, showing advance routes of the Einsatzgruppen in Poland, 1939. Abbreviated references to Einsatzgruppen subunits (EK) include the unit number followed by the Einsatzgruppen designation; for instance, EK3/V refers to Einsatzkommando 3 of Einsatzgruppe V.

47. SDHA II 12 file note, July 8, 1939, BAB, R 58/7154; undated memo by Bruno Streckenbach on the tasks of RSHA Amt I, BAL, B 162/3622.

superiors. Not surprisingly, then, the top officers of the Einsatzgruppen—Streckenbach, Schäfer, Fischer, Beutel, Damzog, Naumann, von Woyrsch, and their EK heads—represented the cream of the crop in Himmler's circle of executive leaders. More often than not, their deployment during "Operation Tannenberg" served as an intermezzo between a rapid prewar career and more prominent functions later in the war, many directly related to the murder of Jews in Poland and other occupied regions.[48]

Einsatzgruppen members hailed from different age cohorts, social groups, and regions. Career policemen who had faced dismissal from their posts if they joined the NSDAP during the Weimar Republic years saw significant career gains after 1933. While some had joined the Nazi movement at an early age before 1933—as members of the NSDAP, Hitler Youth, SA, SS, or another party organizations—others came on board in the year of Hitler's appointment or shortly thereafter, attesting to the close correlation between ideological convictions and opportunistic adaptation as key binding factors in the Nazi system. Sipo and SD men wanted the Third Reich to succeed as much as they wanted to foster their own personal success. Having abandoned universalistic morality and egalitarian humanism, they were mostly concerned with the well-being of their own, ethnically defined "people's community" (*Volksgemeinschaft*). Within this worldview, they readily relegated racially or otherwise defined "outsider" groups to the status of unwanted minorities whose influence on "Aryan Germans" had to be curtailed, if not eradicated.[49] This is what they were expected to do and to varying degrees, depending on their practical work since 1933, were accustomed to doing.

Their desire for a *völkisch* "New Order" and their sense of belonging to a new elite separated Heydrich's officers from mere technocrats or administrative experts driven purely by a professional ethos of getting results.[50] The imposing collection of doctorates among the Einsatzgruppen commanders provides a potent reminder that higher education and intellectual dexterity do not prevent a person from becoming an agent of genocide. Far from social misfits, these men had internalized the antisemitism and radical nationalism prevalent

---

48. For more detailed biographical information on Einsatzgruppen personnel, see Klaus-Michael Mallmann, Jochen Böhler, and Jürgen Matthäus, *Einsatzgruppen in Polen. Darstellung und Dokumentation* (Darmstadt: WBG, 2008), 19–46.

49. Claudia Koonz, *The Nazi Conscience* (Cambridge, MA: Harvard University Press, 2003), 4ff., 221ff.

50. Harald Welzer, *Täter: Wie aus ganz normalen Menschen Massenmörder werden* (Frankfurt am Main: S. Fischer, 2005), 48ff., 68ff.

at German universities during the Weimar era. The *völkisch*-oriented Deutsche Hochschulring, after World War I the strongest political students' association, explicitly understood itself as part of the "German people's community" and remained closed to Jews with the argument that the "Jewish way is not the German way."[51] The lessons these young academics learned instilled a right-wing militant outlook in them in which political opponents had to be crushed by force, not persuaded with reasoned argument.[52]

Violently opposed to the Versailles Treaty, which they regarded as the root cause of all post–World War I problems, and convinced of Bolshevism's Jewish origins, they embraced the Nazi ideal of a new Germany committed to a degree of ethnic purity and political activism that went beyond what traditional German conservatives envisioned.[53] Most shared German state philosopher and jurist Carl Schmitt's insistence on the incompatibility between friend and foe, insider and outsider, German and un-German, which made policies of inequality not only desirable but necessary.[54] Ideological indoctrination in Himmler's apparatus constantly drove home the Nazi notion of a racially homogenous ethnic body and the myth of an "international Jewish conspiracy."[55] In fact, few Einsatzgruppen members required convincing that Bolshevism was a Jewish plot to conquer the globe, even if they harbored no personal feelings against individual Jews. Seeing themselves and the country as victims of a gigantic assault both from within and from the outside world, they regarded violence as a legitimate defense against the alleged perpetrators of the past world war

---

51. Cited in Michael H. Kater, *Studentenschaft und Rechtsradikalismus in Deutschland 1918–1933. Eine sozialgeschichtliche Studie zur Bildungskrise in der Weimarer Republik* (Hamburg: Hoffmann & Campe, 1975), 22; Konrad H. Jarausch, *Deutsche Studenten 1800–1970* (Frankfurt am Main: Suhrkamp, 1984), 117–63; Michael Grüttner, *Studenten im Dritten Reich* (Paderborn: Schöningh, 1995), 19–61.

52. Wildt, *Generation des Unbedingten*, 137–42.

53. Peter Gay, *Weimar Culture: The Outsider as Insider* (New York: Harper & Row, 1970); Boris Barth, *Dolchstosslegenden und politische Desintegration: Das Trauma der deutschen Niederlage im Ersten Weltkrieg 1914–1933* (Düsseldorf: Droste, 2003).

54. See Koonz, *Nazi Conscience*, 58–61.

55. Jürgen Matthäus, "Antisemitism as an Offer—the Function of Ideological Indoctrination in the SS- and Police Corps during the Holocaust," in *Lessons and Legacies VII: The Holocaust in International Perspective*, ed. Dagmar Herzog (Evanston, IL: Northwestern University Press, 2006), 116–28; Jürgen Matthäus, "Die 'Judenfrage' als Schulungsthema von SS und Polizei. 'Inneres Erlebnis' und Handlungslegitimation," in *Ausbildungsziel Judenmord? "Weltanschauliche Erziehung" von SS, Polizei und Waffen-SS im Rahmen der "Endlösung,"* ed. Jürgen Matthäus et al. (Frankfurt am Main: Fischer Taschenbuch Verlag, 2003), 35–86.

and a new one in the making.[56] Yet, during the Polish campaign, Heydrich's officers saw a much bigger threat coming from Polish nationalists, intellectuals, and other leaders of the ethnic majority than the one posed by Jews. These men's conviction that Poland was not a legitimate state and that Poles were as inferior as they were dangerous was a variation on the Nazi racial theme, infused with long-standing anti-Slavic stereotypes widely shared among German nationalists.[57]

If we look at the personal biographies of Einsatzgruppen commanders, World War I and its violent aftermath played a large role in shaping their outlook: ten of the twenty-eight leaders of the Einsatzgruppen and Einsatzkommandos—almost a third—had been frontline soldiers. Beyond this, almost all had joined a right-wing paramilitary organization (the so-called Freikorps) after the war ended, and some had participated in the German-Polish struggle at the Reich's post-1918 eastern border.[58] Illegal right-wing activities and years in the Nazi underground struggle had also clearly left their mark on those Austrians who, after the German takeover of Austria in March 1938, took on leadership roles in the Sipo/SD.[59] Similarly important was the involvement of later Einsatzgruppen officers in the Nazi police state after its emergence in January 1933. In their police work against Hitler's actual or would-be enemies, they had long helped fight alleged "professional criminals" ("*Berufsverbrecher*"), "aliens to the community" ("*Gemeinschaftsfremde*"), "asocials" ("*Asoziale*"), and Jews. Although only a few commanders—for example, Beutel and Woyrsch—had

---

56. Claus-Ekkehard Bärsch, *Die politische Religion des Nationalsozialismus: Die religiöse Dimension der NS-Ideologie in den Schriften von Dietrich Eckart, Joseph Goebbels, Alfred Rosenberg und Adolf Hitler* (Munich: W. Fink, 1998), 333–42; Wolfram Meyer zu Uptrup, *Kampf gegen die "jüdische Weltverschwörung": Propaganda und Antisemitismus der Nationalsozialisten 1919–1945* (Berlin: Metropol, 2003); Jeffrey Herf, *The Jewish Enemy: Nazi Propaganda during World War II and the Holocaust* (Cambridge, MA: Belknap Press of Harvard University Press, 2006).

57. Szarota, "Poland and Poles"; Roschke, *Der umworbene "Urfeind"*.

58. See David Clay Large, *Where Ghosts Walked: Munich's Road to the Third Reich* (New York: W. W. Norton, 1997); Gerhard Paul and Klaus-Michael Mallmann, "Sozialisation, Milieu und Gewalt: Fortschritte und Probleme der neueren Täterforschung," in *Karrieren der Gewalt: Nationalsozialistische Täterbiographien*, ed. Klaus-Michael Mallmann and Gerhard Paul (Darmstadt: WBG, 2004), 1–32.

59. Jürgen Gehl, *Austria, Germany, and the Anschluss, 1931–1938* (London: Oxford University Press, 1963); Bruce F. Pauley, *Hitler and the Forgotten Nazis: A History of Austrian National Socialism* (Chapel Hill: University of North Carolina Press, 1981); Peter R. Black, *Ernst Kaltenbrunner: Ideological Soldier of the Third Reich* (Princeton, NJ: Princeton University Press, 1984), 69ff.

themselves conducted or ordered the murder of opponents of the regime prior to the beginning of World War II, all had actively pursued the ideal of transforming German society into a racially homogeneous community. They had been involved in earlier Nazi attempts to "solve the Jewish question" in the form of enforcing social segregation, stigmatization, and isolation, most violently in the concentration camps but also in day-to-day police actions.[60] The military campaign in Poland, with its explosion of deadly violence, transformed the life of all these men as well as the institution for which they worked. It created a murderous dynamic that helped to transcend established behavioral borders and overcome their remaining moral scruples about genocide.[61]

Given the mix of factors involved, it is only partly possible to reconstruct how Einsatzgruppen officers, once deployed, decided what course of action to take. Although Hitler had initiated the dynamic that radicalized the process, commanders in the field made use of the far-reaching powers vested in them without waiting for clear directives from their superiors. Heydrich visited his field units, but we do not know exactly when. Similarly unclear are communications coming from Himmler, who in his special train ("Sonderzug Heinrich") remained in close proximity to Hitler's headquarters and thereby had countless opportunities to talk to the leader of the Third Reich. After the war, two participants in the meeting held on August 18 at Prinz-Albrecht-Strasse, Einsatzgruppe IV commander Lothar Beutel and his Wehrmacht liaison officer, Dr. Ernst Gerke, stated that no clear directive to kill the Polish intelligentsia had been issued. Instead, Himmler and Heydrich stated that executions were in order within the overall goal of "pacifying" the occupied area. Given that Beutel and Gerke incriminated themselves by admitting that their superiors had issued no direct orders to kill, they were likely telling the truth.[62]

By contrast, as mentioned above, less than a week into the campaign, Einsatzgruppe z.b.V. was equipped with clear directives that removed any restrictions on the use of force: Himmler ordered that "Polish bands" were to be

---

60. Michael Mann, "Were the Perpetrators of Genocide 'Ordinary Men' or 'Real Nazis'? Results from Fifteen Hundred Biographies," *HGS* 14 (2000): 336; Michael Wildt, *Hitler's Volksgemeinschaft and the Dynamics of Racial Exclusion: Violence against Jews in Provincial Germany, 1919–1939* (New York: Berghahn, 2012); Armin Nolzen, "The Nazi Party and Its Violence against the Jews, 1933–1939: Violence as a Historiographical Concept," *YVS* 31 (2003): 245–85.

61. See Wildt, *An Uncompromising Generation*, 240–41.

62. Dorothee Weitbrecht, "Ermächtigung zur Vernichtung: Die Einsatzgruppen in Polen im Herbst 1939," in *Genesis des Genozids. Polen 1939–1941*, ed. Klaus-Michael Mallmann and Bogdan Musial (Darmstadt: WBG, 2004), 57–70. See document 2.

combatted ruthlessly, executions should be carried out, and "Polish insurgents who are caught in the act or with weapons are to be shot on the spot."[63] The commander of the 14th Army welcomed the actions of the Einsatzgruppe without reservations.[64] Two days later, when there were reports of "fights with bandits" (*Bandenkämpfe*) in Częstochowa and an Order Police battalion was brought in, Kurt Daluege, chief of the German Order Police, stated, "The commander of the battalion has been given the order to implement drastic measures, including measures used in the Upper Silesia industrial area to hang partisans from the lampposts." And on September 7 Daluege informed his subordinates, "The Reichsführer-SS [Himmler] has ordered by telephone that the police and not the army implement executions in the whole area."[65] As we will show, the events in Bydgoszcz accelerated the spiral of violence.[66]

ESCALATING VIOLENCE

To react swiftly and forcefully to the situation unfolding behind the front line, leaders in Berlin needed information. This is why the Einsatzgruppen reported from the field twice daily. A week into the war, during a conference of RSHA department heads lead by Best, the lessons of early Einsatzgruppen activities for the future seemed clear: "The leading layer of society in Poland is so far as possible to be rendered harmless," the minutes stated. This implied executions. However, at this point RSHA officers defined the scope of killings fairly narrowly: while "Polish looters" were to be shot, in the case of the Polish elite, "it was decided that the leadership on no account can be allowed to remain in Poland, that it will be sent to German concentration camps, whereas for the lower strata, temporary concentration camps will be established behind the Einsatzgruppen on the border, from where they can be pushed into what remains of Poland." At the same time, Best and his colleagues wanted to make use of the opportunity to forcibly reduce the number of Jews in the Reich by "pushing

---

63. Himmler to Woyrsch, September 7, 1939, BA-MA, RH 19 I/191; CdO to BdO attached to 4th Army, September 16, 1939, BA-MA, RH 20-4/856.

64. Special directive no. 14 of Commander 14th Army, September 12, 1939, BA-MA, RH 20-14/129.

65. CdO notes, September 5 and 7, 1939, USHMMA RG 68.046M (BAB, R 19/334), reel 31:294–97; BDC-SSO file Kurt Daluege.

66. See documents 11 to 22; also Günter Schubert, *Das Unternehmen "Bromberger Blutsonntag": Tod einer Legende* (Cologne: Bund-Verlag, 1989); *Pierwsze miesiące okupacji hitlerowskiej w Bydgoszczy*, ed. Tadeusz Esman and Włodzimierz Jastrzębski (Bydgoszcz: Bydgoskie Towarzystwo Naukowe, 1967).

Polish Jews out of Germany."[67] Within the parameters of these goals, they left the choice of methods open.

Events moved quickly in the direction of greater violence. On September 8, Admiral Wilhelm Canaris, head of Wehrmacht Intelligence (Abwehr), informed General Karl-Heinrich von Stülpnagel that Heydrich had complained about the lack of swift action on the part of the military courts in Poland. Heydrich's criticism culminated in the following sentence: "We want to save the little people, but the aristocracy, priests, and Jews must be killed."[68] A day later Halder informed a small circle that, according to one participant, "it is the intention of the Führer and [Hermann] Göring to annihilate and wipe out the Polish people. The rest of what was said cannot even be hinted at in writing."[69] On September 12, Canaris met with Wilhelm Keitel, chief of the Wehrmacht High Command (Oberkommando der Wehrmacht, OKW), and, according to the postwar testimony of a Wehrmacht officer present, "warned against the measures which had come to his knowledge, namely the proposed shootings and extermination measures directed particularly against the Polish intelligentsia, the nobility, the clergy, and in fact all elements which could be regarded as leaders of a national resistance." Keitel was not surprised, for "these things had been decided upon by the Führer, and [. . .] the Führer, the Commander-in-Chief of the Army, had let it be known that, should the Armed Forces be unwilling to carry through these measures, or should they not agree with them, they would have to accept the presence at their side of the SS, the Sipo and similar units who would carry them through. A civilian official would then be appointed to function with each military commander. This, in outline, was our discussion on the proposed shooting and extermination measures in Poland."[70]

Keitel was hinting at the creation of chiefs of civil administration (*Chefs der Zivilverwaltung*, CdZ): civil servants allocated to the local army commanders who—forming the link between the Wehrmacht and the Einsatzgruppen—were to ensure the smooth establishment of a functioning administration. In reality, in Poland in 1939, the chiefs of civil administration did more than watch

---

67. SDHA I 11 note, September 8, 1939, USHMMA RG 14.016M (BAB, R 58/825), fiche 1:1–4. Heydrich was not present during the meeting on September 7.

68. Helmuth Groscurth, *Tagebücher eines Abwehroffiziers 1938–1940: Mit weiteren Dokumenten zur Militäropposition gegen Hitler*, ed. Helmut Krausnick and Harold C. Deutsch (Stuttgart: Deutsche Verlags-Anstalt, 1970), 201.

69. Groscurth, *Tagebücher*, 202.

70. Interrogation of Erwin Lahousen, November 30, 1945, IMT 2:447. On Canaris and Keitel, see Michael Mueller, *Canaris. Hitlers Abwehrchef* (Berlin: Propyläen, 2006); Samuel W. Mitcham, "Generalfeldmarschall Wilhelm Keitel," in *Hitlers militärische Elite*, ed. Gerd R. Ueberschär (Darmstadt: Primus, 1998), 1:112–20; Megargee, *Inside Hitler's High Command*, 56–57.

over the allocation of police forces in their operational areas. Appointed by Hitler partly on the basis of their Nazi credentials, they also oversaw the ruthless oppression of any kind of real or alleged resistance on the part of the civil population and the implementation of the first anti-Jewish measures, using the Einsatzgruppen and other police formations as their executive forces.[71]

After the campaign, Heydrich explained as the logical consequence of directives received from Hitler a development that in reality had been driven from above and below. In a letter to Orpo chief Daluege on July 2, 1940, Heydrich asserted that "the orders underlying the police actions were extremely radical (e.g., orders to liquidate the circle of Polish leaders, which went into the thousands)" and could not be shared with the military. Consequently, the Sipo/SD chief stated, "from the outside, the actions of the police and the SS appeared to be arbitrary, brutal acts of their own volition." Furthermore, reprisals—according to Heydrich, "self-defense, arising from understandable bitterness against the Polish cruelty"—triggered "unbelievable, uncontrollable acts of revenge, which were blamed on the SS and the police."[72] The picture Heydrich painted of the dutiful execution of the Führer's orders by the Einsatzgruppen, whose men other German agencies singled out as convenient scapegoats, obscured the interplay of multiple factors that drove German policy toward greater violence, particularly the eagerness of Himmler's officers in the field to excel.

A report by Generaloberst Walter von Reichenau in charge of the 10th Army about a serious incident in his area of command attested to the importance of local actors. During the night of September 18, an officer of the "Leibstandarte Adolf Hitler," a Waffen-SS unit formally under Reichenau's command, executed fifty Jewish civilian prisoners in Błonie. Because the officer claimed to have acted in accordance with higher orders, Reichenau asked for instructions from his superior at Army Group South (Heeresgruppe Süd). Its commander, General Gerd von Rundstedt, denied the existence of such an order and recommended that the Waffen-SS men involved be court-martialed. However, when Reichenau telephoned Hitler, he was told that the matter fell within Himmler's jurisdiction.[73] As demonstrated by this and other protests by army officers

71. Rossino, *Hitler Strikes Poland*, 19–20; Hans Umbreit, *Deutsche Militärverwaltungen 1938/39. Die militärische Besetzung der Tschechoslowakei und Polens* (Stuttgart: Deutsche Verlags-Anstalt, 1977).

72. CdS to CdO, July 2, 1940, USHMMA RG 68.046M (BAB, R 19/395), reel 35:289–94.

73. Commander 10th Army/Ic/AO to Army Group (Heeresgruppe) South, September 19, 1939; Commander Army Group South to Commander 10th Army, September 20, both BA-MA, RH 19 I/112.

against the shooting of Polish civilians by police and SS units, Wehrmacht commanders in the field had not been informed about Himmler's expanded assignment. The operations of his units challenged the military's self-perception as the sole proprietor of executive authority in Poland. Yet Wehrmacht commanders accepted the Reichsführer's interference since he had Hitler's backing and, more importantly, was helping to "pacify" the occupied areas.[74]

With the German military pursuing its own radical agenda against civilians, including mass executions, coordination was required. On September 19, Wagner summoned Heydrich to a meeting.[75] Halder, probably informed by Wagner of the discussion, jotted down the following outcome: "a) Missions [of the SD] must be known to the army. Liaison officers: Himmler/ObdH. b) Spatial cleansing: Jews, intelligentsia, clergy, nobility. c) Army demands: clean up [Bereinigung] after army withdraws and after transfer [of authority] to stable civil administration. Beginning of December."[76] Brauchitsch, on whose behalf the negotiations were conducted, agreed to Hitler's suggestion that a separation of tasks between the Wehrmacht and Sipo/SD be implemented but expected this to wait until after the Wehrmacht had relinquished its authority. At the same time, in addition to Jews, clerics, and the aristocracy, a fourth group, the "intelligentsia"—an amorphous term, highly flexible in its applicability—had become the target of what Halder euphemistically called "spatial cleansing" (Flurbereinigung). As Heydrich put it that afternoon at the third conference of RSHA department heads, it had been determined "that Einsatzgruppen leaders will be subordinated to the army commanders [Armeeoberkommandos], but will take their instructions directly from the chief of the security police." Heydrich had reason to interpret this "as a favorable result of the cooperation with the Wehrmacht,"[77] for he had managed to make the Einsatzgruppen practically independent of the military.

Despite these successes, police field officers continued to encounter Wehrmacht opposition whenever the military saw its prerogatives threatened. One day after his meeting with Heydrich, Wagner demanded the immediate withdrawal of Einsatzgruppe z.b.V., proudly writing his wife about his fight "against invisible forces," namely, Himmler and the Sipo/SD chief.[78] Canaris lent a helping hand in the struggle: during a visit to the 14th Army, he had learned from

---

74. See document 10 and document 41.

75. Wagner, *Der Generalquartiermeister*, 134.

76. Halder, *Kriegstagebuch*, 1:79.

77. SDHA I 11 note, September 21, 1939, USHMMA RG 14.016M (BAB, R 58/825), fiche 1:14–17.

78. Wagner, *Der Generalquartiermeister*, 135.

its intelligence officer of "unrest," "which had arisen in the area partly due to the unlawful actions of the Einsatzgruppe," involving "mass shootings, in particular of Jews" and triggering discontent among soldiers because "young people, instead of fighting on the front, are testing their courage on the defenseless."[79] Protests by the 14th Army made through Wagner had the desired effect, and on September 22 these police units were in fact withdrawn from eastern Poland and transferred back to the Katowice (German: Kattowitz) area.[80]

The friction between the Wehrmacht and the SS stemmed from a struggle for power, not a conflict about goals. There is abundant evidence for crimes committed by the German military against Polish prisoners of war and civilians, especially Jews.[81] The Wehrmacht cooperated for the most part smoothly with the Einsatzgruppen, Order Police battalions, Waffen-SS units, and SS-sponsored Ethnic German Self-Defense (Volksdeutscher Selbstschutz).[82] Furthermore, the army issued explicit requests for "cleansing actions" by police or SS troops.[83] And when Arthur Greiser, a known hater of Poles and Jews, took over the business of chief of civil administration at the seat of the regional military commander (*Militärbefehlshaber*) in Poznań, the latter greeted him with the following words: "There are no disputes about the area of competence, there is only one goal: to work together to make German land German again."[84] At the same time, Heydrich reprimanded the army field police chief (*Heeresfeldpolizeichef*), whose troops had on several occasions "handed persons who should have been shot over to the Einsatzkommandos of the Security Police with the request that Einsatzkommandos do the shooting." Heydrich instead urged the military police to conduct its own executions.[85]

Individual Wehrmacht successes in containing Einsatzgruppen freedom of action notwithstanding, postcampaign planning on the broader goals of

---

79. Note by Oberstleutnant Lahousen regarding his trip to Poland, September 19–22, 1939, IfZ, Nuremberg Document PS-3047; also Groscurth, *Tagebücher*, 209.

80. Commander 14th Army/Ic/AO to Army Group South, September 22, 1939, IfZ, MA 113/6; Rossino, "Nazi Anti-Jewish Policy," 43.

81. Böhler, *Auftakt*, 76–200.

82. Rossino, *Hitler Strikes Poland*, 121–43; Böhler, *Auftakt*, 201–47.

83. Gen. Kdo. Gienanth/Ic/AO to CdZ AOK 8, September 8, 1939, APŁ, 175/10a. See also CdZ AOK 8 to EG III, September 24, 1939; file note AOK 8, September 14, 1939, APP, 298/47.

84. Order Military Commander Posen, September 14, 1939, APP, 298/35; on Greiser, see Catherine Epstein, *Model Nazi: Arthur Greiser and the Occupation of Western Poland* (Oxford: Oxford University Press, 2010).

85. CdS to Chief of Army Field Police (*Heeresfeldpolizeichef* OKW), September 15, 1939, NARA, RG 242, T-312, R. 47.

German policies boosted the role of the police. On September 19, Göring's Ministerial Council for the Defense of the Reich (Ministerrat für die Reichsverteidigung) discussed, in the presence of Heydrich and Daluege, the "question of the population of the future Polish protectorate and the accommodation of Jews living in Germany" as part of the shift in German anti-Jewish policy toward forcible expulsion to the east.[86] Although the practical implementation of this program had not yet been worked out, deportation of German Jews into remote, desolate areas clearly meant wide-scale pauperization, starvation, and epidemics.[87] At the same time, the Gestapo had, since the middle of September, arrested 584 Polish and stateless Jews who had previously held Polish citizenship in the Reich and had taken them to the Sachsenhausen concentration camp.[88] Already on September 14, 1939, during an RSHA department head conference held after Heydrich had come back from a visit to the front, the Sipo/SD chief had addressed the "Jewish question" and referred to Hitler's getting "suggestions" from Göring, "for it is only the Führer who can make a decision that will have a considerable foreign impact."[89]

With leading politicians setting radical goals for long-term German policy in Poland, Himmler's and Heydrich's position strengthened vis-à-vis the Wehrmacht. On September 20, Brauchitsch raised the question of executive authority in the occupation zone during a discussion with Hitler. He told Halder that the "Führer will inform ObdH of all decisions," as will Himmler and Heydrich; in addition, police commanders had to inform the relevant military agencies. Brauchitsch agreed to "resettlement on a grand scale" (*Umsiedlung im grossen*): "Former German areas will be cleared of those [Poles] who moved in after 1918." For every German settler, twice the number of Poles would be expelled. The Jewish population was also the subject of discussion: "Ghetto plans exist in broad outline; details are not yet settled; economic needs are prime considerations."[90] Hitler and his army chief agreed that population

---

86. Protocol of meeting of Ministerial Council for the Defense of the Reich, September 19, 1939, IMT 31:230–32.

87. See Alexandra Garbarini with Emil Kerenji, Jan Lambertz, and Avinoam Patt, *Jewish Responses to Persecution*, Vol. 2: *1938–1940* (Lanham, MD: AltaMira Press in association with the USHMM, 2011), 315–27.

88. See Günter Morsch and Susanne zur Nieden, eds., *Jüdische Häftlinge im Konzentrationslager Sachsenhausen 1936–1945* (Berlin: Hentrich, 2004), 180–81. For a powerful firsthand account by a Polish Jew arrested at that time, see Leon Szalet, *Experiment "E": A Report from an Extermination Laboratory* (New York: Didier, 1945).

89. SDHA I 11, September 15, 1939, USHMMA RG 14.016M (BAB, R 58/825), fiche 1:10–13.

90. *Halder War Diary*, 59.

movements could start only after military operations had been completed in order to avoid "atrocity propaganda" by foreign countries, but "a survey and study about which population groups must be resettled and where" already seemed feasible. Although leaving the task of "spatial cleansing" to the future civil administration, Wehrmacht leaders hoped for Himmler's cooperation on short-term measures, as Halder noted: "Summary police courts. Reviewing authority is Reichsführer-SS."[91] This arrangement was communicated to army commanders in the field on September 21 and formalized two days later during a meeting between Brauchitsch and Himmler.[92] Although Wehrmacht leaders continued to insist on their prerogative, in practice the SS and police chief had gained the upper hand.[93]

Hitler's and Göring's interventions left no doubt that the Nazi leadership was keen to make use of the new possibilities brought about by the German conquest in Poland for a redrawing of the ethnic map far beyond the "Jewish question." On September 21, Heydrich again convened his department heads, this time with all Einsatzgruppen commanders present. They learned that Poland's western provinces were to be annexed to the Reich and that a civil administration with its capital in Kraków was to be established for the remaining parts of German-occupied Poland (later known as the Generalgouvernement). Himmler would be appointed "Settlement Commissioner for the East" (*Siedlungskommissar für den Osten*), and Hitler had approved the deportation of Jews from annexed Poland to the Generalgouvernement, expected to take place in the course of a year. In preparation, ghettos would be established in the cities. Jews were to "disappear from the countryside as small landholders" within the next three to four weeks, thus calling into question the agreement just reached between Hitler and Brauchitsch, whereby population transfers would be postponed until after the end of military hostilities. The "Polish problem" was to be resolved by eradicating what little remained of the Polish prewar middle class and relegating millions to the status of serfs concentrated in the Generalgouvernement.[94] Heydrich confirmed the sweeping action program that he had outlined during the meeting in an express letter sent to the Einsatzgruppen, the Army High Command (Oberkommando des Heeres,

---

91. Halder, *Kriegstagebuch*, 1:81–82; see also Wagner, *Der Generalquartiermeister*, 135. For a slightly different translation, see *Halder War Diary*, 59–60.

92. See document 69; also Hartmann, *Halder*, 139ff., 149ff.

93. See CdS express letter, September 30, 1939, USHMMA RG 14.016M (BAB, R 58/276), fiches 6–9:241; RSHA I 1, October 5, 1939, USHMMA RG 14.016M (BAB, R 58/825), fiche 2:38.

94. See document 68.

OKH), and various other state agencies. The letter called for the establishment of Jewish councils charged with immediately conducting a census, signaling that the SS and police were already claiming jurisdiction over this crucial part of Nazi policy in Poland.[95]

Hitler pushed for speedy and radical action. On September 29, he described to party ideologue Alfred Rosenberg his impressions of the campaign: "The Poles: a thin Germanic layer, underneath dreadful material. The Jews, the worst that one could possibly imagine. The towns caked in filth."[96] The territory under German rule was to be divided into three regions:

> 1. Between Vistula and Bug [Rivers]: all Jewry (also from the Reich), as well as all untrustworthy elements. On the Vistula an impregnable East Wall [*Ostwall*]—even stronger than in the West.[97] 2. On the border up until now a wide belt of Germanization and colonization. This presents a large task for the whole *Volk*: creating a German breadbasket, a sturdy community of farmers, resettling good Germans from all over the world. 3. In between a Polish "form of state" [*Staatlichkeit*].[98]

Roughly a week later, Joseph Goebbels wrote in his diary, "Midday with the Führer. A large gathering. [. . .] The Jewish problem will be the most difficult to solve. The Jews are no longer humans. A beast of prey with a cold intellect that must be rendered harmless."[99]

The Bug River became an important delineation of German influence as a result of the Soviet Union joining its Nazi ally by invading eastern Poland as of September 17. By the end of the month, both powers had agreed on the Bug-San River line as a demarcation of their respective realms of influence. As planned, Germany partitioned its occupied territory into Poland's western regions, to be annexed to the Reich, and a separate fiefdom, Hitler's "form of state," called the Generalgouvernement. The annexed parts comprised the area

---

95. See document 52; also Dan Michman, "Why Did Heydrich Write the Schnellbrief? A Remark on the Reason and on Its Significance," *YVS* 32 (2004): 433–47; Isaiah Trunk, *Judenrat: The Jewish Councils in Eastern Europe under Nazi Occupation* (New York: Macmillan, 1972).

96. Hans-Günther Seraphim, ed., *Das politische Tagebuch Alfred Rosenbergs 1934/35 und 1939/40* (Munich: Deutscher Taschenbuch Verlag, 1964), 98.

97. Reference to the "Westwall," a fortified defense line more than four hundred miles long built in 1938–1939 along Germany's western border.

98. Seraphim, *Das politische Tagebuch*, 99.

99. Joseph Goebbels, *Die Tagebücher von Joseph Goebbels*, part I: *Aufzeichnungen 1923–1941*, ed. Elke Fröhlich (Munich: K. G. Saur, 1998), 7:141 (diary entry for October 6, 1939).

of East Upper Silesia around Katowice,[100] the region around Poznań and Łódź
(later renamed Litzmannstadt) called Reichsgau Wartheland or Warthegau,[101]
the new province of Danzig–West Prussia,[102] and the area around Ciechanów
(German: Zichenau), which was to be added to East Prussia.[103] On October
8, the Generalgouvernement was created, comprising four districts administered from Kraków, Warsaw, Radom, and Lublin, respectively.[104] With Hans
Frank, former supreme chief of civil administration, as *Generalgouverneur*, the
Nazi elite saw this area as a sort of dumping ground for the millions of people
affected by plans, as OKW chief Keitel put it, "to clear the old and new Reich
area of Jews, Polacks and scum."[105] In the minds of the German planners, "Germanization" of the newly acquired territory had to coincide with "de-Jewification" ("*Entjudung*") and "de-Polonization" ("*Entpolonisierung*").[106]

Once this partitioning of Poland had been determined, the idea gained
ground within the RSHA to create a "Reich ghetto" in the Lublin District "in
which all the political and Jewish elements will be put" that were expelled from
the annexed territories and the Reich.[107] For Gestapo chief Heinrich Müller,
the new head of RSHA Office IV, this was the opportunity to draw on the
expertise of SS-Hauptsturmführer Adolf Eichmann, who since early 1938, as

---

100. Sybille Steinbacher, *"Musterstadt" Auschwitz: Germanisierungspolitik und Judenmord
in Ostoberschlesien* (Munich: Walter de Gruyter, 2000), 61ff.; Adam Dziurok, "Zwischen
den Ethnien: Die Oberschlesier in den Jahren 1939–1941," in *Genesis des Genozids. Polen
1939–1941*, ed. Klaus-Michael Mallmann and Bogdan Musial (Darmstadt: WBG, 2004),
221–33.

101. Michael Alberti, "'Exerzierplatz des Nationalsozialismus': Der Reichsgau Wartheland
1939–1941," in *Genesis des Genozids. Polen 1939–1941*, 111–26; Michael Alberti, *Die
Verfolgung und Vernichtung der Juden im Reichsgau Wartheland 1939–1945* (Wiesbaden:
Harrassowitz, 2006), 33ff.

102. Dieter Schenk, *Hitlers Mann in Danzig: Gauleiter Forster und die NS-Verbrechen in
Danzig-Westpreussen* (Bonn: J. H. W. Dietz, 2000).

103. Andreas Kossert, *Preussen, Deutsche oder Polen? Die Masuren im Spannungsfeld des
ethnischen Nationalismus 1870–1956* (Wiesbaden: Harrassowitz, 2001); Andreas Kossert,
Ostpreussen: Geschichte und Mythos (Munich: Siedler, 2005), 301ff.

104. Führer decree, October 8, 1939, BAB, R 43 II/1332; Martin Broszat,
Nationalsozialistische Polenpolitik 1939–1945 (Stuttgart: Fischer Bücherei, 1961), 49ff., 68ff.
After the German attack on the Soviet Union in June 1941, the district of Galicia was added
to the Generalgouvernement.

105. Chief OKW to Wagner, October 17, 1939, IMT 26:380–82; see also Norman M.
Naimark, *Fires of Hatred: Ethnic Cleansing in Twentieth-Century Europe* (Cambridge, MA:
Harvard University Press, 2001).

106. Umbreit, *Deutsche Militärverwaltungen 1938/39*, 190ff.

107. RSHA I 11 note, October 2, 1939, USHMMA RG 14.016M (BAB, R 58/825),
fiche 2:36–37.

head of the Central Office for Jewish Emigration (Zentralstelle für jüdische Auswanderung) in Vienna (a year later also in Berlin and Prague), had established an efficient system of expulsion, thus significantly reducing the number of Jews in the Reich and the Protectorate of Bohemia and Moravia. On October 6, Müller instructed Eichmann to make preparations for the "expulsion of 70,000–80,000 Jews from the Katowice District [. . .] across the Vistula" as a means of gathering experience "so that the evacuation of larger masses can be carried out."[108] Criminal Police chief Arthur Nebé, also a brand-new RSHA office head, thought of another unwanted ethnic group and asked Eichmann for "information on when he could send the Berlin gypsies."[109] After Eichmann had identified the area of Nisko on the San River as an appropriate destination in the Generalgouvernement, transport trains began heading there on October 18, carrying several thousand Jews from Vienna, Moravská Ostrava (German: Mährisch-Ostrau), Katowice, Chorzów (German: Königshütte), and Bielsko-Biała (German: Bielitz).[110]

With Berlin pushing toward "Germanization," the pressure for additional "cleansing measures" on Polish territory annexed to the Reich increased.[111] Those officers most eager to excel set the pace. In the "Reichsgau Danzig-Westpreussen" in particular, the number of executions went up after the new inspector of the Sipo and SD (Inspekteur der Sicherheitspolizei und des SD, IdS), former Einsatzkommando 16 leader Tröger, informed his subordinates at the beginning of October that Himmler had authorized them to "eliminate members of the Polish intelligentsia"; again, the SS chief left it to his officers to determine whom to target within this broad group.[112] In the spring of the following year, lists of the "remaining" members of the intelligentsia circulated, containing the names of "doctors, lawyers, middle and higher public servants, teachers, members of the Polish aristocracy, pharmacists, and influential businessmen and industrialists."[113] Hitler legitimized sweeping violence by issuing

---

108. See document 54.

109. SDHA to Eichmann, October 13, 1939, YVA, 0-53/93. On Nebé's Criminal Police coordinating "gypsy policy," see Henry Friedlander, *The Origins of Nazi Genocide: From Euthanasia to the Final Solution* (Chapel Hill: University of North Carolina Press, 1994), 55, 261–62.

110. Eichmann to Günther, October 15, 1939; file note Günther, October 16, 1939, both YVA, 0-53/93. On the Nisko plan, see Hans Safrian, *Eichmann's Men* (New York: Cambridge University Press in association with the USHMM, 2010), esp. 46–58; Browning, *Origins*, 36–43.

111. See document 41.

112. See document 25.

113. Circular Landrat Bromberg-Land, April 12, 1940, BAB, R 138 I/147.

a blanket amnesty decree on October 4 for crimes committed by German military and SS personnel against civilians in Poland after September 1, 1939.[114] Two days later, on October 6, Hitler declared before the Reichstag that the "most important task" arising from the "collapse of the Polish state" was "a new order of ethnographic relationships, that is, a resettlement of the nationalities." As part of the future "order," he announced "an attempt to regulate the Jewish problems."[115] The next day he appointed Himmler Reich commissioner for the strengthening of Germandom (Reichskommissar für die Festigung deutschen Volkstums), with the dual task of fostering the interests of ethnic Germans and eliminating whatever "inimical influences" non-German groups might exert.[116]

Army officers who observed the effects of the new measures in occupied Poland mainly voiced objections, if they had any, within small circles of like-minded officials. In the second week of October 1939, Ulrich von Hassell heard from Carl Goerdeler—both were members of the conservative elite prominent in the July 20, 1944, attempt to assassinate Hitler—that some Wehrmacht commanders had "returned home from Poland very disturbed [*ganz zerbrochen*] after seeing how brutally we conducted war, especially in the ruins of Warsaw." Hassell had talked to young Germans who had "witnessed villages being surrounded (due to partisans) and set on fire, while the villagers, shocked to the core, wandered around screaming."[117] A few days later he noted full of disgust, "But one can only be ashamed if people fire their revolvers to shoot Jews who have been driven into a synagogue."[118]

Based on the precedents set early on in the military campaign, violence was to be firmly integrated into the emerging structure of the occupation. Arthur Greiser, former chief of civil administration in the Poznań region and now the new head of the civil administration in the Reichsgau Wartheland, attended

---

114. Rossino, *Hitler Strikes Poland*, 118.

115. For extract translations of Hitler's Reichstag speech, see Max Domarus, ed., *Hitler: Speeches and Proclamations* (Wauconda, IL: Bolchazy-Carducci, 1997), 3:1828–48.

116. See Robert Lewis Koehl, *RKFDV: German Resettlement and Population Policy 1939–1945: A History of the Reich Commission for the Strengthening of Germandom* (Cambridge, MA: Harvard University Press, 1957); Götz Aly, *"Final Solution": Nazi Population Policy and the Murder of the European Jews* (London: Arnold, 1999), 24–26, 34; Peter Longerich, *Holocaust: The Nazi Persecution and Murder of the Jews* (Oxford: Oxford University Press, 2010), 155ff.

117. Ulrich von Hassell, *Vom andern Deutschland: Aus den nachgelassenen Tagebüchern 1938–1944* (Zurich: Atlantis, 1946), 88.

118. Hassell, *Vom andern Deutschland*, 91. The quote refers to the murder of about fifty Jews in Krasnosielc by SS men and Wehrmacht soldiers on September 5, 1939; see Böhler, *Auftakt*, 228–30.

the last meeting of the RSHA department heads and the Einsatzgruppen commanders in Berlin on October 14. There Heydrich charged his men with the "liquidation of the Polish leadership" by the end of October, while Greiser promised to obtain a decision from Hitler regarding the continuation of the police's authority to "implement martial law after November 1."[119] When the top leaders of the Third Reich met three days later, Hitler outlined his plans for Poland: "The establishment of a Polish intelligentsia leadership group must be prevented. [. . .] The formation of national cells must not occur." He left no doubt that the Reich had to engage in "a hard ethnic struggle, which will not allow any legal restrictions." With the police empowered to act radically, Keitel was advised that "the Wehrmacht should be glad if it can distance itself from administrative questions in Poland."[120]

Wehrmacht officers adapted to the situation. Generaloberst Wilhelm List, who as commander of the 14th Army had forced the withdrawal of Einsatzgruppe z.b.V. on September 22, silenced his soldiers' criticism of SS and police actions less than ten days later by praising the unit's "extraordinarily successful activities" and advising officers to explain to their men that "further comprehensive support for the Einsatzkommandos in their border and state police missions is in the interest of the troops."[121] It is worth noting that only a few days earlier in Przemyśl—a small Polish city situated west of the German-Soviet demarcation line—Einsatzgruppe z.b.V. and Einsatzgruppe I committed the largest mass shooting of Jews in September 1939, resulting in more than five hundred casualties.[122] In the fight against the enemy, be it on the front line or behind it, Wehrmacht officers and Himmler's men stood shoulder to shoulder. Nine days later, Rundstedt, the new high commander in the east (Oberbefehlshaber Ost), stressed that, in the interest of suppressing unrest, "it is necessary that every attempt at sabotage (for example, disturbance of lines of communication) or insubordination [. . .] be brutally nipped in the bud with the harshest means."[123] On October 25, Brauchitsch called on officers to "refrain from any form of criticism of the actions of the state leadership" and

---

119. RSHA I 11 note, October 16, 1939, USHMMA RG 14.016M (BAB, R 58/825), fiche 2:39–40.

120. Discussion Hitler with Keitel, October 17, 1939, IMT, 26:378–79; Halder, *Kriegstagebuch*, 1:107; note regarding Hitler's plans for German occupation policy in Poland, October 18, 1939, BA-MA, N 104/3.

121. Order AOK 14, October 1, 1939, BA-MA, RH 53-23/12.

122. Jochen Böhler, *Der Überfall. Deutschlands Krieg gegen Polen* (Frankfurt am Main: Eichborn, 2009), 202–4.

123. Order OB Ost, October 10, 1939, BA-MA, RH 53-20/14.

on their wives to be "models of uncompromising belief in national socialism and constantly act in accordance with this point of view."[124] Though his men would have known it already, Brauchitsch reminded them on November 1 that "the Jew is the fiercest enemy of the German *Volk*."[125] And in February 1940 he demanded understanding in a basic order titled "Army and SS" for the "ethnic-political measures ordered by the Führer for the security of German living space in Poland," which "inevitably must lead to what would otherwise be regarded as unusual, harsh measures against the Polish population in the occupied territory." Indeed, a "further intensification of these measures" seemed to be called for, he announced.[126]

Where Wehrmacht generals voiced criticism, they did not question the leadership's or their fellow officers' broader vision. When, at the end of November, Generaloberst Johannes Blaskowitz, Rundstedt's successor as high commander in the east, lambasted "the Einsatzgruppen, which operate almost exclusively as execution squads" and whose members "inevitably succumb to blood lust," Hitler was outraged and recalled Blaskowitz a short time later.[127] The general learned his lesson; in his notes for a presentation to Brauchitsch in February 1940, Blaskowitz defined the Poles and the Jew as "our archenemies in the East" and expressed his belief in the need for a more systematic, though not necessarily less radical, occupation strategy: "It is wrong to kill a few 10,000 Jews and Poles as is happening at the moment, because this will, given the size of the population, neither kill off the idea of a Polish state nor remove the Jews."[128] Similarly, Generalmajor Kurt von Tippelskirch, OKH quartermaster (Oberquartiermeister IV), was troubled not by "ethnic cleansing" per se, but by its effect on military discipline: soldiers might get out of control and no longer follow orders.[129]

When army commanders looked at the bigger picture once the smoke on the battlefield had cleared, the Einsatzgruppen actions appeared to them largely in a positive light, and the SS and police top leadership had enough sensitivity

---

124. Order Brauchitsch to army officers, October 25, 1939, BA-MA, RH 26-12/252.

125. Order Brauchitsch to army officers, November 1, 1939, BA-MA, RH 15/73.

126. Order ObdH, February 7, 1940, IfZ, Nuremberg Document NOKW-1799.

127. OB Ost to ObdH, November 27, 1939, BA-MA, RH 1/58; Hildegard von Kotze, ed., *Heeresadjutant bei Hitler 1938–1943. Aufzeichnungen des Majors Engel* (Stuttgart: Deutsche Verlags-Anstalt, 1974), 67–68. On Blaskowitz, see Richard Giziowski, *The Enigma of General Blaskowitz* (London: Leo Cooper, 1997).

128. Notes OB Ost, February 6, 1940, BA-MA, RH 53-23/23.

129. Klaus-Jürgen Müller, "Zu Vorgeschichte und Inhalt der Rede Himmlers vor der höheren Generalität am 13. März 1940 in Koblenz," *VfZ* 18 (1970): 113.

to acknowledge potential misgivings. In a speech before army generals on March 13, 1940, Himmler assured his audience there was nothing to worry about with regard to either the past or the future. As one participant noted, Himmler told them, "I do not do anything that the Führer does not know about."[130] When in July 1940 General Georg von Küchler, commander of the 18th Army, ordered his men to "refrain from any criticism" of "the treatment of Polish minorities, the Jews, and church matters" in the interest of the "final solution of this ethnic struggle, which has been raging on the eastern border for centuries,"[131] Himmler could not have put it better. Disagreements between Wehrmacht generals and Einsatzgruppen commanders during the Polish campaign could be—and indeed were—overcome through shared ideological beliefs and, as military historian Manfred Messerschmidt put it, "the fatal partial sameness of goals" between the leaders of both institutions.

---

130. Müller, "Zu Vorgeschichte und Inhalt der Rede Himmlers," 95.
131. Order OB AOK 18, July 22, 1940, IfZ, Nuremberg Document NOKW-1531.

PART II

Documents and Context

DIRECTIVES AND INITIAL ACTIONS

BEFORE SETTING foot on Polish soil, Einsatzgruppen personnel knew that the Wehrmacht held the key to opening the gate to future German rule in the east. If not particularly pleased about the idea of non-Wehrmacht units operating behind the front line, German military commanders welcomed police support in enforcing security. Each of the five initial Einsatzgruppen was assigned to one of the five armies that invaded Poland and had to report to that army's intelligence officer (the so-called Ic). When in August Sipo/SD chief Reinhard Heydrich and Wehrmacht quartermaster general Eduard Wagner defined the broader parameters of Einsatzgruppen deployment in the area under military jurisdiction, the resulting agreement articulated the willingness of both agencies to cooperate without providing a clear blueprint for action beyond the German-Polish border.

DOCUMENT 1: **Agreement between the Wehrmacht and Sipo/SD regarding "Guidelines for the Foreign Deployment of the Security Police and the SD," undated (August 1939), USHMMA RG 14.016M (BAB, R 58/241), fiche 4:169–75 (translated from German).**

I. General Matters

1) Mission:

The mission of the Einsatzgruppen and Einsatzkommandos has been determined by agreement with the Army High Command (OKH), as is confirmed in a letter from the Army High Command (6. Abt.-II-Gen-StdH. Nr. 1299/39 g.Kdos) dated July 31, 1939: "The mission of the Security Police Einsatzkommandos is to combat all elements hostile to the Reich and to Germans in enemy territory to the rear of the combat troops."

2) Unified Command:

The Einsatzgruppen and Einsatzkommandos of the Security Police consist of members of the Secret State Police, the Criminal Police, and the Security Service. All members are under the direct command of the Einsatzgruppen and Einsatzkommando commanders, who decide on the deployment of the individual members according to the following guidelines.

3) Relationship with the Wehrmacht:

Constant contact is to be maintained with the army command posts, the Chiefs of Civil Administration [Chefs der Zivilverwaltung, CdZ], the German civil administration, and the German Order Police. The commanders of the Einsatzgruppen and Einsatzkommandos are personally responsible for trouble-free communication with these authorities. The orders dealing with the relationship of the Security Police to the Wehrmacht are to be strictly observed.

4) Personal Conduct:

Each member of the Einsatzgruppen is to be firm but correct in his behavior toward everyone, no matter what the situation. The targeted objectives are to be reached in such a way that complaints are avoided, if at all possible.

5) Communication Links:

The immediate establishment and permanent maintenance of communication links is of the greatest importance. Before the commencement of and during the advance, constant communication is to be maintained via the nearest Gestapo duty station with the Gestapo Office in Berlin.

The Einsatzgruppen must submit a daily report once a day to the Chief of the Security Police, advising him of the following:

location of the Einsatzkommando,

presumed location on the following day,

any unusual incidents,

number of arrests (people of particular importance should be listed by name).[1]

Upon reaching the target destination, the Einsatzkommandos are to use all available resources to establish contact with the relevant Einsatzgruppe. The Einsatzgruppen are to maintain constant communications with the Gestapo Office [Geheimes Staatspolizeiamt] in Berlin.

6) Arrests, Searches, and Seizures:

For every arrest, an entry sheet from the issued form books titled "Arrests" is to be completed, with two carbon copies. The original and one carbon copy are to be sent by the quickest means possible to the commander of the Einsatzkommando. He is to forward the original by the quickest means possible to Gestapo Office II D. The carbon copy remains with the commander of the Einsatzkommando. The second carbon copy stays in the form book, which must be given after use to the commander of the Einsatzkommando.

For every confiscation, seizure, search, etc., an entry sheet from the issued form books titled "Searches," with two carbon copies, is to be completed. The original and one carbon copy are also to be forwarded to the commander of the Einsatzkommando, who, by the quickest means possible, is to forward the original to Gestapo Office I F. For arrests, the same procedure is to be followed as above.

The delivery of confiscated items is to be certified by the recipient by signing the second carbon copy of the search report. Particular care should be given to the proper storage and safeguarding of confiscated items.

7) Handling of Persons under Arrest:

It is strictly forbidden to mistreat or kill detainees, and if other persons are undertaking such action, it must be prevented. Force can be used only to break resistance. Persons under arrest are to be initially gathered together in appropriate holding areas. The commanders of the Einsatzgruppen are to ensure that detainees are transported by the quickest means possible to the most accessible State Police post

---

1. At the beginning of the campaign, the frequency of regular reporting from the field was increased to twice daily but, starting October 6, reduced again to one report per day.

[Staatspolizeistelle],² which should be asked to report the detainees' arrival immediately to Gestapo Office II D.

8) Conduct toward the Population:

All nonofficial association with the non-German population is prohibited. Official duties and obligations are to be carried out in a polite, correct, but firm manner. All sexual relations with women or girls of an alien people [*Frauen oder Mädchen fremden Volkstums*] are a sin against our own blood and a disregard for the alien people. Violations will be severely punished.

9) Economic Activities:

The Regulation on Economic Administrative Service during Foreign Deployment of the Gestapo in Special Cases, dated March 13, 1939 (S-V 2 no. 4631/39-251-13), applies in equal measure to members of the Gestapo, Criminal Police, and SD.

10) Support by the Order Police and the Wehrmacht:

If in special cases the forces of the Einsatzgruppen or Einsatzkommandos are insufficient, the commanders are to request support from the Order Police or, if necessary, from the Wehrmacht. In such cases, the Security Police controls the substantive conduct of the action, while authority over Order Police or Wehrmacht units rests with their commanders.

11) Auxiliary Police Officers:

Reliable German nationals [*Reichsdeutsche*] and ethnic Germans [*Volksdeutsche*] can be appointed as auxiliary police officers where and when required. In this connection, the issued printed forms and armbands [identifying members of the auxiliary police] are to be used. The appointments are to be made by the commanders of the Einsatzgruppen or Einsatzkommandos, who are also responsible for the actions of the auxiliary police officers.

12) Disciplinary Authority during Service:

The commander of the Einsatzgruppe has the power to take immediate measures against members of the Security Police and the SD in the event of serious misconduct that damages the reputation of the Security Police. In this context, he can order preventive detention and can immediately punish minor malfeasance in an administrative penalty proceeding, by issuing warnings and reprimands.

---

2. In the Reich, Staatspolizeistellen coordinated the work of the Gestapo on a regional basis. See George C. Browder, *Hitler's Enforcers: The Gestapo and the SS Security Service in the Nazi Revolution* (New York: Oxford University Press, 1996).

The Gestapo Office is to be immediately informed in cases where preventive detention is imposed.

II. State Police Activities

In the districts allocated to them, the Einsatzkommandos must as a general rule perform all the functions that a State Police post must perform in its district, unless otherwise specified below:

1) Arrests:

Those persons listed in the issued Wanted List [*Fahndungsliste*], emigrants who are Reich citizens, and inhabitants who oppose official German measures or are obviously inclined, on the basis of their position and reputation, to cause unrest are to be arrested. Provided no danger is at hand, the Chief of Civil Administration is to be informed before the arrest of influential persons.

2) Preventive Measures:

Prevention of all activity by organizations hostile to Germans and of all anti-German efforts.

Seizure of their buildings, materials, and equipment.

3) Seizures:

Seizure of police buildings and equipment and all other buildings, equipment, papers, card files, etc., required for the activities of the German police.

Seizure of other important buildings, equipment, archives, and records (of associations hostile to the Reich, and of Jews, Freemasons, Marxists, state authorities, state archives, etc.).

III. Criminal Police Activities

Takeover of all criminal police equipment, buildings, documents relating to police records (fingerprint sheets, personal files, arrest warrants), etc.

Takeover of the penal service of the criminal police.

Monitoring of the work of foreign criminal police, to the extent that such a police force is still permitted.

IV. Activities of SD Personnel

Members of the SD shall be involved in executive measures only if danger is imminent. Their mission is:

Immediate establishment of an intelligence network, resumption of existing intelligence connections, especially with confidential informants within the German minorities or local circles known to be reliable.

Less emphasis should be placed on the evaluation of the intelligence and information than on the quickest and most promising way of passing on the information. This work is to be based on the indexes prepared for the overall campaign on the part of the SD: the <u>object card index</u> (information important for intelligence purposes of organizations, associations, and their locations) and the <u>subject card index</u> (information regarding persons of importance for the creation of an intelligence network: confidential informants, agents, and operatives).

Briefing of the leaders of the Einsatzgruppen about all important intelligence procedures, above all about the form and effect of regulations issued by Wehrmacht offices and civil authorities.

Ensuring the evaluation of confiscated enemy materials. Care is to be taken, when archival collections, etc., are seized, to ensure that the captured materials are appropriately stored; experience has shown that careless storing of the material frequently destroys its value, which lies precisely in the nature of the collection. Wherever possible and necessary, SD members are to be involved in confiscations and seizures in subject areas that are handled by the SD (Catholics, Jews, Freemasons).

In other respects, the special instructions of the SD-Hauptamt, which are handed over along with the material referred to in IV 1, par. 2, shall apply.

This document, like most sources generated by German agencies during the Nazi era, only helps to explain historical reality to a limited extent and raises a number of important questions. Why did it make no mention of executions, and what did it mean that Einsatzgruppen personnel were "strictly forbidden to mistreat or kill detainees" while expected to avoid contact with non-Germans and perform their duties "in a polite, correct, but firm manner"? We know that Heydrich's men behaved in exactly the opposite way. How was this possible, and what were the Einsatzgruppen expected to do within and beyond the broad assignment to prevent "all activity by organizations hostile to Germans and of all anti-German efforts"?

As the document suggests, among the few concrete directives issued from above were lists and other compilations containing the names of tens of thousands of Polish suspects put together by Gestapo headquarters in Berlin on the basis of information gathered from spies and informants, usually ethnic Germans living in Poland. Most individuals on the wanted lists belonged to the Polish intelligentsia—teachers, priests, doctors, artists, writers, politicians—or had in the early 1920s been members of Polish insurgent organizations that had fought against German paramilitary units, some of whose members in 1939 filled the ranks of the Einsatzgruppen. These Poles would become the first targets of killings conducted by Heydrich's men.

A widespread consensus existed among the elites in Nazi Germany that a Wehrmacht victory should and would bring about the demise of Poland as a political entity. Prior to the German attack, the idea of ruthless persecution or physical elimination of parts of the Polish population seemed too radical and potentially dangerous for inclusion in written guidelines shared between the participating agencies and distributed down through the lower levels of the hierarchy. Very much in line with the institutional culture established by Himmler and internalized by his SS- and policemen well before the war, Berlin leaders put the decision regarding which methods to apply into the hands of unit commanders. As discussed in part I, they were expected and trained to act autonomously, on the basis of general guidelines from their superiors and their own assessment of conditions on the ground.

At a meeting on August 18, 1939, at Sipo/SD headquarters in Berlin, the assembled Einsatzgruppen commanders learned from their leaders what was expected of them. Because no minutes of the conference exist, the only available sources are postwar interrogations of the participants. In the mid-1960s, West Berlin prosecutors interrogated Lothar Beutel, former commander of Einsatzgruppe IV.[3] Usually, defendants suspected or accused of mass murder in the former occupied territories tried to justify themselves with reference to orders from above that they had to follow. Beutel gravely incriminated himself by admitting that neither during this preattack meeting nor later had he received such an order and that his superiors left executive decisions to him and his fellow commanders. This increases the credibility of his testimony, since he obviously had no interest in denying the existence of superior orders that would have helped in his defense.

DOCUMENT 2: Interrogation of Lothar Beutel, former commander of Einsatzgruppe IV, in West Berlin, July 20, 1965, BAL, B 162/Vorl. Dok. Slg. Leitzordner Einsatzgruppen in Polen II (translated from German).

Around the middle of August 1939, a conference took place here in Berlin on Prinz-Albrecht-Strasse, to which the future leaders of the Einsatzgruppen were invited, among others. At the conference, Heydrich and Himmler sketched out the missions of the Einsatzgruppen along general lines. At that time, we were informed that our primary mission was to provide security for the area to the rear of the combat element. In addition, we were to prevent and oppose any resistance and ensure the safety of the rear forces. Details were provided only to the extent that

---

3. For biographical information on Beutel, see Part I, p. 10n34.

we were told everything was permitted for the purpose of countering resistance movements and groups; that is, both executions and arrests were authorized. The decision about which action to take rested with the implementing units, that is, with the Einsatzkommandos subordinated to the Einsatzgruppe staff unit [*Gruppenstab*]. If I remember correctly, the Einsatzkommando leaders were also present during the discussions. There was no detailed discussion at that time of explicit measures against the Polish intelligentsia. There were allusions to such steps, however, and it was obvious that the driving force of the resistance was to be sought among the members of the Polish intelligentsia. The extent and the nature of the measures were determined in the first days of the Polish campaign, in the first weeks to be more precise, and were based on the events of the day. That is, a decision was only made on the spot as to what was necessary, again with the implementing units, that is, the Einsatzkommandos, naturally making the necessary decisions. [. . .]

As commander of the Einsatzgruppe, I never received any written orders at all; at least I cannot recall having done so. In my opinion, the Einsatzkommando leaders and Einsatzgruppe staff section chiefs [*Abteilungsleiter*] could not have received orders from Berlin, at least not at the beginning. It was not technically possible. We stayed only a short time at each place, and there was no organized radio and Teletype communication. At most, short radio messages about Einsatzgruppen movements may have been sent during the advance. Later, when the Einsatzgruppe had become somewhat stationary, instructions did indeed come from Berlin via radio and Teletype. [. . .]

I can recall that once, in September, I was ordered to Berlin for a discussion. It may have been on September 21, 1939. The discussion was led by Heydrich. Besides me, the other commanders of the Einsatzgruppen participated, and I am no longer certain whether it was at this discussion or at the one in August that von Ribbentrop described the foreign affairs situation. I can recall that at this conference it was stated, among other things, that resistance in Poland in the future would decrease if as few as possible members of the Polish intelligentsia survived. I cannot recall, however, that direct orders to kill the intelligentsia were given at this conference. The talk was in general terms, of "safeguarding" ["*Sicherstellung*"]. The purpose of this had already been made clear, however, by the remark previously mentioned: the fewer the survivors, the less the resistance.

The path taken by the Einsatzgruppen after the start of the German military attack would lead them into uncharted territory. How, for instance, could their Berlin superiors be sure the carte blanche they issued to field officers would be used in the regime's interest? No doubt these officers had worked well for the Sipo/SD prior to 1939 and seemed keen on further career advancement. One means chosen by Himmler and Heydrich to prepare unit commanders for their tasks was a two-week training course held in June 1939 at the Bernau SD School near Berlin.[4] The group of lecturers assembled comprised SDHA department heads and experts, among them Herbert Hagen, the SD's "specialist on Jews" (*Judenreferent*), who presented on the topic "Jewry as a General Political Opponent: Its Significance in Poland." Other SD officers spoke about the role of churches, Freemasons, Polish politics, economics, minorities, and Bolshevism. However, the amount of information seems to have been too much for many course participants to digest.[5] Later Heydrich decided to cut down on abstract lessons for Einsatzgruppen officers; they would learn more, he told them, "when you are active at the front."[6]

The mechanisms and processes cultivated among Einsatzgruppen members through shared experiences became as important for the course of further events as their prewar socialization and practical lessons. Research into the behavior of Nazi functional elites has shown how important peer pressure and other group dynamics—some obvious, others subtle—were in shaping the attitudes and actions of individuals.[7] While on high alert awaiting deployment, the men of Einsatzgruppe II in Opole (German: Oppeln) spent their evenings for the most part drinking, listening to the radio, or going to the movies together. On the afternoon of August 27, 1939, they saw the Hungarian-German film *Between River and Steppe* (*Zwischen Strom und Steppe*), a clichéd depiction of life in a small Hungarian fishing village blended with an ideological message. In

---

4. Outline for Bernau training course, undated (ca. May 1939), USHMMA RG 14.016M (BAB, R 58/827), fiche 3; Włodzimierz Borodziej, *Terror und Politik: Die deutsche Polizei und die polnische Widerstandsbewegung im Generalgouvernement 1939–1944* (Mainz: Philipp von Zabern, 1999), 29.

5. SDHA I/2 to SDHA III, July 7, 1939, USHMMA RG 14.016M (BAB, R 58/827), fiche 3.

6. SDHA I 11, September 13, 1939, USHMMA RG 14.016M (BAB, R 58/825), fiche 1:7–9.

7. Christopher R. Browning, *Ordinary Men: Reserve Police Battalion 101 and the Final Solution in Poland* (New York: HarperPerennial, 1998), 69, 80, 82–84, 93, 99–100; Thomas Kühne, *Belonging and Genocide: Hitler's Community, 1918–1945* (New Haven, CT: Yale University Press, 2010), esp. chaps. 2–3.

it, a gypsy stabs a homeless tramp—a "Nordic type" named Silo—from behind on the bank of the River Theiss (Hungarian: Tirza; Romanian: Tira). Simple, poverty-stricken fishermen care for him until he recovers. Silo, in return, shows them the benefits of civilization, teaches them to swim, and advises them not to barter but to ask for money for their produce. With the help of an ethnic German master carpenter, he builds them a new boat. In a fight he kills his assailant, the lover of a gypsy-witch temptress.[8] Twenty-seven-year old SS-Hauptsturmführer Erich Ehlers, staff officer in Einsatzgruppe II, was probably not alone in his assessment, confided to his diary, that the movie gave the men a "foretaste of the 'conditions in the East.'"[9]

DOCUMENT 3: Diary notes by SS-Hauptsturmführer Erich Ehlers, Einsatzgruppe II, for August 19 to September 1, 1939, CAW (translated from German).

[. . .]

Aug. 19. Receipt of equipment: steel helmet, gas mask, officer's footlocker, field-gray uniform, etc.

Aug. 21. At night, 23:28, departure from the [Berlin-]Friedrichstrasse station with regular express train. Destination of E.Gr. II [Einsatzgruppe II] is initially Oppeln.

Aug. 22. 7:17, arrival in Oppeln. Quarters: "Forms Hotel."—Newspaper reports: German-Russian Non-Aggression Pact.

[glued in: portion of bill for room 31, Forms Hotel, Oppeln]

Aug. 23. Performance of duties at the U.A. [*Unterabschnitt*, local SD office], at Sedanstrasse 6; 13:30–20:20 duty officer.

[. . .]

Aug. 25. On heightened alert! Now we just slept at the duty station of the U.A.—on the floor.

Aug. 26. 9:30 [a.m.], immunization with typhus vaccine, resulting in two "corpses."[10] 14:00 duty officer.

Aug. 27. At the movies in the afternoon. *Zwischen Strom und Steppe*, providing a foretaste of the "conditions in the East."

---

8. *Zwischen Strom und Steppe* was directed by Geza von Bolvary, based on the novel with the same title by Michael Zorn, and produced in Germany/Hungary in 1938.

9. Erich Ehlers (b. 1912 in Kiel) had joined the SS in 1933 and from 1934 worked at the SDHA. He took part in the first Einsatzgruppen deployment in Vienna and Prague in 1938–1939 and on July 15, 1939, gave a lecture titled "Jews and Freemasons" as part of an SD training course (NARA, BDC-SSO file Erich Ehlers).

10. Reference to two officers getting sick as a result of the vaccination.

Aug. 28. In the morning the second group was immunized, in the evening we emptied a bottle of cognac together. Duty officer until 14:00.

Aug. 29. 10:30–15:00, travel to Leobschütz [Polish: Głubczyce] and Neustadt [Polish: Prudnik]. On the way we saw many troops. There's something in the air! Starting at 21:00 duty officer.

Aug. 30. In the afternoon, travel to Gross-Strehlen [Polish: Strzelin] and Gleiwitz [Polish: Gliwice]. Everywhere, uniforms are plentiful. Visited the memorial on the Annaberg [Polish: Góra Świętej Anny].[11] In the evening it was already quite cool.

Aug. 31. Still uncertainty and waiting. Polish radio is very agitated [*aufgeregt*].

[photo (removed); caption:] Annaberg

Sept. 1. The invasion of Poland is beginning, but not for us. We wait and hear the Poles' cries of fear: *Uwarga! Uwarga!* [*uwaga*: "danger," "watch out," "attention"] *Stefan! Karol*, etc. Kattowitz [Polish: Katowice] radio station soon falls silent.

Expectations and fears associated with the attack contributed to shaping behavior. After the war, Einsatzgruppen members remembered having been given to understand "that the wells might be poisoned and the ethnic Germans in Poland were in great danger, and that our advance, or rather, the advance of Wehrmacht units into Poland was a race against time to save the lives of the ethnic Germans"; once in Poland, they were told, "there [would be] well-trained paramilitary units" expected to act as partisans behind the German lines.[12] Among the German military, precampaign perceptions about what to expect beyond the border were similar. With the whole Polish population regarded as hostile and the Nazi leadership having decided to wage a ruthless war, the mere suspicion of resistance sufficed to trigger ruthless measures on the part of the invaders. Although no organized partisan movement existed in Poland in 1939—one Einsatzgruppen officer said that it was "as if the population was paralyzed. No one thought of resistance"[13]——commanders used the

---

11. Reference to a hill located southeast of Opole where a battle between Polish and German paramilitary units took place in May 1921.

12. Interrogation of Horst W. (former member of Einsatzgruppe IV), June 23, 1965, BAL, B 162/Vorl. AR-Z 13/63, 4:694; see also interrogation of Hubert S. (formerly of Einsatzkommando 1/I), February 5, 1971, BAL, B 162/Vorl. AR-Z 302/67, 2:405.

13. Interrogation of Georg Schraepel (formerly of Einsatzgruppe I), April 16, 1964, BAL, B 162/3622, 224.

ongoing shooting behind the front (mostly caused by dispersed Polish soldiers or friendly fire) or mere allegations of attacks on Germans as a pretext for violent "reprisals."[14]

As shown by document 4, a file note by a chief of civil administration at the end of the first week of the campaign, security concerns would remain a shared interest between Wehrmacht authorities and the Einsatzgruppen. By stressing the omnipresence of "gangs," "partisans," and "bandits" and the need to intensify "pacification," Sipo and SD officers—in this case Hans Fischer,[15] commander of Einsatzgruppe III (in the document identified by his civilian rank, not by his SS officer status)—could legitimize the use of violence as an indispensable means for anchoring German rule.

DOCUMENT 4: **Notice by the Chief of Civil Administration of the 8th Army, September 6, 1939, APŁ, 175/10 b (translated from German).**

Commander of the Einsatzgruppe, Oberregierungsrat Fischer, hereby informs:

Proof has been obtained that partisans [*Freischärler*] are shooting German troops in Army rear areas. Thus the [Einsatz-]Gruppe is on edge.

Cattle are running around everywhere, not being looked after. No one to catch them.

Criminal elements are roving about behind the front.

German police forces are urgently needed. Systematic use of auxiliary police is desired.

The posted notices of the Supreme Commander, especially the demand to surrender weapons, are displayed only along the advance routes. The villages and farms not on the routes are unaware of the orders. Owners of weapons therefore could not be punished for possessing firearms. Here police protection is also absent.

Polish gang leaders caught without weapons and therefore not shot immediately must be shot once it is certain that they, acting as gang leaders, have organized armed resistance by some portion of the civil population after withdrawal of the Polish troops. [. . .]

---

14. Jochen Böhler, *Auftakt zum Vernichtungskrieg: Die Wehrmacht in Polen 1939* (Frankfurt am Main: Fischer Taschenbuch Verlag, 2006), 57–60.

15. For biographical information on Fischer, see p. 10n33.

One day later, military units in the area of the 8th Army were authorized to shoot armed civilians and "assassins" instead of handing them over to the Einsatzgruppen, since the evidence against them was not expected to be sufficient for further investigations.[16]

The available record suggests that German expectations of Polish resistance triggered the first shootings. As they approached Częstochowa (German: Tschenstochau), Einsatzgruppen and the Wehrmacht anticipated violent opposition from the local population.[17] The city was seat of the Jasna Góra Monastery, home to the Black Madonna icon credited with many miracles and a symbol of Polish national desire for freedom; during the 1919–1921 German-Polish conflict in Upper Silesia, the monastery had served as the logistical base for the Polish guerrillas. On September 4, soldiers of Infantry Regiments 42 and 97 shot more than two hundred Polish and Jewish men, women, and children in the city as bloody revenge for what were most likely two incidents of friendly fire.[18] The Einsatzgruppen were rather hesitant to report details about their mass shootings during the first days of the 1939 campaign and only referred to allegedly singular "incidents" with relatively small numbers of victims in their daily reports and diary entries. Erich Ehlers had barely touched Polish soil when his unit got involved in what came to be referred to as "executive action" in and near Częstochowa. In his diary, following his impressionistic descriptions before crossing the border and a copy of Himmler's September 1 order to all SS men to do "more than their duty," Ehlers noted the execution of people he called "cutthroats" (*Rasiermesserhelden*; literally: "razorblade heroes"), among them Jews, as if they had stepped out of a gangster novel. When and by whom the accompanying—and, after the war, highly incriminating—photographs were removed from his diary can no longer be ascertained.

DOCUMENT 5: Diary notes by SS-Hauptsturmführer Erich Ehlers, Einsatzgruppe II, for September 1 to 5, 1939, CAW (translated from German).

Sept. 2. We're supposed to get going, too. But things got stuck at "supposed to." 11:00, scheduled departure time, 12:40 back to the command headquarters.

16. Daily order no. 2 by Chief of Civil Administration at Eighth Army, September 7, 1939, APP, 298/49.

17. See Böhler, *Auftakt*, 36–41; interrogation of Horst W., June 23, 1965, BAL, B 162/ Vorl. AR-Z 13/63, 4:694.

18. Böhler, *Auftakt*, 98–106.

Sept. 3. In the afternoon, at the movies after a great meal at "Form" [Hotel] (4 RM). In the evening, duty officer. At noon, abortive attempt to depart.

Sept. 4. Departure of the headquarters personnel of Einsatzgruppe II with cars and trucks, in the direction of the border. First stop in Lublinitz. Two Einsatzkommandos have been located in the local school for deaf-mutes since the previous day. There, three Polish cutthroats [*Rasiermesserhelden*] were handed over to us. Execution in the woods on the Lublinitz-Tschenstochau road. One of them still ate a piece of bread, even after the pit had been dug and the guns were already pointed at him.

Noon: Arrival in Tschenstochau, a so-called large city. We were billeted in the "Handlowy Bank" on Piłsudski Street. Midday meal at the Hotel Polonia. Shortly after 14:00 there is shooting all over the place. Rifles and machine guns operated by stealthy rooftop snipers. A good bit of trouble's brewing. I'm commander of the guard and duty officer. We supply two double sentries and one rooftop sentry. The watchword is: Be alert! We all sleep fully dressed in our uniforms.

In the afternoon: one cutthroat.

Sept. 5. In the afternoon: Execution of two Jew[ish] cutthroats in the grounds opposite the command headquarters.

[Photograph missing]

[caption:] Commanders, from left: Breun, Raser, Schmidt.

Shooters, from left: Penning, Kock, Gegenwart, Leube, Westphal, Becker.

I stood at front right and had brought the condemned men before the shooting squad.

Execution squad at attention!

[Photograph missing]

[caption:] A few minutes later! Racial comrades [*Rassegenossen*, meaning fellow Jews] cover the corpses with earth. (I stood to the right, next to the Jew!)

Einsatzgruppe II stated that "in the end it cannot be determined who shot at whom" in Częstochowa and partly blamed the jumpiness of military authorities for the massacre of civilians.[19] Nevertheless, in the two weeks that followed, the unit executed seventy-two people labeled as "hostages," "insurgents," or

---

19. CdS daily report for September 6, 1939, USHMMA RG 15.007 (BAB, R 58/7001), reel 2, file 1:6.

"partisans";[20] on September 17 in Lubliniec (German: Lubinitz), it shot 182 civilian prisoners alleged to be "insurgents, looters, etc."[21]

What attributes or behavior would have made a Polish civilian a security threat in the eyes of German soldiers and policemen? On September 3, Himmler advised his men that "insurgents" (*Aufständische*) were "all persons who individually or communally attack members of the German occupation forces, or *Volksdeutsche* [ethnic Germans], or who threaten institutions and properties critical to protecting the lives of these persons in the occupied territories" and encouraged taking hostages from among "leading figures from the local Polish political administration."[22] The violence of the war made the German occupiers susceptible to suspecting persons who met this vague description, especially among those deemed racially or otherwise "undesirable." After the war, Polish authorities gathered evidence of Nazi crimes by interrogating thousands of eyewitnesses. Roman Tynczyk gave a graphic report on what happened near his hometown of Ślesin (German: Schlüsselsee), east of Poznań (German: Posen), at the beginning of September 1939.

DOCUMENT 6: Testimony by Roman Tynczyk, 1939 inhabitant of Ślesin, June 1, 1970, BAL, B 162/Vorl. AR-Z 124/78, vol. 3:407–8 (translated from German).

One day shortly after the invasion of the German troops, I was sitting with three colleagues in the ditch on the road that leads from Ślesin to Sępolno [German: Sompolno]. Suddenly we noticed some people who were fleeing from Ślesin. They said that German gendarmes were picking up Poles. Two of my colleagues and I thus hid in the reeds along Lake Mikorzyń-Wąsowski. Franciszek Waszak from Rozopole did not hide with us. He remained behind, telling us that he was born in Hamburg and that the Germans would do nothing to him. At most they would offer him a cigar. From my hiding spot in the reeds, I saw Germans in black uniforms arresting people on the road. They also arrested Franciszek Waszak. I saw how they pulled a young Pole off a cart, while they let the old man sitting on the cart go free. After a time, I heard a lot of shots. That day the Germans shot 18 Poles in Różopole. I did not see the shooting. But when I left my hiding place, I saw a fairly large fresh grave in the marsh

20. CdS daily reports for September 8–17, 1939, USHMMA RG 15.007M (BAB, R 58/7001), reel 2, file 1:17–113.

21. See document 10.

22. Secret order by Himmler, September 3, 1939; cf. Alexander B. Rossino, *Hitler Strikes Poland: Blitzkrieg, Ideology, and Atrocity* (Lawrence: University Press of Kansas, 2003), 66.

grasses. The corpses were only lightly covered with earth, which was "moving," and that indicated that some of those who were shot were still alive. After about six weeks, local Jews exhumed the corpses, put them in a box, and transported them to a mass grave in the Roman Catholic cemetery. Among the dead was Franciszek Waszak.

Gdańsk (German: Danzig) and its surrounding region had been a center of German culture since the Middle Ages and became an extraterritorial "free city" after World War I; most of its inhabitants were ethnic Germans rather than Poles. After 1933, its city government had grown increasingly dependent on the German Reich and become dominated by Nazi Party members. Sharing one border with eastern Prussia and open to the Baltic Sea, Gdańsk was easy prey for invading German forces, which had already taken control of the city on September 1, 1939. Acts of ruthless revenge conducted by local German members of the police—from whose ranks Einsatzkommando 16 was recruited on September 12, 1939—accompanied the first arrests of Polish and Jewish citizens.

DOCUMENT 7: **Testimony by Władysława Winiecka, 1939 inhabitant of Danzig, September 29, 1973, BAL, B 162/Vorl. AR-Z 51/75, vol. 1:112–13 (translated from German).**

[. . .] My brother was a Polish activist and belonged to almost all the Polish organizations in the Gdańsk area. He was also president of the Gdańsk Polish community. On September 1, 1939, immediately after the outbreak of the second world war, my husband, Jan Winiecki, born around 1881, probably in Juncewo, Żnin [German: Znin] District, son of Jozef and Michalina, was arrested by Gestapo functionaries who were unknown to me and was locked up in the Viktoria School. A week later my brother Roman, too, was arrested and locked up in the same school. A few days later I visited my husband in the Viktoria School. At that time I learned from him and his fellow prisoners, whose names I no longer remember, that my brother Roman Ogryczak had been taken by Gestapo officials, led by Antoni Reiwer,[23] to the third floor, where he was beaten severely, almost to death. Then Antoni Reiwer and the other Gestapo officials, whom they did not know, threw my brother down onto the stone floor of the ground floor. My sister-in-law was able to get his body released. I saw his corpse.

---

23. The authors have been unable to locate information on Roman Ogryczak. The Gestapo man was most likely Anton Reiwer (b. 1896 in Culm in West Prussia), a World War I veteran who during World War II became an SS-Obersturmbannführer. See NARA, BDC-SSO file Anton Reiwer.

My brother's face and head were badly crushed. [. . .] My brother's corpse was buried in the Gdańsk Cemetery in a location known as the "Little Rabbit Mountain." After a while, my husband was taken to the Oranienburg-Sachsenhausen concentration camp, where he was murdered in June 1940.

Given the intensity and rapidity of the campaign, German documents not surprisingly often convey a distorted image of the fate of those targeted in the course of "pacifying" the occupied territory. For instance, Einsatzgruppen reports did not mention the town of Limanowa (German: Ilmenau) in southern Poland. Yet we can glimpse what happened there immediately after the German occupation through the testimony of witnesses who saw what members of one Einsatzkommando—discernible from other German forces by their uniforms—did to some of the town's inhabitants.

DOCUMENT 8: Testimony by Zofia Semik on German violence in Limanowa, May 13, 1977, BAL, B 162/Vorl. AR-Z 304/77-K-:14–15 (translated from German).

Before World War II, I lived with my husband, Jan Semik, and my four children in Limanowa. My husband ran the chimney-sweep business. In early September, when the real town administrator left Limanowa, the function of deputy town administrator was assigned to my husband. On September 12, 1939, around 3:00 p.m., Germans entered our house. There were six of them, in green coats with black epaulettes, with visored caps and skulls on the caps. [. . .] The Germans had a list with names of Limanowa inhabitants, and at the top of this list was my husband, Jan Semik. The other names on the list were those of Jews, rich craftsmen, and businessmen from Limanowa. [. . .] I was able to get into a room on the ground floor of the rectory, and in this room I saw Germans sitting behind a table. There were several of them, and men who were beaten and bloody were lying on the floor. Among them I recognized my husband. His face was bleeding, and one eye and some teeth were knocked out. The other men on the floor were Jews, craftsmen, and businessmen from Limanowa. [. . .] The guard standing at the door to this room shoved me out of the room and punched me in the face and threw the six-month-old baby in my arms against the church wall. [. . .] Previously—I was thrown out of the rectory after that—I heard the Germans sitting behind the table read out the name of my husband. Falling onto the road, I fainted. When I came to after some time, I noticed a truck in front of the rectory and Germans with machine guns, who were leading my husband and ten Jews to the truck. They had been held in the rectory together with my husband,

and I gave their names earlier [in this testimony]. I saw the vehicle drive off in the direction of Mordarka. As I learned later, my husband's hunting dog ran after the truck, and behind the dog, my 7-year-old son, Łukasz. My son came across my brother Władysław Lesiecki—he is no longer alive—and told him that the dog was chasing the truck carrying my husband, and that the vehicle was headed in the direction of Mordarka, near the quarry. My brother went to Mordarka, and when he came to my house around 5:00 p.m., he told me that the Germans had murdered my husband and ten Jews, and that the corpses were in the quarry at Mordarka.

Once in the war zone, German soldiers and policemen were prone to seeing local residents through the lens of racial prejudice and prewar propaganda. The fact that Jews figured prominently in the photographs taken during Einsatzgruppen actions highlights that they appeared as a special group within a large population deemed hostile. Like the written German documentation produced at the time, these photographs do not always allow us to draw conclusions about what happened next to the persons depicted. This applies to the images in document 9 taken by photographers of a German propaganda unit in southern Poland.

DOCUMENT 9: **Photographs of Jews arrested by Sipo/SD in the area of Ustronie/Opatów, undated (September 1939), Bundesarchiv Bildarchiv Bild 101I-380-0069-34, 39.**

Wehrmacht commanders, eager to assert their executive authority over Heydrich's men, would on occasion intervene against Einsatzgruppen activities. Thus, on September 12, a few days after the German army had occupied Lubliniec in Upper Silesia, Einsatzgruppe II moved in and took over roughly 180 Polish civilians and young recruits locked up in the local court prison. The next day Wehrmacht Major Rudolf Langhaeuser, staff officer of Army Group South (Heeresgruppe Süd), had an argument with Einsatzgruppe II officers who cited execution orders.

DOCUMENT 10: **Notes for a report by Army Group South (Oberquartiermeister IV) for Oberbefehlshaber von Brauchitsch, September 17, 1939, BAL, Dok. Slg. USA 15:26a (translated from German).**

The Ic [enemy intelligence officer] of Army Group South, Major i. G. [im Generalstab] Langhaeuser, has reported the following by telephone:[24]
    On September 12, while the headquarters in Lublinitz was being moved forward, 180 civilian prisoners were handed over to Einsatzgruppe Tschenstochau. On the evening of September 12, it was learned in

24. See also the witness statement by Rudolf Langhaeuser, April 30, 1967, BAL, B 162/16660.

conversation that these people were to be shot by the Einsatzgruppe. The Ic immediately ordered the people to be handed over to the local Wehrmacht commander [*Ortskommandant*]. This order was carried out.

On September 13, the Ic had a heated argument with an [SS] Untersturmführer who was demanding that the prisoners be handed over. Handover was denied. The Ic immediately went to the commander of the Einsatzgruppe in Tschenstochau (Obersturmbannführer Dr. Schäfer). The latter explained that he had received an order from the Reichsführer-SS to shoot all members of Polish insurgent organizations. In Tarnow [Polish: Tarnów] and Kattowitz [Polish: Katowice], the shootings have already taken place. The Ic succeeded in keeping the prisoners in Lublinitz under the guard of the local Wehrmacht commander there.

The Commander of Army Group South has received no information whatsoever regarding the order of the Reichsführer-SS.

On September 17 at 10:00 a.m. Dr. Best of the Berlin Gestapo, in reply to a query from the Chief of the Army Military Police [Heeresfeldpolizeichef], stated that no order from the Reichsführer-SS calling for the summary execution of insurgents had come to his attention. Only pointed directives in accordance with the wishes of the Führer had been issued, calling for actions against insurgents to be taken. He would look into the matter, however.

At 12:15 p.m., two senior police officers informed Major Kossmann (quartermaster general) that the order to shoot all Polish insurgents immediately (without trial) had been issued directly from the Führer's train [mobile headquarters] to the Einsatzkommandos of the Gestapo and commanders of the Order Police.

Einsatzgruppe II shot 182 prisoners from the Lubliniec prison.[25] Without support from his Wehrmacht superiors, Major Langhaeuser was unable to prevent the executions, even though he could prove that Schäfer's claim to be acting on Himmler's orders was an invention. Elsewhere Einsatzgruppen leaders did not face opposition from the army when relentlessly pushing for radical action. Their activism provided fuel for an escalation of violence, sometimes even side by side with the armed forces.

---

25. CdS reports for September 20, 1939; for September 19–20, see Rossino, *Hitler Strikes Poland*, 85.

The atrocities in the city and surroundings of Bydgoszcz (German: Bromberg) offer a case study of the factors driving the German course of action in the early phase of the attack on Poland. After World War I, the formerly German city had become part of the Second Polish Republic, causing many citizens of German nationality to leave. In 1939, about ten thousand of its remaining inhabitants—6.4 percent of the city's overall population—were of German origin. On the morning of September 3, 1939, a Sunday, exhausted Polish troops retreated through the streets of Bydgoszcz, when suddenly shots were fired, the origins of which have never been established. The soldiers immediately suspected ethnic Germans and, with the assistance of Polish civilians, subsequently killed approximately 350 of them—mostly men—within the city borders and several hundred more on the outskirts of Bydgoszcz.[26]

After the Wehrmacht had taken over the city on September 5, the German propaganda machine immediately seized upon the "Bloody Sunday of Bromberg" ("*Bromberger Blutsonntag*") and hugely inflated the number of *Volksdeutsche* victims. In and around Bydgoszcz, the killings triggered a violent German backlash. Roland Freisler, the state secretary in the Reich Ministry of Justice, visited the city on September 9 to see whether special courts would work according to legal protocol. He was assured that commanding Wehrmacht officers had no problem with the fact that "the troops have spoken" by shooting several hundred civilians "for carrying arms or resisting."[27] The first detachment of Einsatzgruppe IV—Einsatzkommando 1/IV—reached Bydgoszcz after the retreat of the Polish troops on September 5. Side by side, Wehrmacht soldiers and Einsatzgruppen men arrested suspects, as documented in the photographic record they themselves created.

---

26. See Paweł Kosiński, "Ofiary pierwszych dni września 1939 roku w Bygoszczy," in *Bydgoszcz 3–4 września 1939: Studia i dokumenty*, ed. Tomasz Chinciński and Paweł Machcewicz (Warsaw: IPN-Komisja Ścigania Zbrodni przeciwko Narodowi Polskiemu, 2008), 253–328; Rossino, *Hitler Strikes Poland*, 62–73; Włodzimierz Jastrzębski, *Der Bydgoszczer Blutsonntag: Legende und Wirklichkeit* (Poznań: Westinstitut, 1990; Doris L. Bergen, "Instrumentalization of 'Volksdeutschen' in German Propaganda in 1939. Replacing/ Erasing Poles, Jews, and Other Victims," *German Studies Review* 31 (2008): 447-70.). Women and children were among those killed, but their number cannot be established with any degree of certainty. For the files of a wartime German investigation into the Bydgoszcz killings, see BA-MA, RW 2/51.

27. War diary, Commander 580th Rear Army Area, September 9, 1939, BA-MA, RH 23/167.

DOCUMENT 11: **Photograph of Polish clergy and prominent citizens arrested by members of Einsatzgruppe IV, police, and German soldiers on the Bydgoszcz market square, undated (September 9–11, 1939), USHMMPA WS# 50837.**

According to the leader of EK 1/IV, thirty-one-year-old SS-Sturmbannführer Helmuth Bischoff,[28] "fate destined that [his] Einsatzkommando was the first to arrive in this unhappy city and to see the countless victims and it was the first to take revenge." Writing later in 1939, Bischoff claimed that he and his men underwent "an inner transformation" to an extent they never would have imagined a week earlier: "In this short time we became as hard as steel; we were won over by an immoveable conviction: a nation that commits such acts of cruelty has lost forever its right to be one of Europe's people of culture."[29] Yet the transformation, if any, was hardly surprising. When he entered Bydgoszcz, Bischoff could not have overlooked the impact of Luftwaffe air raids and the extent of Wehrmacht executions of civilians and prisoners of war. He had

---

28. Helmuth Bischoff (1908–1993) joined the Nazi Party in 1930, studied law, and in November 1935 took over command of the Gestapo office in the Silesian town of Liegnitz (Polish: Legnica). From August 1940 to September 1941, he was head of the Gestapo in Posen (Polish: Poznań). In February 1945 he became KdS z.b.V. for Mittelbau-Dora in the Harz Mountains in Germany, where he was responsible for subterranean V-weapon production and for countless executions of forced laborers.

29. Helmuth Bischoff, EK im Polenfeldzug, undated (ca. 1939), IPNW, NTN 196/180.

personally heard at the above-mentioned conference in Berlin on August 18, as another participant recalled after the war, that the men were expected to excel in the "fight against saboteurs, partisans, Jewry, the Polish intelligentsia, and the punishment of attacks on the ethnic German minority in Poland."[30]

Like other field officers handed the authority to act as the situation required, Bischoff decided to make use of his executive power. In a police action he led personally on September 5 in the neighboring town of Nakło (German: Nakel), Bischoff shot, in broad daylight, a civilian suspected of looting, explaining that he had no time "to deal with such criminals." During the night of September 7–8, when a German order policeman and a Wehrmacht soldier were shot dead by unknown assailants, he and his men swore "bloody revenge! Our decision to deal radically with this rabble was unshakeable."[31] Bischoff's report—an intended contribution to a chronicle of Bydgoszcz under German rule that was never published—provides an extraordinary glimpse not only of early German terror in Bydgoszcz but also of Bischoff's reflections on this period and his attempt to highlight his own leading role in a situation that he already perceived as having historic importance.

DOCUMENT 12: **Report by Helmuth Bischoff, leader of Einsatzkommando 1/IV, on his deployment in Bydgoszcz, September 7 and 8, 1939, undated (late 1939), IPNW, NTN 196/180 (translated from German).**

[. . .] [September 7, 1939]

After uninterrupted and brisk shooting by unknown Polish snipers also went on during this night on almost every street in Bromberg and in particular near our office building, which was surrounded by garden plots, we went to the local commander at the city hall the following morning to urge him to undertake forceful and draconian deterrent measures. Unfortunately, the first local commander, the energetic General von Gablentz, had already been replaced and had moved on with the forces. In his place we found a helpless little man put into a major's uniform, who carried out his duty as in peacetime, in long trousers. This gentleman was appalled by the demands made of him by the Security Police along with the Commander of the Order Police, General von Mülverstedt. In reply to our demand that 50 hostages be shot in public,

---

30. Interrogation of Ernst Gerke, September 15, 1965, BAL, B 162/Vorl. Dok. Slg. Einsatzgruppen in Polen I.

31. Bischoff, EK im Polenfeldzug.

he declared that he would have 10 hostages shot if he received another report that once again a German soldier or police officer had been shot down from behind by the Poles. If, on the other hand, we ourselves were prepared to accept responsibility for such measures, then he would do nothing to stop us; he, however, could not be responsible for such a drastic step. This information was quite enough for us, and after briefly and meaningfully looking each other in the eye, we took leave of the local commander. Steps were immediately taken to prepare for the execution of hostages, to be selected from among the prisoners from every walk of life. After the Poles even had the colossal gall to shoot at us from the church at the market square at noon, the first executions of hostages took place at last, in full public view, in the market square. Eight rooftop snipers who were hauled out of the church, as well as the priest, were shot along with them. This pious gentleman had solemnly and expressly assured me only the previous day that everything was fine in his church and that there were no strangers on the church grounds.

[September 8, 1939]

When night fell on the third day of our stay in Bromberg, we fully expected new attacks, and so we resorted to a measure born of necessity to protect our quarters. In broad daylight, around 5:00 p.m., 14 Jewish and Polish male hostages were already standing before the men's quarters in front of the hotel entrance. They themselves and the Polish passers-by were well aware that with every shot fired that night in our street, one of them would be killed. Because even this did not discourage the Polish snipers, the fate of the hostages was sealed.

For Bischoff and his men, the brutal repression of any sign of Polish defiance was legitimate, while attacks on ethnic Germans in Bydgoszcz came in handy to provide further justification. Search and raid parties—often including local residents willing, for whatever reason, to provide useful assistance to the invaders—swept through the city.

DOCUMENT 13: Photograph of a group of SS, police, and ethnic German auxiliaries preparing to conduct a search during the "pacification" of Bydgoszcz, undated (September–November 1939), USHMMPA WS# 15872.

When the Commander of the Wehrmacht's 580th Rear Army Area (Korück 580), SS-Brigadeführer Walter Braemer, took over control in Bydgoszcz on September 8, he was eager to perpetuate the violent momentum generated during the first days of the German occupation.

DOCUMENT 14: War diary of the Commander of the 580th Rear Army Area regarding the situation in Bydgoszcz on the morning of September 9, 1939, BA-MA, RH 23/167 (translated from German).

During the night of September 8–9, 1939, there was repeated shooting in the city. One member of Anti-tank Unit [Panzerabwehr-Abteilung] 218 was seriously wounded.

Mopping-up operations [*Säuberungsaktionen*] by the individual troop units to date have resulted in the following:

200–300 Polish civilians have been shot. Information from the Bromberg town commander [*Ortskommandantur*]. Acting Mayor Kampe estimates the number of those shot at 400 or more. No precise details are available. Carried out by police, SD, Einsatzgruppe, and field elements, primarily Luftwaffe Signal Communications Regiment [Flieger Nachrichten Regiment] 1.

Between 400 and 500 civilians interned, taken off the street at random by the troops occupying Bromberg. Number will increase to 1,400 by September 10, 1939. Includes many refugees flooding back.

Braemer adjusted quickly to the opportunities opening up for radical reprisal actions. September 10, 1939, marked a new stage in the escalation process but was only dimly reflected in the reports generated by the military commander.

DOCUMENT 15: **War diary of the Commander of the 580th Rear Army Area regarding the situation in Bydgoszcz on September 10, 1939, BA-MA, RH 23/167 (translated from German).**

During the night of September 9–10, 1939, there was shooting at German soldiers at 2 locations on the city outskirts, with the shots fired from outside and at one location in the city. 1 soldier wounded.

I order the shooting of 20 hostages at the market square. Order carried out at midday. [Handwritten note: Renewed public notice to the population.]

The mopping-up operation in the roughest neighborhood of the municipality has resulted in:

about 120 shot

900 arrested (nasty mob) [*übler Mob*].

These detainees are being separated from the other internees. At the disposal of the special courts, for sentencing.

Public notice about this, addressed to the city's residents.

Announcement of the hostages' execution as ordered.

Similarly sketchy were the written reports compiled by the RSHA in Berlin. As described in part I, Heydrich preferred to discuss important matters orally with Einsatzgruppen commanders, whom he summoned to Berlin for this purpose several times during the Polish campaign. In the case of Einsatzgruppe IV, document 16, a report from September 9, 1939, falls short of fully describing the violent actions pursued by German units in Bydgoszcz.

DOCUMENT 16: Daily report by the Chief of the Sipo/SD special office "Operation Tannenberg," September 9, 1939, USHMMA, RG 15.007M (BAB, R 58/7001), reel 2, file 1:23–27 (translated from German).

[. . .]

Einsatzgruppe IV:

The following measures were introduced for the City of Bromberg:

From 18:00 on, the whole population is to remain indoors at home.

The selling of distilled liquor is prohibited.

A requirement for carrying identity cards has been introduced and will take effect immediately.

Looters will be executed.

Because of the continuing nightly shooting by Polish inhabitants, hostages have been placed in front of every building serving as officers' quarters and in the market square. They will be shot immediately if further partisan attacks take place.

[. . .]

According to an RSHA report dated Sunday, September 10, 1939, "A thorough mopping-up operation will take place in Bromberg in the next few days. The complete city area of Bromberg will be systematically combed through. Each flat will be searched. If weapons are found, severe measures are to be implemented; likewise if there is any resistance."[32] Braemer had indeed ordered a raid in the workers' district of Szwederowo (German: Schwedenhöhe) that day. Local Wehrmacht and police units, including all of Einsatzgruppe IV, were instructed "that everyone is to be shot who is met carrying a weapon of any description" or "who in some way resists."[33] The two images presented in document 17, photographed by German participants, depict scenes from one such action near Bydgoszcz.

---

32. CdS daily report, September 10, 1939, USHMMA RG 15.007M (BAB, R 58/7001), reel 2, file 1:38–42.

33. War diary, commander 580th Rear Army Area, September 9, 1939, BA-MA, RH 23/167.

DOCUMENT 17: Photographs of Polish hostages arrested and executed by Einsatzgruppe IV and German Order Police during the "pacification" of Bydgoszcz, September 10, 1939, USHMMPA WS# 15753, 15752.

Once their superiors had opened doors for radical action, some field officers followed this route more violently than others. By Sunday afternoon, Bischoff's men, together with Order Police and Wehrmacht soldiers, had shot between fifty and sixty Poles at Szwederowo.[34] By the end of the day, the total number of people killed by Einsatzgruppe IV had increased to more than 240.[35] After the war, former members of Bischoff's unit gave different accounts of the executions.

DOCUMENT 18: Interrogation of Bruno G., former member of Einsatzkommando 2/IV, regarding "reprisals" in Bydgoszcz, December 1, 1964, BAL, B 162/Vorl. AR-Z 13/63, vol. 1:128–29 (translated from German).

[. . .] SS Stubaf. [Sturmbannführer] Bischoff addressed us in a speech, saying roughly the following. His speech was constructed in such a manner that he first referred to the Bloody Sunday on which many ethnic Germans were murdered, in some cases savagely, by Poles. His further remarks were to the effect that he intended to induce us to take a form of revenge. This was to be done by having members of EG [Einsatzgruppe] IV search preassigned streets or houses, looking for "suspicious" Poles. Bischoff also stated clearly that Poles "who make themselves suspect in any way" are to be shot at once. He also declared that this action [*Aktion*] was not ordered by anyone higher up, and his exact words were more or less, "In this action, anyone can prove he's a real man." [. . .] I can also still recall that ethnic Germans came to the collection point to have a close look at the Polish prisoners assembled there. If an accusation was made by an ethnic German against a Pole, the latter was assigned to a separate prisoner detachment. These prisoners were later taken to the Artillery Barracks. [. . .]

For obvious reasons, examples of Einsatzgruppen atrocities are rare in postwar statements by former members, but they can be found in individual cases such as the one described in document 19. Like all such judicial sources, this one raises questions about its accuracy and reliability, especially regarding the role of the person being interrogated. The war diary of the Commander of the 580th Rear Army Area Einsatzgruppen confirms mass shootings at Szwederowo on September 10, 1939, however, and several postwar testimonies of former Einsatzgruppen members refer to Bischoff's speech.

---

34. Rossino, *Hitler Strikes Poland*, 69–72.

35. War diary, commander 580th Rear Army Area, September 10, 1939, BA-MA, RH 23/167.

DOCUMENT 19: **Interrogation of Erich M., former member of EK 1/IV, regarding "reprisals" in Bydgoszcz, November 30, 1964, BAL, B 162/Vorl. AR-Z 13/63, vol. 1: 117ff. (translated from German).**

[. . .] I also can recall an incident on a Sunday, it must have been the Sunday following the so-called Bloody Sunday, September 10, 1939, when all the Einsatzgruppe IV members, that is, the two Einsatzkommandos, as well as the police units, had to assemble. Bischoff delivered a speech, conveying more or less that the Poles had instigated the Bloody Sunday the previous Sunday, and that we now had to take revenge. [. . .] Several smaller detachments were formed to search streets or houses; each was led by an EG IV member. We were given instructions to shoot any Polish males we encountered, regardless of whether they were armed or not. I would like to mention here, however, that Bischoff mentioned in his speech that any executions undertaken during this action [*Aktion*] could not be covered up by him, for it had not been ordered from above. [. . .] After this action, it was discussed by members of the EG IV among themselves. A certain Ernst V., SS-Hauptscharführer and criminal policeman from the Schneidemühl Stapo, said the following: he and his detachment forced their way into a Polish home. He found an old man lying in bed. The man was about to get out of the bed. V. indicated to him that he should stay where he was. Then he shot the old man in bed. [. . .] I also witnessed another shooting: this also took place during the Sunday action in Bydgoszcz. I saw a male Pole coming out of an apartment house. A certain Gerhard M., SS-Oberscharführer and Kripo man, also from the Schneidemühl Stapo, produced his pistol and shot that same Pole from behind. He hit him in the back but did not kill him. Since he was not killed right away, I assume that a member of the Order Police, using a P08 [Parabellum "Luger"] pistol, finished him off. [. . .] The action was to end at 13:00. Then each individual detachment leader was to report the number killed to an officer of the Order Police. [. . .] I made a "nil" report [*Fehlanzeige*], and the police officer asked me whether we really had found no one in our search. I replied that this was not the case but that we had had no reason to shoot anyone. On this occasion, I glanced at the list the police officer held in his hand and saw that according to the reports on hand from the individual detachments, around 700 Poles were listed as having been shot. I asked the police officer whether this number referred to those who had actually been shot, and he replied in the affirmative. He made a derogatory remark to me, since I allegedly was the only detachment leader who could show no proof of shootings.

The proceedings in Bydgoszcz during the first days and weeks of occupation were a crucial testing phase for the Einsatzgruppen, one watched closely by the Berlin leadership. Having largely succeeded in giving their men on the ground a free hand and expecting them to act autonomously, SS and police leaders in Berlin would interfere only if absolutely necessary. When on the evening of September 10, 1939, Himmler himself ordered the arrest of more hostages in Bydgoszcz, he officially sanctioned the ruthless actions taken by the Einsatzgruppen and made it clear that Bischoff's subordinates had correctly interpreted and implemented his speech.

DOCUMENT 20: **Daily report by the Chief of the Sipo/SD special office "Operation Tannenberg," September 11, 1939, USHMMA RG 15.007M (BAB, R 58/7001), reel 2, file 1:46–49 (translated from German).**

[. . .]
Einsatzgruppe IV:
[. . .]
The thorough mopping-up action [*durchgreifende Säuberungsaktion*] in Bromberg, announced because of the persisting attacks on Germans, began on September 10, 1939, at 6:30 a.m. and is being successfully continued. The Reichsführer-SS, on the basis of the report of the numerous instances of surprise fire directed at German troop transports, activities, and military patrols in Bromberg, has ordered that 500 hostages be taken, primarily from the Polish intelligentsia of Bromberg and also from communist circles, and that decisive action be taken by shooting hostages at the slightest attempt at revolt and resistance.
[. . .]

Given the disparity between the less than three thousand men comprising the Einsatzgruppen in Poland, on the one hand, and the huge number of people arrested and executed, on the other, the Sipo and SD quickly solicited the help of local auxiliaries to ensure control over the area. In the occupied western territories, the ethnic German civilian militia (Volksdeutscher Selbstschutz, or Ethnic German Self-Defense) formed by the SS and commanded by Himmler's adjutant, SS-Oberführer Ludolf-Hermann von Alvensleben, played an important role once the fighting was over.[36] On September 20, Himmler personally attended executions conducted by the Self-Defense near Bydgoszcz. Like the commanders of the Einsatzgruppen and the Einsatzkommandos, von Alvensleben and his men understood the message and widened the range of victims. He reported to Berlin on October 5 that the "severest measures had to be taken against 4,247 former Polish citizens."[37] In the Fordon "Death Valley" eight miles east of Bydgoszcz, the regional Self-Defense, together with men from Einsatzkommando 16, shot between fourteen hundred and three thousand people between the end of September and the end of October 1939. Another mass-execution site near Bydgoszcz was the Tuchola [German: Tuchel] Forest, where on October 27, 1939, a group of SS and Selbstschutz men shot forty-five Poles, including the priest Piotr Sosnowski.

DOCUMENT 21: Photographs of Polish prisoners executed by SS and Volksdeutscher Selbstschutz in the Tuchola Forest near Bydgoszcz, October 27, 1939, USHMMPA WS# 50093, 50097, 50840.

---

36. See Rossino, *Hitler Strikes Poland*, 135; Christian Jansen and Arno Weckbecker, *Der "Volksdeutsche Selbstschutz" in Polen 1939/40* (Munich: Oldenbourg, 1992). Despite an identical mission and, in part, close cooperation with the local security police contingents, the Selbstschutz was an autonomous unit, which obtained its orders not from the RSHA but from the head of the regional administration and from Alvensleben, who in turn obtained them from Himmler (Jansen and Weckbecker, *Der "Volksdeutsche Selbstschutz,"* 113–14, 163–72).

37. Dieter Schenk, *Hitlers Mann in Danzig: Gauleiter Forster und die NS-Verbrechen in Danzig-Westpreussen* (Bonn: J. H. W. Dietz, 2000), 156–57.

From the first day of the invasion, the Einsatzgruppen acted aggressively against the Polish intelligentsia and the local Jews. A later section will focus specifically on the German persecution of Jews in 1939. It is important to note, however, that the occupier's violence, not limited to a narrow range of targets, engulfed a broad number of groups regarded and treated as "enemies of the Reich." In Bydgoszcz, Jews were among the victims of Einsatzgruppen and Self-Defense brutalization and murder. In this local setting in the first weeks of the war, the notion of solving the "Jewish question" by ridding the city of its Jewish residents seems to have already crossed the minds of those fighting for the Germans.

DOCUMENT 22: Interrogation of Ewald S., former member of the Selbstschutz in Bydgoszcz, August 6, 1962, BAL, B 162/3268:478–82 (translated from German).

[. . .] Poles and Jews were housed, that is, locked up, in the artillery barracks at that time. So far as I can remember now, members of the Wehrmacht took about 100 of the detainees from the stables and handed them over to the Gestapo and to us Selbstschutz men. The arrested were loaded onto two trucks, one of which could hold about 50 to 60 people and the other between 30 and 40. [. . .] The Poles and Jews had to lie down in the trucks, presumably so they could not be seen by the local population during the trip. We Selbstschutz men were allowed to stand and had to guard these people. The journey took us to trenches that had been dug in the forest near Tryszczyn [German: Trischen]. The trenches had been dug by the Poles before the beginning of the war. On the road, near the trenches, we stopped, and the tailboards of the trucks were opened and the prisoners were forced out onto the ground. The Poles were gathered about 50 to 100 meters [55 to 109 yards] away from the road in a small hollow. There they had to lie on the ground. In groups of 15 at a time, they were forced into the trenches and were shot there by gray-uniformed members of the Wehrmacht or Gestapo. [. . .] On the day in question, it must have been in the first few days of October 1939, the two trucks drove three times from the artillery barracks to Tryszczyn. On this day, probably around 250 Poles, all men, were shot. [. . .] With regard to the Jews, all I know is that in the first few days of October 1939, banners appeared in the Bydgoszcz streets with the slogan "This city is free of Jews!" I assume, therefore, that the vast majority of the Jews had already been liquidated. [. . .]

Word of the violent events spread fast. In 1970, a former German order policeman stated that in 1939, executions among Polish civilians near Bydgoszcz ranged "in the hundreds, if not the thousands. The executions went on for weeks." At the time, he added, "it was the talk of Bydgoszcz that the Polish intelligentsia was being wiped out."[38] Toward the end of 1939, Lily Jungblut, the wife of a German manor owner living near Inowrocław (German: Hohensalza) in the Poznań province, felt prompted to act against the ongoing targeting of the city's Polish residents. Although she had been a member of the

---

38. Interrogation of Edmund S., December 3, 1960, BAL, B 162/16663.

Nazi Party since 1930, the brutality of the German police and Self-Defense units obviously shocked her to such a degree that she wrote a letter to Hermann Göring, the second man in the Nazi hierarchy, and invoked the region's centuries-long German-Polish history to help her Polish neighbors.

DOCUMENT 23: **Letter by Lily Jungblut, near Inowrocław, to Hermann Göring, December 6, 1939, USHMMA RG 14.021M (BAB, R 43 II/1411 a), fiche 4 (translated from German).**

[. . .] Is it, as is claimed, truly the will of our Führer and of the government to systematically wipe out the entire Polish population of German extraction? Based on the untrue claim that the "responsibility for the murders of ethnic Germans is borne exclusively by the intellectual leadership of the Polish population [*Polentum*]," as the *Deutsche Rundschau* in Bromberg states on September 12, 1939, thousands and thousands of innocent people in these circles have been shot; all teachers, both male and female, male and female doctors, lawyers, notaries, judges and state prosecutors, merchants and landowners—to the extent that they were still alive—have been arrested by the Danzig Gestapo, taken by the thousands from the schools in front of the children, from the positions in which the Wehrmacht had installed them again, from their medical and dental offices, from the hospitals, from the country estates, wherever they happened to be at the moment, and locked up in jails and prisons. [. . .]

And today the same tragedy is beginning for the small farmers and laborers. [. . .]

What glory do ethnic Germans and trustees earn when they have almost all the crucifixes and Crosses of Mary along the roads sawed down and broken to pieces, and when they invade the workers' homes, pull down images of the saints from the walls, and trample them, thereby profoundly insulting the pious Catholic rural population? [. . .]

As a result of her letter, Jungblut was arrested in early January 1940 by the Bydgoszcz Gestapo—the very policemen who, as members of a subunit of EK 16, had replaced Einsatzgruppe IV at the end of September and escalated mass murder in the region. She was released after another high-ranking official intervened on her behalf.[39]

---

39. See Schenk, *Hitlers Mann*, 169–70, and Martin Broszat, *Nationalsozialistische Polenpolitik 1939–1945* (Stuttgart: Fischer Bücherei, 1961), 46–47.

German violence initially followed gender lines in that it primarily targeted men for execution as "enemies of the Reich" and left their families, as in the cases of Władysława Winiecka and Zofia Semik, featured above,[40] to cope with the massive and enduring consequences of Nazi rule over the area. Nazi racial ideology reviled the notion of sexual intercourse between "Aryan" Germans and Jews or "Slavic" Poles; in reality, rape and other forms of sexual violence became a standard feature of the German occupation in Poland. Jewish women were also targeted, but such incidents rarely were recorded.[41] The photograph presented in document 24, taken in the Poznań region, shows that even when it came to executions, women became engulfed in the dragnet of German "reprisal" and "pacification" measures.

DOCUMENT 24: Photograph of Polish men and one woman lined up for execution in the forest near Szubin, October 21, 1939, USHMMPA WS# 50096.

---

40. See document 7 and document 8.

41. See document 23 and document 32; also Alexander B. Rossino, "Destructive Impulses: German Soldiers and the Conquest of Poland," *HGS* 7 (1997): 357–58. Cf. the second volume of a series of "Black Books" published with support from the Polish government-in-exile on German atrocities, *The German New Order in Poland* (London: Hutchinson & Co., 1942), 103–11, 221–23; Myrna Goldenberg and Amy Shapiro, eds., *Different Horrors, Same Hell: Gender and the Holocaust* (Seattle: University of Washington Press, 2013); and Sonja M. Hedgepeth and Rochelle G. Saidel, eds., *Sexual Violence against Jewish Women during the Holocaust* (Lebanon, NH: University Press of New England, 2010).

EXPANDING THE SCOPE OF VIOLENCE

The pattern of Einsatzgruppen executions in Poland evolved in a different direction from that taken by the Wehrmacht: German army units initially acted with great harshness toward a civilian population it deemed prone to partisan warfare, but soon the number of shootings declined dramatically.[42] While military commanders issued orders designed to stem the wave of Wehrmacht violence, the Berlin leadership encouraged the ruthless persecution by the SS and police of Polish elites, Jews, and other "undesirable" groups. Both developments were interconnected, as one agency, the military, receded into the background at the same time that others—the civil administrations in the annexed territories and the Generalgouvernement (with Himmler's men in charge of security matters)—gained prominence in determining occupation policy. At the end of September, the Wehrmacht's top brass readily agreed to let the Einsatzgruppen and civil administrators step up the level of violence directed against civilians, while police and SD were eager to assert their authority in an area destined to become, in the mind of Nazi planners, an inseparable part of the Nazi empire.[43] Wherever they went, the Einsatzgruppen had the local population at their mercy. Ethnic Germans could choose to stand aside or assist in the persecutions; most Poles would try to keep a low profile and survive under the harsh reality of occupation, while Jews would find no place in the German "New Order" from the very start.

In Pomerelia (German: Pommerellen), the Polish region annexed to the Reich as part of "Reichsgau Danzig–West Prussia," ethnic Germans provided valuable support for the Einsatzgruppen, since they knew the area and could identify suspicious Poles.[44] In Gdańsk and other parts of the region, Einsatzkommando 16 with its subunits acted purely as an execution squad targeting mainly Polish educated classes and other "undesirable" groups and individuals.[45] From mid-September, members of the Volksdeutscher Selbstschutz systemati-

---

42. Of the more than sixteen thousand Polish civilians executed in the first two months of the war, an estimated 75 percent were killed during September under Wehrmacht jurisdiction; the number of these executions conducted by Einsatzgruppen remains unknown (Böhler, *Auftakt*, 241–42).

43. See Christopher R. Browning with contributions by Jürgen Matthäus, *The Origins of the Final Solution: The Evolution of Nazi Jewish Policy, September 1939–March 1942* (Lincoln and Jerusalem: University of Nebraska Press and Yad Vashem, 2004), 15–35; Rossino, *Hitler Strikes Poland*, 227–35.

44. CdS daily reports for September 9 and 15, 1939, USHMMA RG 15.007M (BAB, R 58/7001), reel 2, file 1:33, and USHMMA RG 14.016M (BAB, R 58/825), fiche 1:10–13.

45. Schenk, *Hitlers Mann*, 163.

cally participated in the murder of their Polish and Jewish neighbors. According to the militia's commander, Alvensleben, his units killed more than four thousand "former Polish citizens" during the first days of October.[46]

The chief of the political police in Gdańsk since the spring of 1939 had been Dr. Rudolf Tröger, before he became head of Einsatzkommando 16.[47] Starting in mid-September 1939, his unit operated in the Gdańsk area and sent subunits (*Teilkommandos*) to surrounding cities and towns. A *Teilkommando* in Gdynia (German: Gdingen or Gotenhafen) consisted of thirty to thirty-five men under the command of SS-Hauptsturmführer Friedrich Class; Class's colleague Jakob Lölgen commanded another *Teilkommando* active mainly in Bydgoszcz after Einsatzgruppe IV had moved farther eastward.[48] In the late 1960s, one of the former unit members described this transformation.

DOCUMENT 25: Interrogation of Max-Franz Janke, former member of Einsatzkommando 16 stationed in Gdynia, July 10, 1969, BAL, B 162/16658 (translated from German).

[. . .] I myself was the deputy of Criminal Director [Kriminaldirektor] Class in Gdynia. To the best of my knowledge, in the first few weeks, that is, from about mid-September 1939 until early October 1939, no shootings were carried out by the *Teilkommando* in Gdynia. Instead, the *Kommando*'s task at that time was to arrest ethnic Poles accused by people of German descent from the Polish Corridor of having been involved in committing outrages against Germans. The detainees were checked against names on wanted lists. The wanted lists contained the names of Poles who in the last few years had emerged as being actively anti-German. These lists had been prepared by the Political Police in Gdańsk. A large number of those arrested were released again after being

---

46. Jansen and Weckbecker, *Der "Volksdeutsche Selbstschutz"*, 155; see also document 82.

47. For biographical information on Tröger, see p. 12n45.

48. Friedrich Class (1899–1945), a World War I veteran and Freikorpsmember, had joined the police in Gdańsk in 1920. A Nazi Party member from March 1933, he rose rapidly in the ranks of the city's police. In 1940 he became head of the Criminal Police in Graz before moving to RSHA Office V. After serving in World War I, Jakob Lölgen (1897–?) joined the police in 1927 and the NSDAP in 1933 before he was transferred, a year later, to the Gestapo. In 1938 Lölgen was sent to Gdańsk as a counterintelligence specialist and remained there until the war's end. In the only postwar prosecution conducted for the events in Bydgoszcz, a Munich court acquitted him and a codefendant in 1966.

screened, because they were classified as "harmless." But those who were on the wanted lists were sent to Grabowek [German: Grabau], the former camp for Polish emigrants. Around the beginning or middle of October 1939, Dr. Tröger telephoned all the top officers from the rank of criminal detective [*Kriminalkommissar*] upward to summon them to a conference at police headquarters in Gdańsk. At the conference were the aforementioned individual detachment commanders and their deputies, including me, as well as the Criminal Police officers. As I recall, the top detectives who still remained in Gdańsk and had not been immediately called into action were also brought into the conference. Dr. Tröger opened the meeting by speaking to those present along the following lines: "I have just come from the Reichsführer-SS. He has ordered that the Polish intelligentsia is to be eliminated!" Thus Dr. Tröger clearly stated that the members of the Polish intelligentsia were to be killed. He then added that Polish children were not to be allowed to attend secondary schools and that the Polish nation in general was to be kept at the lowest cultural and educational levels. Finally, Dr. Tröger kept back the detachment commanders Class and Lölgen for an internal meeting. I do not know what was discussed there in detail. At any rate, from this point on the arrest and shooting of the Polish intelligentsia in the Danzig–West Prussia area immediately began. In the sector of Einsatzkommando Gdynia, of which I was a member, extensive shootings henceforth took place under the command of Kriminaldirektor Class. [. . .] At the aforementioned Grabowek camp, to start with, those who were considered for execution were singled out and transported to the Wejherowo [German: Neustadt] prison. In the Wejherowo prison, in addition, the members of the Polish intelligentsia from the various districts were collected and initially held. At the end of October 1939, 350 to 370 of the Wejherowo prisoners were shot on one day. Among those shot were also 27 Polish Catholic clerics who had been brought to Wejherowo in the preceding days from the various districts of the former Gdańsk Administrative Region [*Regierungsbezirk*]. On another occasion, between 80 and 90—as I recall, 82—Polish women and men from the Hospital for Epidemic Diseases at Hexengrund near Gdynia, who had venereal diseases, were shot. So far as I know, this execution took place in November 1939. To my knowledge, they were shot because the Navy wanted to establish a torpedo school in the building. So far as I know, Class had ordered the execution because the Navy wanted the building to be vacated.

In the course of "eliminating" actual or potential "enemies of the Reich," the members of EK 16 became experienced executioners. Their victims included "undesirable" hospital patients from places such as Wejherowo or Hexengrund—mentioned by Janke—of whom an estimated seventy-seven hundred were murdered in the occupied Polish territories. Propelled by many local initiatives and plans developed centrally, these killings of persons deemed "unworthy of life" fed the emerging so-called T4 murder program that by August 1941 had claimed the lives of more than seventy thousand people.[49] Decades after the war, local eyewitness Josef Lemke could still recall details of the brutal measures against prisoners in the Danzig–West Prussia region.

DOCUMENT 26: Testimony by Josef Lemke about German atrocities in Wejherowo in late 1939, February 10, 1971, BAL, B 162/Vorl. AR-Z 368/67, Sonderheft vol. 2:168–69 (translated from German).

[. . .] I observed, after German troops occupied Wejherowo, that widespread arrests of Poles followed. I also noticed that those arrested were overwhelmingly members of the intelligentsia and the so-called Westmarken-Verband [a Polish nationalist organization]. [. . .] Those arrested were all taken to the prison in Wejherowo. I also observed that Gestapo trucks often arrived at the Wejherowo prison. Sometimes the trucks already had people on board and traveled from Wejherowo straight into the forest to Piaśnica [German: Piaschnitz]. As a rule the trucks then returned to Wejherowo and loaded up once again with prisoners to travel back to Piaśnica. [. . .] I should add here that I am a cattle dealer and that in this capacity I have traveled a lot around the Wejherowo District. As part of my work, I was often in the Piaśnica area and heard the shooting in the forest. I also saw tents in the forest, which was obviously where the squad that did the shootings was based. Once, when I was a guest in Wejherowo at the Danziger Hof [Hotel], a squad of SS men who had obviously just come from a shooting came into the pub for a drink. Then I heard a few members of the squad boasting of shooting 100 or more Poles again. "The damned brains just squirted everywhere." I did not personally see the shootings, but I can confirm that none of the Poles arrested at that time in October/November 1939 returned to Wejherowo. [. . .]

---

49. Browning, *Origins*, 184–94; Henry Friedlander, *The Origins of Nazi Genocide: From Euthanasia to the Final Solution* (Chapel Hill: University of North Carolina Press, 1994).

The subunit of Einsatzkommando 16 deployed east of Bydgoszcz to the town of Toruń (German: Thorn) in the Danzig–West Prussia region left similar vivid impressions in the minds of those Poles lucky enough to survive the unit's action.

DOCUMENT 27: Testimony by Franciszek Komar about German atrocities in Toruń in November 1939, June 26, 1968, BAL, B 162/3242:1107, 1109, 1111 (translated from German).

[. . .] On October 17, 18, and 19, 1939, the Germans organized systematic hunts on the streets and in the homes of Toruń. During these hunts, around 1,100 to 1,200 people from various occupational groups were arrested (intellectuals, tradesmen, business people, laborers, schoolchildren, and students). They were taken in military vehicles to Fort VII.[50] I was arrested in my home on October 17, 1939. [. . .] On October 30, Fort VII was taken over by the Gdańsk Gestapo and the local Selbstschutz. [. . .] Court officials and Gestapo functionaries then began to question the prisoners, using the personal data sheets on hand. Tables were set up in the hall on the ground floor for this purpose and a card index was created. This was the seat of the murder squad and the interrogation room. Here the Poles were evaluated and selected for extermination in Barbarka, for transport to a concentration camp, or for release. Many prisoners were interrogated multiple times. In November 1939 death sentences were carried out every Wednesday. The victims were driven in their underwear to the Barbarka woods to be shot. As I remember it, and according to the 1939 calendar, the executions took place in the Barbarka Forest on each Wednesday during November, and there were about 340 victims: Wednesday, November 8, 42 people; Wednesday, November 15, about 65 people; Wednesday, November 22, about 75 people; Wednesday, November 29, about 150 people. [. . .]

Barbarka was a small village northwest of Toruń (about 1.5 miles from Fort VII). In 1939, the Barbarka Forest became the execution site where, between October and December, Einsatzkommando 16 and Self-Defense members murdered several hundred Poles and Jews.

---

50. Part of the nineteenth-century fortification of Toruń, where Einsatzkommando 16 and Selbstschutz detained members of the intelligentsia.

DOCUMENT 28: **Photograph of Poles executed by Gestapo and Selbstschutz members in the Barbarka Forest near Toruń, October 1939, USHMMPA WS# 50849.**

As in Bydgoszcz, mass violence against Polish civilians in Toruń occurred within the context of prior atrocities committed against ethnic Germans that created a heated climate of revenge. Different groups in the population invariably perceived the increasing pressure differently. After the war, Richard Otto Dey, in 1939 a Protestant clergyman and member of the German minority in Toruń, attested to the key role that Einsatzgruppen members had played in the process.

DOCUMENT 29: **Testimony by Richard Otto Dey regarding German atrocities in Toruń, July 24, 1962, BAL, B 162/3240:662–63 (translated from German).**

[. . .] I can say with certainty that the first large-scale arrests of the Polish intelligentsia in Toruń began as early as September 13 or 15. I would like to add that the arrests had in part begun even earlier. At first, one heard of isolated arrests. Soon they became mass arrests. I can recall that the first prisoners from the Polish intelligentsia were held in the court jail in Toruń. Later, the number of prisoners was so great that this building became inadequate for the purpose. As I recall, the prisoners did not start coming to Fort VII until about mid-October. I can say with certainty that the Fort VII internment camp as such did not exist before October 15, 1939. I am certain of this because before the date I mentioned, the prisoners were taken from the jail to do work. Among other things, they had to carry the corpses—40 of them[51]—laid out in the Protestant church on the market place [*Neumarkt*] from the church to the identification room, and from there to the town hall square [*Rathausplatz*], where the ceremony took place. It took place in the last days of September 1939. The prisoners all came from the court jail and were, without exception, members of the intelligentsia. After this ceremony and the subsequent burial, a large execution in Toruń must have occurred. As to that, I have to describe an event: On the evening before the service, after the 40 corpses laid out had been identified, an SS man in black uniform with SD markings appeared in my office. He had the insignia of an SS-Führer, I mean he held an officer's rank. He demanded that I give him the keys to the church in which the bodies were laid out. I declined his request, asking why he would want to be alone in the church with its strong odor of decaying corpses and saying that it was my responsibility to ensure that the bodies were undamaged and ready for the state funeral planned for the following day. He told me he had to have the keys and had to spend the night with the bodies so that he would be fully charged with rage for the action the next day. I did not give him the keys. However, I heard that he managed to get into the church nonetheless and spent the night with the corpses. [. . .] On the day of the state funeral, I heard for the first time the slogan that for each murdered German, 10 Poles were to be killed. This statement was later repeatedly used in propaganda speeches. Accordingly, 400 Poles should have been killed on this day. I heard rumors that there actually was a big execution on this day. I cannot say anything about the number of the victims. This execution is said to have taken place in the Barbarka Forest. [. . .]

After Einsatzgruppe IV had left Bydgoszcz in mid-September to be replaced by units of EK 16, it proceeded eastward and on October 1 reached its final destination, Warsaw. It established headquarters in the Polish capital on the premises of the former Ministry of Education and Cultural Affairs on Szucha Avenue.[52] The building soon became a symbol of German occupation terror in the capital city.

---

51. Presumably a reference to ethnic Germans killed in Toruń before the German conquest of the city.

52. See also Regina Domańska, "Policja bezpieczeństwa dystryktu warszawskiego i jej więzienie 'śledcze' Pawiak," *BGK* 27 (1978): 145.

DOCUMENT 30: **Photograph of German police headquarters on Szucha Avenue, Warsaw, undated (November 1939), Bundesarchiv Bildarchiv 121-0286.**

The threat of violence was just one facet of German rule Poles had to face. The report presented in document 31 describes the desperate situation of the Warsaw population after the military campaign as seen by Sipo/SD officers. It reflects how the men used their ideologically freighted perspective to legitimize what they had already done and what they expected to do.

DOCUMENT 31: **Activity report by Einsatzgruppe IV in Warsaw, October 10, 1939, APŁ, 175/41 (translated from German).**

[. . .]

1.) Catastrophic food situation, less a shortage of food than the absence of means of transportation and lack of a regulated and appropriate distribution system. The consequence of the catastrophe is price gouging. Especially by the Jews, and there is also hoarding by them. But Poles are also engaging in price gouging, making those who are better off pay higher prices. [. . .]

3.) Weapons are definitely still hidden among the civilian population.

4.) Provocations by teenage Polish elements. RFSS: in heavily guarded labor gangs for cleanup work.[53] [. . .]

6.) List of the citizens' militia [*Bürgerwehr*] shows the elite of Warsaw, who naturally have to disappear! [. . .]

14.) On October 8, 1939, a total of 354 clergymen and teachers were arrested; because of their demonstrated Polish chauvinism, they represent a danger, not to be underestimated, to the security of the German troops, German civilian officials, and the German civilian population.

15.) In cooperation with the Order Police, the numbers of arrests of Jews for unbelievable price gouging are on the increase. [. . .]

21.) Almost everywhere there is agreement on the arrest of the Jews. Leading figures in Warsaw, too, are heard to ask again and again, "When will the Jew disappear completely from Poland?"

22.) A message provided here by the Polish landowner Radezki on the Russian invasion of Poland is of interest.[54] The report states above all that the Russians are destroying all valuables and are slaughtering the Polish intelligentsia. Russian officers are allegedly telling the Polish population that Stalin has said there will only be peace in Poland if the Polish intelligentsia, Poland's capitalists [*das polnische Kapital*], have been destroyed.

[. . .]

As before, the Sipo/SD included local women among those they deemed dangerous and singled out for execution. The photographs presented in document 32 depict the arrival of female prisoners from the Pawiak and Mokotów prisons at Palmiry, a mass murder site north of Warsaw.

---

53. See document 63.

54. The Soviet occupation of eastern Poland started on September 17, 1939.

DOCUMENT 32: Photographs of women about to be shot by German police in the Palmiry Forest near Warsaw, undated (October–December 1939), USHMMPA WS# 50646, 50642, 50069.

Violence against women and girls was part and parcel of the system of persecution established by the occupiers and their local helpers. Its prevalence stands in marked contrast to the silence or scarcity of records on incidents of sexual abuse and rape. As the statement presented in document 33 by a Polish woman from a town in the Poznań District shows, it remained difficult for women to talk about abuse even at a remove of three decades. Few, if any, settings were conducive to sharing such highly personal and traumatic experiences.

DOCUMENT 33: **Testimony by Marianna Kazmierczak regarding German atrocities in the autumn of 1939 in Zakrzewo, October 12, 1971, BAL, B 162/Vorl. AR-Z 26/72, vol. 2: 222–23 (translated from German).**

[. . .] During the whole occupation I lived in Zakrzewo, Poznań District. A few months after the occupation of these areas by Germans, I started working for the German Kassei (Kassej), who ran a grocery shop, a restaurant, and a textile shop in Zakrzewo. I sold things in the shop and served guests in the restaurant. It was in the fall of 1939 when Kassei told my father, Franciszek Baum, that the next day clerics and university students would be shot in the forest. [. . .] On the morning of that day, Germans in uniforms with skull insignia appeared in the restaurant. Also present were local Germans in black SS uniforms and brown SA uniforms, altogether more than 30 men. I had to serve them all, carry schnapps and beer. Finally they were half drunk, and the mood was very merry, as if they were intoxicated. They sang and danced. They rode (slid) around on chairs through all the rooms and in Kassei's private quarters. There were no German women among them. Such drinking bouts were repeated after every mass shooting. The shootings took place often, sometimes several times a week. The drinking bouts went on into the late hours, sometimes longer, sometimes shorter. I heard that the clothes of those who had been shot were distributed among the Germans. [. . .] At the beginning of the war, I was not quite 18. The uniformed Germans were brutal to me. Once, I correct myself, it was several times, they grabbed me when I was outside and tried to rape me, but I was able to fend them off and free myself. In general they thought I was a German because I had long braids.

Women also tried to intervene on behalf of spouses and family members directly threatened with death. As the wife of a landowner in the Poznań region made clear well after the war, these efforts rarely succeeded, given the ruthlessness of German policies and the uncompromising attitude of key functionaries.

DOCUMENT 34: Testimony by Paula von Karlowska regarding violence in Gostyń, January 14, 1965, BAL, B 162/Vorl. AR-Z 268/67:41–42 (translated from German).

[. . .] Many of the large landowners in the Gostyń District, including my husband Stanisław von Karlowski, owner of Szelejewo Manor, and other prominent members of this circle were arrested on October 19, 1939, taken to Gostyń, and locked in the cellar of the municipal office there. The prisoners were not even given straw; there was just a concrete floor on which they had to lie. They were not fed either, but we were allowed to bring them food. On October 21, when we brought the prisoners breakfast, the guards pressed us to hurry; I feared the prisoners would be transported to a concentration camp, but what happened was much worse. Around 10:00 in the morning, the prisoners were assembled at the main square and murdered, shot in the back of the neck. Two of the prisoners are said to have been saved because they were so old. The priests were locked in the rectory and were not allowed to give the martyrs any comfort. This murder squad then went from one place to another, from one shooting to another. When we—the prisoners' wives—heard of the terrible fate threatening our loved ones, we wanted to ask the district head

[*Landrat*], a Dr. Reichel or Reichelt from Wrocław [German: Breslau], to intervene. But we were told that he was out of town. My husband, the son of a landowner from the Poznań District, was educated in Berlin and was decidedly a Germanophile; for this reason he was often treated with hostility by the Poles. [. . .]

In the mind of Einsatzgruppen officers and in line with their prewar experiences in Germany, control and order in occupied Poland depended not only on the use of terror but also on surveillance of the population. To find out what issues were discussed and what the prevailing mood was among Poles, the Sipo/SD roped in informants from among German administrators and the local population. In late September, Criminal Detective Franz Tormann, a member of an Einsatzgruppe VI unit stationed in Środa Wielkopolska (German: Schroda) in the Poznań region, sent the report presented in document 35 to his superior. Although Tormann legitimized the persecution of Poles by claiming they were engaged in conspiratorial activities, he chose not to comment on the arrest of thirteen Jews, thereby illustrating how the persecution of Jews—regardless of their behavior—had already become a matter of course.

DOCUMENT 35: **Situation report by Einsatzkommando 1 subunit stationed in Środa Wielkopolska to Einsatzkommando 1/VI, September 22, 1939, APP 305/2 (translated from German).**

[. . .] During my visit to the farm of Miss Juan, I was informed by the [probably Wehrmacht] captain who was quartered there that there are rumors among the population of Santomischel [Polish: Zaniemyśl] that the Poles have won a great battle! They have only to persevere for three more days and all will be saved again. This rumor appears to have spread in Schroda, too, on a large scale. The population's mood is what might be expected. The former mayor, Polki, from Schroda, whose membership card for the Union of Insurgents of Greater Poland [Verein Aufständischer Grosspolens] was found, has been arrested. A memorial book prepared on the occasion of a flag consecration by the insurgents in 1938, listing the names of the participants in the ceremony, was found in the office of the printer Malicki, who is alleged to have prepared an inflammatory pamphlet against the Führer. Leading figures from Schroda who had fled have now returned, including the provost Dr. Janitizki and the post office manager Polchnopek, who are being labeled as great German haters. Several ringleaders were arrested: a certain Tomaszewski from the Augustenburg

Manor farm, Piesiak from Sockelstein [Polish: Sokolniki] near Wreschen [Polish: Września], and Tuczinski from Wreschen, who also had a double-action revolver with the appropriate ammunition in his home. In addition, 13 Jews were arrested in Wreschen. There were 17 arrests in Schroda. In accordance with the order received here today, the detainees will be sent there in a group during the course of tomorrow, as prescribed, after questioning. A car was requisitioned today. I request a submachine gun.

Terror and violence not only served the immediate German interest in "pacifying" the region but also had a longer-term effect on enforcing compliance. After their killing spree in Bydgoszcz, Einsatzgruppen officers reflected on the mood of the population through the filter of their prejudices against "the Poles" and their expectation of future threats from those quarters.

DOCUMENT 36: Situation report by Einsatzkommando 16 subunit stationed in Bydgoszcz, September 26, 1939, IPNW, NTN 196/179 (translated from German).

[. . .] At the moment the Polish population in Bromberg is still very depressed, because not one Pole had counted on such a defeat. The Pole, however, and in particular the generation that was active before 1918 on behalf of the Polish Confederation, has experience in organizing in the dark, and the younger generation, owing to its chauvinistic upbringing, will very quickly gain these skills. Anyone who knows the Polish national psyche, therefore, is aware that we will soon face Polish resistance movements [*Aufstandsbewegungen*] or the attempt to form them. As yet, only very few areas of the liberated territory could be thoroughly combed, and naturally that greatly favors the gathering together of scattered Polish soldiers and bands to organize the Polish population for resistance or for fighting a running battle. Special attention is to be given to the returning Polish refugees, because there is a possibility here for transporting ammunition and weapons. The importance of taking this measure is especially evident when one sees how strong the flow of returning Polish refugees now is. There can be no doubt, either, that a great many Poles, before fleeing, hid or buried any weapons and ammunition on hand and will take them out again after their return. The Polish worker will be the first who must be satisfied. For him, it is mainly a matter of finding work again and having a livelihood. As for the Polish Catholic Church, the middle class, and the intelligentsia, there will always be the risk that they will form groups and unite the Poles.
  [. . .]

On the basis of their investigations, Einsatzgruppen subunits would carry out "reprisal" executions with the semblance of orderly legal proceedings camouflaging their randomness. After the war, former inhabitants of Środa Wielkopolska and Leszno (German: Lisssa) elaborated on how these court proceedings really worked and what consequences they had for the accused, who in this case seem to have been all men.

DOCUMENT 37: Testimony by Stanisław Szałapieta regarding a summary trial by Einsatzkommando 2/VI held on October 20, 1939, in Środa Wielkopolska, November 14, 1972, BAL, B 162/Vorl. AR-Z 380/77, vols. 1–2:150–51 (translated from German).

[. . .] After a few minutes these Poles were led out into the prison yard and the next group of 10 was led into the courtroom, and after a few minutes led out again. Then the third group of 10 was led in. I did not see which of the Germans was sitting in the courtroom. At the time it was said among the court functionaries that the court had convened under the Gestapo officer Sommer. [. . .] Among the Poles led into the courtroom, I easily recognized the following, whom I knew: the lawyer Edward Trauczyński; the businessman Adam Woźny; the high school teacher Marian Gruszczyński; the man in charge of the municipal sewer system, Blaszak; the high school teacher Stanisław Jankowski; the businessman Ignacy Kostrzyński; the teacher from Murzynowo, Konrad Kaniewski; and the engineer at the sugar plant, Michał Szymański.[55] After a certain time, the Poles who had been led out of the courtroom into the prison yard were taken back from the prison yard into the court building in groups of 10, and then through the front door onto the market square. I add here that in the morning, when I entered the court, I saw on the sidewalk, on the right side of the front of the court building as seen from the market square, sand and railroad ties piled up in two layers, one vertical and the other horizontal. After each group of 10 Poles had been led out, you could hear a very loud salvo of shots from carbines, as well as a few single shots. Now I can no longer remember whether I heard Adam Woźny in the first or in the second group of ten. His voice was very familiar to me from the church choir. In the court corridor he sang the national anthem, "Poland Is Not Yet Lost." When he reached the words "March, march, Dąbrowski," the salvo of shots rang out.

Ethnic Germans served on these courts as props in the attempt to create the illusion of legality. Yet they also wielded extensive power in cases where their

---

55. The authors have been unable to locate information on these men.

local knowledge provided the basis for the verdict. In Leszno, according to a postwar statement by a Polish witness, two ethnic Germans on the court "were in effect the prosecution. Their report meant the prisoners were either sentenced to death, a prison term, or released."[56] If the accused were sentenced to capital punishment, the German police would take over.

DOCUMENT 38: **Photographs of men about to be shot by German police in Leszno, October 20, 1939, USHMMPA WS# 50273, 50290.**

---

56. Statement by Marcin Rydlewicz, July 6, 1967, BAL, B 162/Vorl. AR-Z 345/67, 8:1260.

Ethnic Germans played a large role in the persecution of other Poles; it is estimated that roughly half of the up to sixty-five thousand civilians murdered in the last quarter of 1939 were killed by Self-Defense units.[57] However, the picture was far from uniform as local ethnic Germans would not always act as their German superiors desired. From Środa Wielkopolska, the Unterkommando reported with regret that "the ethnic Germans feel bound to put in a good word for the prisoners (Jews and clerics)."[58] More often than not, the Einsatzgruppen managed to make locals complicit in determining the fate of their neighbors, as exemplified by a postwar eyewitness account of an early roundup in Kostrzyn (German: Kostschin) near Poznań.

---

57. Richard J. Evans, *The Third Reich at War, 1939–1945* (London: Allen Lane, 2008), 15.

58. Report by Einsatzkommando I subunit stationed in Środa Wielkopolska to Einsatz-kommando I/VI, October 9, 1939, APP, 305/2.

DOCUMENT 39: **Testimony by Roman Klamrowski on the arrest of inhabitants of Kostrzyn, September 17, 1973, BAL, B 162/Vorl. AR-Z 345/67, vol. 8:1186–87 (translated from German).**

[. . .] Several trucks with Gestapo functionaries arrived in Kostrzyn on the afternoon of September 16, 1939. They went from house to house and took all the men to the market square. My brother Kazimierz and I were among them. I am certain that they were Gestapo functionaries, as they had the skull insignia on their caps. They wore greenish uniforms. Later, on the market square, there was a selection in which the Kostrzyn inhabitants participated—those who were German. [. . .] Some of the assembled Poles were allowed to go home, among them my brother Kazimierz. The rest, about 500, were driven in rows of three in the direction of Swarzędz. Among them was my friend from the boy scouts, Tadeusz Drzewiecki, who was a student at a trade school in Poland. A few minutes before the group was herded in the direction of Swarzędz [German: Schwersenz], Else S. [an ethnic German woman] came up to a Gestapo man and whispered something in his ear. The Gestapo man went straight up to Tadeusz Drzewiecki and began striking him in the face. After the whole column had marched off, the Gestapo men pulled Tadeusz Drzewiecki out of the column, took him to the rear, and began to beat him. For about 3 km [2 miles] he was forced to run around the marching column while being beaten with rifle butts. Drzewiecki was so badly beaten that he was unrecognizable. Near Skałowo, two Gestapo men took Drzewiecki into a field and shot him. I have to add that at this point Drzewiecki could no longer march and kept falling down. The Gestapo men forced him to his feet again with their bayonets. I myself saw Drzewiecki being led into the field. After that I heard shots. [. . .] The next day we were put on trucks and taken to Owińska. From there we went by foot to Biedrusko, where we were held in military accommodations at the troop training grounds. After repeated checking of my personal data, I, like many other prisoners, was allowed to go home. The Germans held back the Jews, the men with tattoos, and the men with prewar criminal records.

Where the interests of locals overlapped with those of German authorities—as in document 40, a case reported in 1967 by a former official of the Reich Labor Service deployed in 1939 in Kórnik (German: Kurnick or Burgstadt), also near Poznań—court proceedings were but a brief formality.

DOCUMENT 40: **Interrogation of Willy Panse regarding court proceedings in Kórnik, May 19, 1967, BAL, B 162/Vorl. AR 2654/65:84–85 (translated from German).**

[. . .] One day in Kórnik, hostages were seized; they were kept in prison cells there, located in the town hall. These hostages were chosen in each case by the local mayor, an ethnic German named Maier. [. . .] One morning when I came to my unit from my quarters, one of my men reported to me that before midday, at 10:00, I think, a court-martial would convene in the Kórnik school and that there would be shootings. At that, I went to the mayor and asked what the reason for this measure was. He told me that the arrested men had planned an uprising on Poland's national holiday, which, as I recall, was in early November.[59] I then went to the school building, where the court-martial was to convene, to take part in the trial and to find out the real reason for it. It seemed strange to me when, on the way from the town hall to the site of the trial, I noticed that sandbags with railroad ties in front of them were already arranged along the wall of the town hall. That proved to me that even before the trial started, shootings were a foregone conclusion. Twenty men were accused, and a female teacher from a neighboring village near Kórnik. Among the 20 men were the Kórnik church provost, a priest from Kórnik, and a vicar from a neighboring village.

Local representatives of other German agencies who tried to intervene in the Einsatzgruppen's summary executions often advanced practical considerations. This is hardly surprising for, at the time, those arguments would have seemed to have the greatest chances of success, while humanitarian concerns ranked low on the priority list of German officials in occupied Poland. From our perspective, it is thus difficult to ascertain whether calls to "act responsibly" merely expressed an interest in the smooth running of the occupation machine or served as camouflage for the moral inhibitions of officials critical of indiscriminate violence. In the report presented in document 41, as well as in many other cases, the need to establish and maintain a functioning administration provided the main, if not the only, impulse for criticizing Einsatzgruppen actions.

---

59. Poland's Independence Day is celebrated on November 11.

DOCUMENT 41: Report by the district head of Lubliniec to the Chief of Civil Administration in Katowice, October 2, 1939, on the relationship with the Sipo/SD, APK, 119/1637 (translated from German).

[. . .] In my report today regarding the seizure of premises by the Sipo Einsatzkommando, I had already pointed out that this entity takes the view that it reports to specific offices of the Sipo in Tschenstochau [Polish: Częstochowa] and Radomsk[o] and not to the Chief of Civil Administration. Therefore, I would like to alert you to the fact that according to information from the head of the Einsatzkommando, SS-Sturmführer [*sic*] Zeidler, the following measures will be introduced in the next few days, measures that seem so invasive to me that I must call this to the attention of the Chief of Civil Administration. I request your guidance as to whether these measures are being taken in concert with the administrative office there and whether possible support by the proper police authorities is thus contemplated. All pro-Polish [*polnisch gesinnte*] clerics, teachers, doctors, and landowners are to be arrested and taken to a camp. Beyond this, the Sipo intends to confiscate their Polish properties. Since there are hardly any pro-German persons in the aforementioned status groups, this measure amounts to a mass arrest of all those in the professional groups listed above. So far as clerics, teachers, and large landowners are concerned, there are no objections on my part. However, I regard the arrest of doctors as irresponsible and have made the commander of the Einsatzkommando aware of my view. The Lublinitz [Polish: Lubliniec] District, with 51,000 inhabitants, currently has only three doctors, of whom only Dr. Skuppe in Koschentin is an ethnic German. The general practitioner, Dr. Kaminsky in Stahlhammer, and the resident physician, Dr. Migdal in Lublinitz, are Poles. There are no Wehrmacht doctors available. The Guttentag [Polish: Dobrodzień] public health officer, Medizinalrat Dr. Menger, is only occasionally available and is presently endeavoring to direct medical care in the district. Therefore I request that any physicians affected by this measure be informed immediately that they will not be arrested. [. . .]

Due to a lack of sources, it is unclear how many people the Einsatzgruppen shot on Polish territory in 1939, particularly since the Selbstschutz or other units often carried out killings in the areas annexed to the Reich on October

8.[60] According to their own statistics, in the first four weeks of the campaign the Einsatzgruppen executed roughly one thousand people. The staggering figure of twenty thousand civilians killed by EK 16 through the end of the year can serve as a clue to the Einsatzgruppen's increasing deadliness in this period. By late December 1939, more than forty thousand civilians had died in the annexed regions as a result of the regime's attempt at "spatial cleansing" (*Flurbereinigung*): roughly thirty thousand in Danzig–West Prussia, ten thousand in the Wartheland, fifteen hundred in East Upper Silesia, and one thousand in the Zichenau region. In the remaining parts of German-controlled Poland, the Generalgouvernement, the Einsatzgruppen executed an estimated five thousand civilians.[61] Most of the victims, especially those killed by execution, were men of military age; we have no firm data to estimate the number of rapes and other kinds of physical abuse that targeted women, children, and other groups within or outside the nebulous German category of "the elite."[62] In all of occupied Poland, two groups of Polish citizens had been targeted in particular by the end of 1939: hospital patients, of whom an estimated seventy-seven hundred were murdered, and Jews, of whom at least seven thousand had been killed.[63] The murder of Jews occurred in the wider context of German occupation policy, to which we now turn.

PERSECUTING JEWS

As we have seen in previous sections of this book, anti-Jewish violence by Sipo/SD units formed part and parcel of a thoroughly racist, expansionist Nazi agenda facilitated by a range of German agencies and supported by small, yet

---

60. See, e.g., the execution of roughly eight hundred Poles by SS-Totenkopfstandarte "Brandenburg" during two days in late September 1939 in Bydgoszcz; Martin Cüppers, "'. . . auf eine so saubere und anständige SS-mässige Art': Die Waffen-SS in Polen 1939–1941," in *Genesis des Genozids: Polen 1939–1941*, ed. Klaus-Michael Mallmann and Bogdan Musial (Darmstadt: WBG, 2004), 99.

61. Czesław Łuczak, *Polska i Polacy w drugiej wojnie światowej* (Poznań: Wydawnictwo Naukowe UAM, 1993), 101; Dieter Pohl, *Verfolgung und Massenmord in der NS-Zeit 1933–1945* (Darmstadt: WBG, 2003), 49.

62. Monika J. Flaschka, "Race, Rape and Gender in Nazi-Occupied Territories" (PhD diss., Kent State University, 2009).

63. Pohl, *Verfolgung*, 123; Dieter Pohl, "Der Völkermord an den Juden," in *Deutsch-polnische Beziehungen 1939–1945–1949: Eine Einführung*, ed. Włodzimierz Borodziej and Klaus Ziemer (Osnabrück: Fibre, 2000), 115; Michael Alberti, *Die Verfolgung und Vernichtung der Juden im Reichsgau Wartheland 1939–1945* (Wiesbaden: Harrassowitz, 2006), 43.

important, parts of the local population. Although a close correlation exists between violence against members of the Polish elite and other groups of "undesirables," Jews formed a particularly obvious, almost "natural" target for officers equally as attuned as Himmler's men to the urgency of the "Jewish question." If any of them had doubts, precampaign guidelines issued by Heydrich's headquarters in Berlin described Jews as "a very great threat" both quantitatively and qualitatively: "In Poland there are more than 3 million of them, and in fact this is the number of observant Jews alone, so Jews represent more than 10 percent of the total population in Poland. Of course, the Jews make up a particularly large part of the urban population. In the towns of the eastern districts, they even constitute a majority. The not insignificant commerce in Poland's eastern portion is almost exclusively in Jewish hands. Regardless," the guidelines concluded, "the Jewish question thus will become a difficult problem."[64]

Documents 42 to 61 provide a glimpse of the scope and consequences of antisemitic measures initiated by the Einsatzgruppen. The units commanded by SS-Obergruppenführer Udo von Woyrsch (Einsatzgruppe z.b.V.) and SS-Brigadeführer Bruno Streckenbach (Einsatzgruppe I) left a particularly bloody trail, killing hundreds of Jews on their way eastward from East Upper Silesia to the German-Soviet demarcation line. Despite the fact that Nazi anti-Jewish violence had complex origins, one aim was to force Jews to flee across the demarcation line into Soviet-controlled territory.[65] Since the Germany-wide pogroms of November 1938, the burning of synagogues combined with acts of physical violence against Jews formed part of the Nazis' program of organized terror. Once they had crossed the border into Poland, Wehrmacht troops as well as Sipo/SD resorted to arson attacks in towns and cities like Będzin [German: Bendzin], Katowice, and Końskie [German: Konskie].[66] But the attacks did not stop there. The author of the account in document 42 of events in Mielec in southeastern Poland was one of many contemporaries who reported on the atrocities.[67]

---

64. Proposal for the deployment of Security Police and SD in preparation for the attack on Poland, undated (before September 1, 1939), RGVA 500-1-36.

65. Alexander B. Rossino, "Nazi Anti-Jewish Policy during the Polish Campaign: The Case of Einsatzgruppe Woyrsch," *GSR* 24, no. 1 (February 2001): 35–53.

66. Situation reports for September 9, 10, and 27, 1939, IPNW, NTN 196/179.

67. For other accounts, see Tatiana Berenstein and Adam Rutkowski, "Prześladowanie ludności żydowskiej w okresie hitlerowskiej administracji wojskowej na okupowanych ziemiach polskich (1.9.–25.10.1939 r.)," *BŻIH* 38 (1961): 28–38.

DOCUMENT 42: Account by Berta Lichtig on the burning of the synagogue in Mielec, undated (ca. 1943), USHMM RG 15.084M (ŻIH 301/1029) (translated from Polish).[68]

[. . .] The "heroes" of the German army immediately put their prowess on display, starting with the synagogue. Wishing to destroy it, they surrounded it, as well as the slaughterhouse and the bathhouse.

They doused the synagogue with gasoline and set it on fire. The Jews in the bathhouse and the slaughterhouse were locked inside, and the buildings were set on fire. Those who tried to escape and save themselves were shot at and thrown back into the fire. Then they fanned out across the city, pulling Jews from their homes and hauling them away, taking advice from the dregs and the scum of the city. [. . .] The people caught in the slaughterhouse were burned alive. They kept up this conflagration for two days. A few nearby buildings burned down. Pictures of saints were placed on the homes and in the windows of Christians. That same evening a different SS detachment caught 20 young people, mostly students from various towns [. . .]. These were boys who had fled and whom the arrival of the Germans caught by surprise. They were loaded on trucks and taken to Berdechów (a village three kilometers [about two miles] from Mielec). There, their arms and legs were broken, and their stomachs were crushed until their guts poured out. As they lay dying, they were shot. One of them fled when he saw what was going on and survived. They pursued him and shot after him. He rushed to Farmer Gawryś, who, seeing the pursuit, led him to a cornfield and hid him there. The corpses of his companions lay about for two days, and it was only after this that Jews from the town came, gathered them up, and buried them. The bodies were missing parts of their limbs. [. . .]

On that same day (when the Germans entered the town), a third SS detachment caught 150 Jews, both young and old, and lined them up against the wall of the yeshiva, with their faces to the wall and their arms up. [. . .] They were held there and weren't allowed to move for several hours. The Jews were already half unconscious, and when the Germans began readying their arms, they prayed, calling out, "Shema

---

68. Berta Lichtig spent over a year in the ghetto in Mielec and later worked in forced labor camps. She appears to have survived the war. See the USHMM Holocaust Survivors and Victims Database.

Yisrael."[69] Just when they were about ready to fire, a cab drove up from a side street. A German officer got out and, upon seeing the Jews lined up, asked what they were doing. He spoke with the torturers and ordered them to disperse. The Jews could not believe that they were alive. They were all mesmerized particularly because they had seen what had happened to the others who had been burned alive. [. . .] The next day (the synagogue, the bathhouse, the slaughterhouse, and the yeshiva, as well as the nearby houses, were still burning), a few girls were rounded up and were ordered to clean the bathroom in Mayor Kazana's home with their bare hands.

After these events, youth of both sexes and middle-aged men fled en masse toward Russia. The remainder, those who did not have the means or the ability, fearfully awaited what lay in store. Smiles vanished from people's faces, their gazes grew somber, they timidly slunk along the walls, only leaving their homes for important reasons. People died from heart attacks, caused by joy as well as despair.

[. . .]

Even former Einsatzgruppen members admitted after the war to targeted destruction of buildings as part of the wave of violence sweeping through the area.[70] In urban settings the dangers to public safety inherent in these acts were large enough to prompt Himmler on September 9 to prohibit the burning of synagogues in the major cities of Kraków, Łódz, and Warsaw, even though he took no exception to the killing of Jews.[71] Photographs of destroyed buildings frequently found their way into the memorabilia collections of German participants in the Polish campaign and its aftermath. The image in document 43 depicts the ruins of a building wrecked by bombs in Będzin in Upper Silesia, with the synagogue destroyed by Einsatzgruppe z.b.V. visible in the background.

---

69. "Hear, [O] Israel"; title of a Jewish prayer.

70. Interrogation of Hubert S., February 5, 1971, BAL, B 162/Vorl. AR-Z 302/67, 2:411.

71. RFSS to BdO and BdS with 14th and 10th Army, September 9, 1939, BA-MA, RH 20-14/132; RFSS to Woyrsch, September 7, 1939, BA-MA, RH 19 I/191.

Document 43: Photograph of an SS officer and civilian posing in front of the ruins of the Great Synagogue in Będzin destroyed by Einsatzgruppe Woyrsch on September 10, 1939, undated (1939–1940), USHMMPA WS# 18542.

For those directly targeted, as well as for the Polish population in general, the wave of violence sweeping the region made it difficult to determine to which German agency the persecutors belonged. It appears, however, that from early on Einsatzgruppen and Wehrmacht units worked jointly toward a common goal, as a resident of Dynów (German: Dünhof) near the San River testified in 1969.

Document 44: Testimony by Jakub Gąsecki on German anti-Jewish atrocities in Dynów, January 21, 1969, BAL, B 162/Vorl. AR-Z 302/67, 3:498–99 (translated from German).

[. . .] I have lived in Dynów, Brzozów District, Rzeszów region, all my life. I no longer remember the exact day and month, but it was in 1939 immediately after the Germans invaded Dynów when I saw Germans in dark uniforms with skull insignia, as well as Germans wearing German soldiers' uniforms, haul some grown Jewish men out of their houses in Dynów and apprehend others on the Dynów streets. These Jews—there were about 60 of them—were finally taken away by the Germans in two trucks to the so-called Zurawiec, a forest near Dynów. At the same time, the Germans told the weeping Jewish women that these Jews had been transported across the San River to Jawornik Ruski to work. Meanwhile these Jews in reality were shot at once by the Germans, close to the forest. [. . .] About two or three days later, around 90 male Jews were rounded up close to the Dynów elementary school by Germans in the same uniforms. From there, these Jews were taken in vehicles to the so-called *Księże pole* (priests' field), which was located behind the Catholic rectory in Dynów. Immediately thereafter, shots were heard in this location.

In Dynów, the Sipo/SD transformed its brutal anti-Jewish actions into a public spectacle designed to strike terror into the hearts of the Jews and drive them across the river into Soviet-occupied territory.

DOCUMENT 45: Testimony by Sacher Grünbaum on German anti-Jewish atrocities in Dynów in September 1939, June 11, 1945, USHMMA RG 15.084M (ŻIH 301/4534) (translated from Polish).[72]

The Germans entered Dynów on September 11, 1939. A few days later, during the new year holiday Rosh Hashanah itself, a group of Gestapo men drove up, got out of their cars, and immediately began rounding up Jews off the street.[73] When word of this spread around the city, the Jews hid in their houses, and the Gestapo men broke into their homes, dragged the Jews out, and led them away with their hands up to the school building, where they held them for the entire day. The Jews stood with their faces turned to the wall and their hands up. The Gestapo men beat them with the butts of their pistols when anyone lowered his hands for just a moment. After a few hours they drove the Jews into a single hall, and in the evening they loaded them into automobiles and drove them out of the city. There they lined them up in rows of ten persons and shone the headlights of the cars on them, and then fired at them with machine guns. In this way they murdered 170 Jews on that night. Some of them were Jews from Dynów, some were refugees from Brzozów, Krosno, Jasło, Nowy Sącz, and Gorlice [German: Brzozow, Krossen, Jassel, Neu Sandez, and Görlitz].

---

72. Born in Dynów in 1926, Grünbaum provided his postwar testimony in Przemyśl. See ŻIH, *Holocaust Survivor Testimonies Catalogue* for RG 301 (Warsaw: ŻIH INB, 2007), 5:190.

73. Grünbaum does not specify whether women were among those rounded up and killed on this occasion.

My father, Eisig Grünbaum, died during the massacre. The merchant Jacob Guttman was wounded but escaped with his life. He played dead at the execution site. Then, when night came, he dragged himself crawling on his stomach to the neighboring field, where he subsequently fled across the San to the neighboring village.

The next day, that is, the second day of Rosh Hashanah, a detachment of Gestapo men entered the Dynów synagogue. They gathered up prayer scrolls and prayer books into a single heap, doused them with gasoline, and lit them on fire. In this way, the synagogue burned down, as did two other houses of prayer, along with their prayer scrolls and collections of Talmudic writings. Two Jews who lived in the little house next to the synagogue were thrown into the burning synagogue and were burned alive. It was the baker's assistant Israel Kehr and Józef Rogel, who made shoe uppers.

A few days later, during the Sukkot festival, a local [Polish] policeman, at the command of the Gestapo, announced amid beating drums that the Jews were required to assemble within 15 minutes on the market square, under the penalty of death. The purpose of the gathering was not announced. After the Jews had assembled, they were surrounded by German soldiers and Gestapo men and driven in the direction of the San River as the local orchestra played. Shooting at random to frighten them, they forced all the Jews to cross the river, and since the water was deep and the current strong, several older women drowned during the crossing. In this way, the Jews of Dynów, after losing nearly everything that belonged to them, left behind their native city, where their ancestors had shared a common fate with the Polish population for several hundred years. [. . .]

The initial need to label Jews as a "security threat" soon became redundant in what historian Alexander Rossino has called the most murderous crescendo of the Polish campaign. Around September 20, when they reached Przemyśl, a small southeastern Polish city located immediately at the demarcation line, men from Einsatzgruppe I and Einsatzgruppe z.b.V., most likely assisted by Wehrmacht soldiers, perpetrated the largest single murder action against civilians of the Polish campaign, killing more than five hundred Jews.[74] As one eyewitness recalled in 1946, the victims were "mostly from the intelligentsia"; the killers "left the women and children in peace then. They robbed all the Jewish shops,

---

74. Estimates range from five hundred to eight hundred victims, but some sources report more than nine hundred; see Jochen Böhler, *Der Überfall: Deutschlands Krieg gegen Polen* (Frankfurt am Main: Eichborn, 2009), 199–207.

emptying them. German trucks drove up in front of the shops and took all their belongings, took them to Germany and robbed their houses."[75] Document 46 presents the account of another resident of the city.

DOCUMENT 46: Account of anti-Jewish violence in Przemyśl, cited from Bruno B. Shatyn, *A Private War: Surviving in Poland on False Papers, 1941–1945* (Detroit, MI: Wayne State University Press 1985), 121–22.

[. . .] Several days after the arrival of the Germans I was driving along Mickiewicz Street, one of the main thoroughfares in Przemyśl, when I saw a ragged line of people running down the middle of the street, all with their hands clasped behind their necks. I pulled over to one side and stopped my truck. Around a hundred people ran past, and as they did I saw that they were Jews. They were half naked and crying out as they ran, "Juden sind Schweine" ("Jews are swine"). Along the line, revolvers in hand, German soldiers were running, young boys about eighteen years old, dressed in dark uniforms with swastikas on the sleeves, with light blond hair and rosy faces. When someone fell behind or broke pace, they beat the victim with the butts of their revolvers or with whips, or simply kicked him. Poles gathered on the sidewalks, incredulous, some crossing themselves at this monstrous sight. The faces of the old Jews were contorted with pain, and the young boys were crying, but the Germans ran along the street almost joyfully, drunk with power. As I later found out, the soldiers had fallen on the Jewish section of town that morning and had driven all the men and boys out of their houses with blows and kicks. They made them do calisthenics for several hours in the street, and now they were driving them toward the railway station and on, until they crossed the city limits.

I returned home, shaken. Only in the afternoon, when I had calmed down somewhat, did I go out again to return my truck to the power station. Now a new horror met my eyes: distraught, weeping women were running toward the cemetery, for they had heard that all the Jews taken in the morning had been shot in Pikulice, the first village outside town. I put a load of these wailing women in my truck and headed for Pikulice. Right at the edge of the village, beside a small hill, a swarm of people had gathered. I drove up and stopped. What I saw surpassed all belief; it was a scene out of Dante's hell. All the men driven through the streets in the

---

75. Testimony by Marian Bień, August 17, 1946, USHMMA RG 15.084M (ŻIH 301/138).

morning lay there dead. Some men from the nearby houses told me what had happened. The Jews had been driven up to the side of the hill and ordered to turn around. A truck was already standing there. A canvas had been lifted off a heavy machine gun, and several bursts of fire rang out, sweeping back and forth. Then a few more shots were fired into the few bodies that were still writhing. All was still. The soldiers climbed into the truck, and drove away.

I went quietly up to the little hill. The corpses were lying on their backs or sides in the most contorted positions, some on top of others, with their arms outstretched, their heads shattered by the bullets. Here were pools of blood; there the earth was rust colored with blood; the grass glistened with blood; blood was drying on the corpses. Women with bloodied hands were hunting through the pile of bodies for their fathers, husbands, sons. A sickish sweet smell pervaded the air.

I felt something inside me die, as though my heart had turned to stone. I was choking from the smell, from the sight, from the cries filling the air. I saw everything, but I could not grasp what I saw. Before my eyes I had an image of the laughing young Germans, the proud representatives of Hitler's New Order. [. . .]

For Jews across German-controlled Poland, that "New Order" held a bleak future. As a survivor from Przemyśl stated, "There was not one day in which there were not shootings or people were not severely mistreated."[76]

To the invaders, the setting looked entirely different. Among the topics of photographs taken by Einsatzgruppen members deployed behind the front line was the "strangeness" encountered in Poland, often epitomized by images of Jews dressed in traditional attire, combined with the Germans "bringing order" to the newly occupied territories. We can only speculate about the motives of the photographers and album owners; it is fair to assume, however, that they saw their wartime activities as a source of pride and considered their memories worth sharing with their circles back in Germany.[77] Of the many photographic images produced by Sipo/SD men in Poland, only a few have survived.[78]

---

76. Testimony by Izak Eisner, April 25, 1960, BAL, B 162/1397:70ff.; similarly for Łódź, see Frederick Weinstein, *Life on the Precipice of Hope and Fate* (New York: Self-published, 2000), 30ff.

77. See Alexander B. Rossino, "Eastern Europe through German Eyes: Soldiers' Photographs, 1939–1942," *History of Photography* 23 (1999): 313–21; Judith Levin and Daniel Uziel, "Ordinary Men, Extraordinary Photos," *YVS* 26 (1997): 265–93.

78. The photographs of executions removed from the diary of Erich Ehlers (see document 5; these photographs can serve as examples).

Among them is the photo album compiled by Hermann Baltruschat, who was a member of EK 3/V. The first pages of this album illustrate the anti-Jewish measures taken by this Einsatzgruppe in the Ciechanów (German: Zichenau) region of northern Poland in late September 1939. They complement what the unit reported to Berlin headquarters.[79]

DOCUMENT 47: Photo album pages by SS-Oberscharführer Hermann Baltruschat of Einsatzgruppe V regarding "Jewish actions" in Raciąż and Płońsk, undated (late September 1939), IPN (captions translated from German). [To better see photos, go to rowman.com/isbn/9781442231412 © Agency Agreement, IPN.]

"Action against 6,000 Jews in Plonsk [Płońsk]."

79. The Polish Institute of National Remembrance and the German Historical Institute in Warsaw are currently preparing an edition of the album for publication in German, Polish, and English.

"Action against Jews in Raciąc [Raciąż]."

"Raciąc, Plonsk."

After the war Jews from Raciąż remembered scenes of the roundups, their preparation, and their consequences that were not depicted on Baltruschat's neatly arranged album pages.

DOCUMENT 48: Excerpts from the memorial book for Raciąż, *Gal'ed li-ḳehilat Ratsyonz'*, ed. Efrayim Tsoref (Tel Aviv: ha-Irgun shel 'ole Ratsyonz', 1964) (translated from Yiddish).

[Avrom Yeshaia Altus, "When the Nazis Invaded Raciąż," 350–51]

At the beginning of September, the SS men called once again for the rabbi of the city and the supervisor of the Jewish community. "All the Jews of the city must gather on the market square" was now the new order. Levi-Itsik, the *shames*, went and banged on the doors of every house and store with his wooden hammer: "Jews, out in the street! Order of the SS! Those who don't come out will be shot!"[80]

At eleven in the morning, all the Jews of Raciąż were already on the market square. Those who were late were made to stand to a side. The late ones were: my brother Yosef-Leyb Kuzhtseba, of blessed memory, and Rotman, Knaster's son-in-law, and they were beaten for not coming on time. The "torture action" of bullying us soon began. They forced us to do "physical exercises," a means of offending and debasing our self-worth. They ordered us to lie on the ground, and they kicked us and stepped on us with their boots. They also forced the elderly to run across the entire length of the market square and beat them with the butts of their rifles. And this continued until lunchtime, when they let us go, about a thousand Jews, with the announcement to gather once again on the square later in the afternoon.

On that day something happened that we saw as a sign of God: the SS officer had ordered us to go home via the opposite side of the square. [. . .] There was confusion in the mass of Jews, and the officer whipped out his revolver and shot right into the bewildered crowd. But a miracle happened, and the bullet hit the shooter instead, in his hand.

When we came back in the afternoon [. . .] the SS men let loose their wrath on us because of what had happened to their officer [. . .]. The SS

---

80. In the traditional Jewish communities of Eastern Europe, the *shames* (synagogue caretaker, beadle) would bang on the door of each house on Friday evening to announce the coming of the Sabbath.

men took Mendl Plinsker's son-in-law, Itche Rozenthal, the tailor, out of the rows of Jews. They tied the hands of the rabbi's son, Avrom, with string and ordered the rabbi to take leave of his son because he would be sent off with the others to Płońsk. The Germans beat up one of them so badly that he was entirely covered in blood. We were all quite shaken. Our eyes darkened from shame and from pity.

[Hayim Fogel, "The Lives of Raciąż That Are No More," 224:]

Yom Kippur eve, 1939

The Jews of Raciąż begin to arrange how to organize quorums for prayer and in which places to conduct the "Kol Nidre" service.[81] But the German assassin was plotting something else for them. All of a sudden, a number of cars came by with the "Gestapo." We heard shots being fired, and we soon heard that two had been wounded—Hanah Freyda Vis, of blessed memory, and Reb Israel Teitelbaum, of blessed memory. The keys to the synagogue and study house were taken, and the *shames*, Reb Levi Yitshak, of blessed memory, once again announced with his hammer that all Jews from 14 years of age must present themselves with shaved beards and appear tomorrow, Yom Kippur, at eight o'clock in the morning. [. . .]

Most shaved their beards, and their appearance was frightening. [. . .] With fear and trembling we gathered at eight in the morning in the town's market square and were forced to line up in rows of five. Several cars of Gestapo arrived, with firearms in hand, and they began to beat us with murderous blows. They checked to see we were all cut and shaven, and woe to him who was not shaven. And the Germans began their work—they sheared and burned. We stood exhausted for hours under murderous blows, accompanied by derisive calls such as, "Jewish pig! War mongers!" It was now two o' clock in the afternoon. The German captain ordered us to leave the market square, and he ordered the younger ones to return at four in the afternoon, each with a broom in hand. [. . .] Afterward we presented ourselves at the market square with brooms. We were divided into groups. One group went to clean the church grounds. And after this humiliating work on Yom Kippur, we gathered once again in the evening in the yard of the Polish school for a roll call. We were divided into two large groups. All whose names were called would pass between two lines of Germans who rained murderous blows down on them. After that an order was given to go home and bring back all the wine or tobacco that we

---

81. The service on the eve of Yom Kippur.

had. And if not, they would organize a search, and in any place where they found wine, the owner would be killed. Wines were brought and all types of alcohol. Cantor Granat, of blessed memory, was given the "honor" of drinking and, with a heaping share of blows, was forced to sing. [. . .]

Organized theft of Jewish property followed a pattern first visible from Nazi prewar measures in the Reich, where the forced emigration of Jews was combined with their exploitation.[82] In Poland, as indicated by Einsatzgruppen members after the war, Sipo and SD men adopted methods to extract Jewish wealth that combined public humiliation with visible, often sexualized violence.[83]

DOCUMENT 49: **Interrogation of Kurt G., former member of Einsatzkommando 1/IV, regarding anti-Jewish violence in Białystok, November 13, 1965, BAL, B 162/Vorl. AR-Z 13/63, vol. 4:767 (translated from German).**

[. . .] Our EK was deployed in Białystok to round up all male Jews between about 15 and 60 years of age in a schoolyard. They stood there for several hours with their arms in the air, but were then released. No shootings took place. I assume they were released because in the meantime it had become known that the city would be handed over to the Russians. The next morning we left Białystok. In Pułtusk [German: Ostenburg], the entire EK of Bischoff,[84] whom I saw there in person, was deployed to round up all the Jewish inhabitants in the market square. The Jews were allowed to take along everything they could carry. Then they were led to a large meadow, where the SS took away their gold, silver, valuables, and money. As I later learned from the SS man O. (he came from Saxony), he was given rubber gloves during this action and, with a few other comrades, had to search the genitals of the Jewish women, looking for hidden objects. After that the Jews were chased away across a bridge (I

---

82. See Martin Dean, *Robbing the Jews: The Confiscation of Jewish Property in the Holocaust, 1933–1945* (Cambridge: Cambridge University Press in association with the USHMM, 2008).

83. Similar scenes that took place toward the end of the war in Hungary; see Zoltán Vági, László Csősz, and Gábor Kádár, *The Holocaust in Hungary: Evolution of a Genocide* (Lanham, MD: AltaMira Press in association with the USHMM, 2013).

84. SS-Sturmbannführer Helmuth Bischoff, head of EK 1/IV (see p. 52n28).

guess, across the Bug) in an easterly direction. The river was at that time the demarcation line between the German-occupied and Russian-occupied territory.

In Raciąż in October 1939 more violence followed the roundups around Yom Kippur described in the postwar memorial book.

DOCUMENT 50: Excerpt from the memorial book for Raciąż, *Gal'ed li-ḳehilat Rat-syonz'*, ed. Efrayim Tsoref (Tel Aviv: ha-Irgun shel 'ole Ratsyonz', 1964) (translated from Yiddish).

[Avrom Yeshaia Altus, "When the Nazis Invaded Raciąż," 351–53]

On the first day of Sukkot, 1939, the SS men once again called for the rabbi and the supervisor of the Jewish community, also the antisemitic city president, and informed them that all Jews must leave Raciąż over the course of four days and, specifically, before the third day of khol ha-mo'ed,[85] which fell in October [in] 1939.

[An account follows of a committee of Raciąż Jews who attempted to prevent the expulsion by giving the German authorities a large sum of money.]

A month later [. . .] they demanded another 25,000 złoty of ransom money from the Jews. The entire bribe that the Nazis had extorted from the Jews was nothing more than a trick until they were ready to execute their final, brutal "actions." On November 9, 1939, they called together all men into the study house [*beys-medrish*] and all the women into the synagogue, with the order to bring all the jewelry that they had and all their money. They undressed one woman until she was naked and forced her to dance for them. They also desecrated Torah scrolls. They detained the women in this way until around morning, and letting them go, they announced that they must leave the city in one or two hours, taking with them no more than one bundle per family and go on their way wherever fate would take them.

Hirsh-Volf Norzhemski took his own life when his wife was trampled to death in the panic that broke out in the push toward the exit of the

---

85. The intermediate days of Jewish festivals such as Sukkot, during which relatively more work is permitted.

study house, as the Nazis began shooting.[86] One girl also took her life then.

In the morning, the Jews of Raciąż were led to the railway station, to the accompaniment of a military orchestra, and there they were pushed into train cars, under conditions of terrible crowding, to be sent to Warsaw.

Raciąż was no exception. A Jewish doctor in Kraków reported after the war that "lawlessness was evident from the very first day. We were witness to attacks, raids, beatings, and orthodox Jews having their beards cut off, passers-by having their jewelry stolen; we were witness to the theft of furniture from apartments and goods from businesses."[87] In the Lublin area, members of Einsatzkommando 3 systematically robbed Jews, not sparing wedding rings, which they tore from women's fingers with brutal force.[88] Already in mid-September, the Einsatzgruppen had committed to "the exclusion of Jewry from economic life" and largely ignored their own caveat that their "immediate removal will probably result in chaotic conditions (the decline of economic goods, an immediate cessation to whole economic sectors e.g. the food industry, etc.)."[89] Later came "more shootings; beards and side locks, together with the skin, were ripped out; forced labor began; people were thrown out of the better dwellings; there were 'fur raids' and 'gold raids,'" recalled a Jewish survivor from Tarnów.[90]

---

86. As written, although there may be some confusion in reference to the study house as opposed to the synagogue.

87. Aleksander Biberstein, *Zagłada Żydów w Krakowie* (Kraków: Wydawnictwo Literackie, 2001), 16; see also Andrea Löw, "'Wir wissen immer noch nicht, was wir machen sollen': Juden in Krakau unter deutscher Besatzung bis zur Errichtung des Ghettos," in *Deutsche-Juden-Polen: Geschichte einer wechselvollen Beziehung im 20. Jahrhundert: Festschrift für Hubert Schneider*, ed. Andrea Löw, Kerstin Robusch, and Stefanie Walter (Frankfurt am Main: Campus, 2004), 119–36.

88. Klaus-Michael Mallmann, Jochen Böhler, and Jürgen Matthäus, *Einsatzgruppen in Polen: Darstellung und Dokumentation* (Darmstadt: WBG, 2008), 75.

89. CdS daily report, September 17, 1939, USHMMA RG 15.007M (BAB, R 58/7001), reel 2, file 1:91–113.

90. Testimony by Josef Dobrucki (no date), BAL, B 162/2149, 269ff.

DOCUMENT 51: Photograph of the public humiliation of Jewish civilians conducted by members of the German Order Police in Sosnowiec (Upper Silesia), undated (1939–1940), USHMMPA WS# 74401.

Although Einsatzgruppen units resorted unevenly to murder as a means of terrorizing Jews in Poland, all of them acted according to the same principles: isolating, registering, and arranging the mass exodus of the Jews. With the transition between different authorities, firmer guidelines seemed necessary to facilitate long-term planning for how the "Jewish question" would be handled in the broader context of Nazi racial policy. Immediately after the conference at the SD Main Office held on September 21, 1939,[91] Heydrich informed the Einsatzgruppen chiefs of the short- and long-term goals for dealing with the Jews in German-controlled Poland.

DOCUMENT 52: Express letter by Reinhard Heydrich to the Einsatzgruppen on the "Jewish Question in the Occupied Territory," September 21, 1939, USHMMA RG 14.016M (BAB, R 58/954), fiche 4:181–85 (translated from German).

Express letter
To the Heads of all Einsatzgruppen of the Security Police
Subject: *Jewish Question in Occupied Territory*
    I refer to the conference that took place in Berlin today and again point out that the *planned total measures* (that is, the final goal) are to be kept *top secret*.
    A distinction must be made between
        1) the final goal (which requires a longer time frame), and
        2) the stages in the fulfillment of this final goal (which can be carried out in the short term).
    The planned measures require the most thorough preparation with regard to both the technical and the economic aspects.
    It is obvious that the tasks ahead cannot be determined from here in all their details. The instructions and guidelines below also serve the purpose of urging the chiefs of the Einsatzgruppen to engage in practical considerations.

I.

The first prerequisite for the final goal is initially to concentrate the Jews from rural areas in the larger cities.
    This is to be done expeditiously.
    In the process, a distinction must be made:
    1. between the areas of Danzig and West Prussia, Posen, eastern Upper Silesia,[92] and

---

91. See document 68.
92. These were the parts of Poland (with roughly ten million inhabitants) to be annexed to the Reich.

2) the remaining occupied territories.[93]

As far as possible, the area referred to under 1) is to be cleared of Jews; at least, the aim should be to establish only a few cities of concentration.

In the areas referred to under 2), as few concentration centers as possible are to be set up, to facilitate the subsequent measures. Here it must be borne in mind that only those cities which either are rail junctions or at least are situated on railroad lines should be selected as concentration points.

As a matter of principle, Jewish communities of *fewer than 500 persons* are to be dissolved and the people transported to the nearest city of concentration.

This directive does not apply to the area of Einsatzgruppe I, which, located east of Kraków, is roughly bounded by Polanica, Jarosław, the new demarcation line, and the previous Slovak-Polish border. Within this territory, only a provisional census of the Jews is to be carried out. In addition, the councils of Jewish elders discussed below are to be established.

II.

Councils of Jewish Elders

1) In each Jewish community, a council of Jewish elders is to be established, composed, if possible, of remaining influential individuals and rabbis. The council of elders is to consist of up to 24 male Jews (depending on the size of the Jewish community).

It is to be held *fully responsible*, in the literal sense of the word, for the exact and punctual implementation of all directives already issued or to be issued in the future.

2) In cases of sabotage of such directives, the councils are to be informed that the most severe measures will be taken.

3) The Jewish councils must carry out a provisional census of the Jews in their local areas, broken down where possible according to sex (and age groups), a) up to 16 years of age, b) from 16 to 20 years, and c) over 20, and according to the principal occupational classes, and must report the result in the shortest time possible.

4) Dates and deadlines for departure, available means for departure, and, finally, departure routes are to be announced to the councils of elders. Thereafter they are to be held personally responsible for the Jews' departure from the countryside.

---

93. Most of the area administered as the Generalgouvernement (with eleven million inhabitants).

The reason to be given for concentrating the Jews in the cities is that Jews have played a most significant part in the attacks by snipers and in the looting activities.

5) The councils of elders in the cities of concentration are to be held responsible for suitably housing the Jews who move in from the countryside.

For general security police considerations, the concentration of the Jews in cities will probably necessitate orders banning Jews from certain parts of town altogether and forbidding them, for example, to leave the ghetto, to go out after a certain evening hour, etc.—always with due regard for economic requirements, however.

6) The councils of elders in the concentration cities are also to be held responsible for providing appropriate food to the Jews during transport to the cities.

No objections are to be raised if the departing Jews take their movable goods with them, to the extent that this is technically possible.

Jews who fail to comply with the order to move into the cities are to be granted a short grace period in cases where this is justified. They are to be advised that the most severe punishment will ensue if they should fail to comply within this additional period.

III.

All requisite measures are, as a matter of principle, always to be taken in the closest consultation and cooperation with the German civil administrative authorities and appropriate local military authorities.

In carrying them out, it is to be borne in mind that securing the economies of the occupied territories should not be impaired.

1) First and foremost, the needs of the army must be taken into account; for example, it will hardly be possible to avoid leaving behind Jewish tradesmen here and there at first, people who absolutely must stay behind to supply the troops, for lack of other possibilities. In these cases, however, in consultation with the appropriate local German administrative authorities, the prompt Aryanization of these businesses is to be sought, and then the moving of the Jews is to resume.

2) For the preservation of German economic interests in the occupied territories, it is self-evident that Jewish-owned branches of industry and industrial enterprises that are of vital or strategic importance or are relevant to the Four Year Plan must be kept going for the time being.[94]

---

94. The Office of the Four Year Plan, led by Göring, coordinated the German wartime economy.

In these cases, too, prompt Aryanization is to be sought, and then the moving of the Jews is to resume.

3) Finally, the food situation in the occupied territories is to be taken into account. For example, land belonging to Jewish settlers, wherever possible, is to be provisionally put into the care of the neighboring German or even Polish farmers to be worked along with their own land, so as to ensure harvesting of the crops still out in the fields or growing of new crops.

4) With regard to this important issue, contact is to be established with the agricultural expert of the Chief of Civil Administration.

In all cases in which the interests of the Security Police, on the one hand, and those of the German civil administration, on the other hand, can be brought into accord, I am to be informed by the speediest means before the specific measures in question are carried out, and my decision is to be awaited.

IV.

The chiefs of the Einsatzgruppen will report to me on an ongoing basis regarding the following matters:

1) Numerical overview of the Jews present in their areas (if possible, broken down into the categories indicated above). Here the numbers of Jews being evacuated from the countryside and the numbers of Jews already in the cities are to be stated separately.

2) Names of the cities that have been designated as points of concentration.

3) The deadlines set for moving the Jews to the cities.

4) Overview of all Jewish-owned branches of industry and enterprises within their areas that are of vital and strategic importance or are relevant to the Four Year Plan.

If possible, the following facts are to be ascertained:

a) Nature of the enterprises (also information on their possible conversion into enterprises that are truly essential or vital to the war effort or relevant to the Four Year Plan).

b) Which of these enterprises are to be Aryanized with the greatest urgency (to eliminate all possibility of harm)? What type of Aryanization is proposed? Germans or Poles (this decision depends on the importance of the enterprise).

c) How large is the number of Jews employed in these enterprises (including Jews in leading positions).

Can the enterprise readily be kept going after removal of the Jews, or does continuance of operations require allocation of German or Polish workers? On what scale? To the extent that Polish workers must be used, care must be taken to ensure that they are brought in mainly from the former German provinces so that the Polish element there can begin to be broken up. These requirements can be carried out only through the involvement and participation of the German labor offices that have been set up.

V.

To achieve the goals that have been set, I expect total commitment of all forces of the Security Police and the SD.

The chiefs of neighboring Einsatzgruppen are to establish contact with each other immediately so that the territories in question will be covered completely.

[. . .]

Historians regard this document as a key source for this early period in Holocaust history and have discussed it extensively.[95] We should not overlook, however, that German measures on the ground often followed a much less structured, more varied, and unpredictable pattern than implied by Heydrich's letter. In towns and cities where, prior to the German arrival, Jews had organized a council that was to represent the community vis-à-vis the occupier, council members found themselves hostages to Nazi demands. The report in document 53 by an inhabitant of Kraków on the arrival of what he referred to as the "Gestapo" provides an inside glimpse of the mechanics of German anti-Jewish policy.

DOCUMENT 53: **Testimony by Leon (Leib) Salpeter, Kraków, on the formation of the Jewish council, undated (ca. 1945), USHMMA RG 15.084M (ŻIH 301/832) (translated from Polish).**[96]

[. . .] The transitional council was constituted by forming a steering committee . . . and it began its work in the community building at 41 Krakowska Street.

A few days later, the community was informed that representatives of the Kraków Gestapo would be coming for a conference. Three

---

95. See Dan Michman, "Why Did Heydrich Write the Schnellbrief? A Remark on the Reason and on Its Significance," *YVS* 32 (2004): 433–47.

96. Leon (Leib) Salpeter (b. 1897?) survived a long series of camps and may have been a pharmacist by training. See the USHMM Holocaust Survivors and Victims Database.

limousines appeared, and three officers with several Gestapo men stepped out of them. By way of greeting, they slapped the vice president in the face because no one had been awaiting their arrival in front of the building. Then Oberscharführer Siebert declared:

We come as victors and not to help the Jews.

I recognize the community as the sole representative of the Jews, in the person of the chairman.

Jews can intercede at the Gestapo office (2 Pomorska Street) and nowhere else, and Jews are subject exclusively to the authority of the Gestapo.

The community is to provide relief for the Jewish poor and for refugees. To this end, it has the absolute right to impose taxes on Jews and baptized Jews. [. . .]

Adolf Eichmann, a mid-ranking officer in Heydrich's RSHA who in the course of the war became the chief executioner of the "Final Solution" in vast parts of German-dominated Europe,[97] had attended the meeting convened by Heydrich on September 21. Afterward, he began to develop large deportation schemes in conjunction with regional Nazi officials. His ambitious expulsion plans and those of his superiors (among them Gestapo chief Heinrich Müller[98]) marked the attempt to devise anti-Jewish measures that complemented the broader goals of Nazi ethnic policy concentrated in Himmler's hands, all built around the "imperative" to get rid of the Jews in the annexed Polish territories and in the process find ways to resolve the "Jewish question" elsewhere, too.

DOCUMENT 54: File note by RSHA "resettlement" expert SS-Hauptsturmführer Adolf Eichmann, October 6, 1939, YVA O-53/93 (translated from German).

During a consultation with SS-Oberführer Müller on October 6, 1939, SS-Obf. Müller ordered as follows:

Get in contact with the office of Gauleiter Wagner in Kattowitz.[99]

Discussion with this office regarding the expulsion of 70,000 to 80,000

---

97. See David Cesarani, *Eichmann: His Life and Crimes* (London: William Heinemann, 2004); Hans Safrian, *Eichmann's Men* (New York: Cambridge University Press in association with the USHMM, 2010).

98. Heinrich Müller (1900–1945?), a World War I veteran and from 1919 a career policeman, joined the Nazi Party in 1939 and became head of RSHA Office IV (Gestapo).

99. Josef Wagner (1899–1945), Nazi Party Gauleiter for Silesia from January 1935 to November 1941.

Jews from the Kattowitz District. For now, these Jews are to go eastward across the Vistula for expulsion. Simultaneously Jews from the Mährisch Ostrau [Czech: Moravská Ostrava] area can also be taken along for expulsion. Ditto for all Jewish immigrants from Poland who are there, seeking refuge in connection with the events of recent times. These actions will serve primarily as a means of gathering experience so that the evacuation of larger masses can be carried out on the strength of the experience thus gained.

SS-Obf. Müller is to be kept informed daily by Teletype.

As part of the RSHA's "Nisko plan," almost five thousand Jews from Poland, Austria, and the Protectorate of Bohemia and Moravia were deported and put into a "Jewish reservation" (*Judenreservat*) in the Lublin area in October 1939. At the end of the month, Himmler stopped the initiative, for it clashed with his broader plans. For the time being, historian Christopher R. Browning writes, "Priority was given to the consolidation of Lebensraum through ethnic German resettlement, and a solution to the Jewish question was either postponed or sought in forms other than deportation eastward."[100] Centrally devised plans for solving the "Jewish problem" in German-controlled territory ran into competing priorities. As a result, the initiative shifted back to the local representatives of the occupying power.

Following on the heels of the Wehrmacht, Sipo and SD men further escalated the violence initiated by the military and often spearheaded the anti-Jewish thrust: at the end of October, the first ghetto was established in the Generalgouvernement by the Einsatzgruppen in Piotrków Trybunalski (German: Petrikau).[101] On October 27, Einsatzgruppe z.b.V. provided guards when the Jews were deported from Katowice to Nisko.[102] In mid-November 1939, EK 16 proudly reported that the Bydgoszcz region was "free of Jews."[103] Einsatzgruppe V was particularly active: a week after the beginning of the military campaign, its men started appointing Jewish "representatives," as well as regis-

---

100. Browning, *Origins*, 43.

101. See Ben Giladi and Martin Dean, "Piotrków Trybunalski," in *The United States Holocaust Memorial Museum Encyclopedia of Camps and Ghettos, 1933–1945*, Vol. 2: *Ghettos in German-Occupied Eastern Europe*, ed. Martin Dean (Bloomington: Indiana University Press in association with the USHMM, 2012), 279–83; Jacek Andrzej Młynarczyk, *Judenmord in Zentralpolen: Der Distrikt Radom des Generalgouvernements 1939–1945* (Darmstadt: WBG, 2007), 112.

102. Mallmann, Böhler, and Matthäus, *Einsatzgruppen in Polen*, 86.

103. Situation report by EK 16, November 17, 1939; IPNW, NTN 196/179; see also document 22.

tering and seizing Jewish property, then proceeded with expulsions. At the end of September, Einsatzgruppe V cabled to Berlin that the Jews would now "be pushed across the demarcation line in large columns."[104] Terrorizing Jews into fleeing eastward into Soviet-occupied Poland did not have the desired effect; as a result of the very limited opportunities for escape, the vast majority of the roughly 2 million Jews on German-occupied Polish territory—1.7 to 1.8 million—were still there at the end of 1939.[105]

German-perpetrated or -instigated robbery, abuse, and murder shaped a perception among the local population that the new overlords saw Jews as the lowest of the low. As a woman who in 1939 lived in Radomyśl Wielki, in the Rzeszów region in southeastern Poland, confirmed after the war, this fed the appetite among some Poles for goods in the possession of Jews to which the Germans had laid no claim.

DOCUMENT 55: **Testimony by Helena Aussenberg about German atrocities in Radomyśl Wielki, October 15, 1945, USHMMA RG 15.084M (ŻIH 301/1145) (translated from Polish).**[106]

[. . .] The Germans entered Radomyśl Wielki in 1939. The next day they chased Jews together with Poles into the church, where a few people were shot. The people were held there the whole night; they were released in the morning. The next day, they began rounding up Jews from apartments, from off the streets, and from paths—and they were driven onto the market square. There, people's shoes, clothes, and even underwear were taken and distributed to farmers. One farmer pointed to my brother's clothes. At the command of a German, my brother removed his clothes and gave them to the farmer. The people assembled on the square were then ordered to tidy up and clean the square, to pull the grass out with their teeth, and to collect papers and garbage with their bare hands. They were beaten terribly.

There was no permanent Gestapo presence in Radomyśl Wielki, but the Gestapo would come from Mielec and shoot, beat, and rob. The

---

104. Situation report Einsatzgruppe V, September 29, 1939; IPNW, NTN 196/179.

105. Browning, *Origins*, 12.

106. Helena Aussenberg (b. 1914), a seamstress, was from Radomyśl Wielki. She escaped the ghetto there and joined a Jewish partisan unit in the woods. In late 1944, she crossed the front into Soviet territory and was injured in a minefield. See ŻIH, *Holocaust Survivor Testimonies Catalogue* for RG 301 (Warsaw: ŻIH INB, 2000), 2:82.

Jews were sent to perform forced labor on nearby farms, but at night they returned to their homes.

The Jewish Council [*Judenrat*] issued lists of Jews who had to report for forced labor. Some did report and were sent to the Pustkowie labor camp. [. . .]

Germans raked in most of the profits resulting from the dispossession of the Jews, but on occasion their Polish neighbors also benefited. Although occupation officials tried to stake a claim to the spoils of expropriation, many local residents quickly got the message that they could gain from Nazi anti-Jewish measures.[107]

DOCUMENT 56: Daily report by the Chief of the Sipo/SD, September 20, 1939, USHMMA RG 14.016M (BAB, R 58/7002), reel 2, file 2:5–10 (translated from German).

[. . .] Einsatzgruppe VI:

Today a search operation for weapons is being conducted in part of the city of Posen. The following are being deployed: 1,000 men from the Security Police, Order Police, and Wehrmacht.

[. . .]

The Jews address themselves very energetically to securing any tangible items still available. The hope is to prevail in this regard by using special commissioners to liquidate businesses whose Jewish owners have fled. In the city of Posen a total of 40 Jewish businesses are closed. Also, the planning of such measures is prompted in particular by the fact that Polish employees of Jewish businesses are taking advantage of the situation to profit from the stock left behind by their employers who have fled.

[. . .]

Not many eyewitness reports on the murder of Jewish individuals in 1939 were recorded during wartime. One early report claiming to be based on an eyewitness account was documented in 1941 by the staff of the Ringelblum Archive, the secret underground archive of the Warsaw Ghetto initiated by Emanuel Ringelblum. It describes the shooting of the Jewish journalist and writer Lipe Kestin and his son in the course of what can be identified as a

---

107. See Jan T. Gross, *Neighbors: The Destruction of the Jewish Community in Jedwabne, Poland* (Princeton, NJ: Princeton University Press, 2001); Idem., *Golden Harvest: Events at the Periphery of the Holocaust* (New York: Oxford University Press, 2012).

typical Einsatzgruppen massacre of Jews in the town of Łuków, about 75 miles southeast of Warsaw.[108] When the Warsaw Ghetto was liquidated, members of the Ringelblum Archive buried the documents in metal containers so they would survive the war.

DOCUMENT 57: **Anonymous report on the murder of the Jewish journalist Lipe Kestin in October 1939 in Łuków, April 21, 1941, USHMMA RG 15.079M (ŻIH Ring. I/1019) (translated from Yiddish).**

The murder of Lipe Kestin, z'l[109]

It is possible that others have already recorded the story of the bestial murder of the well-known Jewish journalist and writer Lipe Kestin, but let us, too, fulfill the responsibility of registering the tragic end of L.K. according to an eyewitness account.

L.K. left Warsaw together with other journalists on the night of September 6–7, 1939. They went on the road toward Shedlets [Polish: Siedlce], like many other hundreds of thousands. This "road of hell" has already been well documented, and we will not describe it here. Dark fate drove L.K. and his 18-year-old son to Lukov [Polish: Łuków]. The Germans caught up with him there. On the second day, L.K. was standing together with his son on a lawn in front of a bakery, hoping to get a piece of bread. At that moment, about 20 German military personnel rode into the city on several motorcycles. The motorcycles came to a stop, and there could soon be heard, "Jews—out front!" About 70 Jews were told to go to the marketplace, and there they were ordered to stand with their faces to the wall; soon the salvo of a machine gun was heard. For a whole day, the Jews of Lukov holed up in their hovels, scared to leave. When they finally

---

108. Lipe Kestin (aka Kestkind, b. 1889), was a noted Yiddish author and journalist, popular among Jewish circles in Warsaw and elsewhere in Poland. At the outset of the German invasion in September 1939, he fled Warsaw with his eighteen-year-old son. The Germans killed them soon thereafter, but the accounts of their deaths vary widely. One account does not give the precise day of their deaths but claims the Germans took Kestin and his son out of their apartment in Łuków and shot them in the street. A third account mentions in passing that Kestin was killed in Mińsk Mazowiecki in a German bombing of the city. See Abraham Zak, "Der Moment tsvishn beyde velt milkhomes," in *Di Yidishe prese vos iz geven*, ed. David Flinker, Mordekhai Tsanin, and Shalom Rozenfeld (Tel Aviv: Yeltfarband fun di Yidishe zshurnalistn, 1975), 102; Yonas Turkov, *Azoy iz es geven: Hurbn Varshe* (Buenos Aires: Tsentral-farband fun Poylishe Yidn in Argentine, 1948), 26. The document printed here seems the most reliable in terms of dating Kestin's murder.

109. "Of blessed memory."

came out to the marketplace, they could only mourn for the 70 martyrs. Among the fallen were Lipe Kestin and his son, who in the last minute had tightly embraced each other and so had died. This was on October 19, 1939.

The randomness and violence of German measures made it even harder for local Jews to figure out what the occupiers ultimately sought. As a former inhabitant recalled in 1945, in the town of Cisna in southeastern Poland (then in the Lesko region), humiliation was rampant, but without a comprehensible purpose. Robbery obviously served material interests; yet the way they stripped Jews of their possessions made it clear the Germans were not content with mere monetary gain.

DOCUMENT 58: **Testimony by Moses Zwas about early anti-Jewish measures in Cisna, May 31, 1945, USHMMA RG 15.084M (ŻIH 301/280) (translated from Polish).**[110]

When the Germans came, Cisna had 150 Jews. The mistreatment already began during the first days of their stay in our village—beatings and searches in our houses by the Gestapo. A week later they rounded up all the men, harnessed us to carts, and ordered us to put the things that had been looted from our homes on the carts and to pull the carts around the village several times for the amusement of the Christian population. We suggested horses for the task, but they refused. So we had to endure being kicked and beaten with whips almost until the evening.

The next day I was rounded up along with a few other respected Jews to clean all the toilets in Christian homes. I was assigned to perform such tasks later, too, since, as the Germans asserted, it was most suitable for a bearded Jew (I was Orthodox).

At this time, the Germans issued a prohibition on lighting candles on Fridays and assembling for prayers. One Friday, the Germans burst in as a few other Jews and I were secretly reciting prayers in a small, out-of-the-way room in my home. With a mocking laugh they began to ask us

---

110. Moses Zwas (b. 1892 or 1896 in Cisna) was sent to the Lesko ghetto. His wife and child perished in the Bełżec camp, while he was transferred to the forced labor camp at Zasław. He survived the war by escaping in 1942 to Hungary, where he lived illegally. He provided this testimony in Bucharest and ultimately emigrated to the United States. See ŻIH, *Holocaust Survivor Testimonies Catalogue* for RG 301 (Warsaw: ŻIH INB, 1998), 1:109.

various Talmudic questions, and we had to pray in their presence. They then grabbed us by our beards with wild sadism and beat us about our heads with clubs. The next morning, they ordered us to report to the Gestapo.

We all showed up punctually, all dressed up (it was a Saturday), prepared for the worst, even death. But they didn't do anything to us at the time, they didn't even beat us, but they ordered us, as was typical in the past, to go clean the toilets. This no longer affected me; I calmly completed my work.

A decree then came from the German authorities that a Jewish council had to be constituted within a few days. I was offered the position of the elder, but I declined, promising my cooperation.

The next Saturday they conducted a meticulous search of all Jewish homes. They took all the prayer shawls and religious [*biblijne*; literally "biblical"] books, drove all the Jews onto the market square, and ordered them to set on fire, in turn, all the items that had been taken. The Jewish women and children had to circle around and dance and sing, "We rejoice as the filth burns [German used here: 'Wir freuen sich wie das Dreck brennt']." The men had to sway back and forth and pray aloud. All of this took place under terrible blows from the whip and under the guard of machine guns.

The next day, Sunday, we all, even women and children, had to report for work. They once again assigned us to clean toilets; some had to clean ditches and break stones. We had to work quickly and accurately under German supervision. The local Christian population, as well as those who had come to church from surrounding villages, watched us with delight. [. . .]

The threat of arrest was ever present as both the civil administration and the Sipo/SD were keen on preventing "Jews from avoiding the planned measures by constantly moving home" as part of an envisaged "solution of the Jewish problem."[111] After the war a woman living in Krasnystaw in eastern Poland in the vicinity of Lublin described how one's situation could change from one day to the next.

---

111. Situation report Einsatzgruppe III to the Supreme Army Command (Armeeoberkommando) 8, September 26, 1939, APŁ, 175/10a.

DOCUMENT 59: **Testimony by Pola Ajzensztajn regarding anti-Jewish violence in Krasnystaw and Rejowiec, September 30, 1946, USHMMA RG 15.084M (ŻIH 301/1885) (translated from Polish).**[112]

[. . .] At the outbreak of the war there were about 5,000 Jews in Krasnystaw. The Germans entered the town in September 1939. My entire family (my husband, two children, and my mother) and I were immediately taken from our home. All our furniture was taken away. This was done by the ethnic German [*folksdajcz,* a Polonized form of the German *Volksdeutsche(r)*] Gayde, who was given many items, including our mill together with the house, for his loyal service to the Germans on Polish territory. The abuse began almost immediately. True, the SS did not set up in our town, but they visited it continually. There were robberies and murders on a daily basis. One day they shot 15 people. They broke into homes at night and compelled us to work amid beatings. The conditions were terrible, so we decided to move to nearby Rejowiec. It was peaceful there initially. But after three weeks, things became even worse. SS and SD men came from Chełm two or three times a week (Mondays, Thursdays, and Saturdays) and put on their "little games." [. . .]

Despite the problems inherent in large-scale resettlement plans that had become visible during the "Nisko experiment," Himmler continued to consider the "solution of the Jewish question" in the context of his broader goals for the "Germanization" of the annexed parts of Poland. To this end, the Einsatzgruppen were told to gather the necessary demographic data while combing the countryside.

---

112. Pola Ajzensztajn (b. 1908 or 1910 in Rejowiec) survived forced labor, while her parents and children were murdered in Trawniki. She survived an evacuation march at the end of the war and gave her testimony in Lublin. See the USHMM Holocaust Survivors and Victims Database.

DOCUMENT 60: Express letter by Einsatzgruppe z.b.V., Katowice, to the Sipo Berlin, November 8, 1939, USHMMA RG 11.001M (RGVA 500-1-431), reel 6 (translated from German).

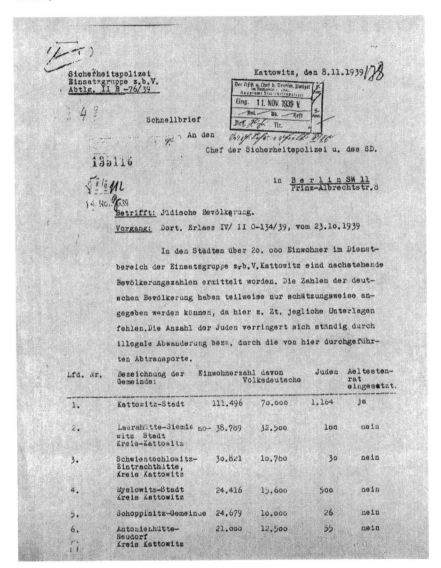

Sicherheitspolizei
Einsatzgruppe z.b.V.
Abtlg. II B -76/39

Kattowitz, den 8.11.1939

Schnellbrief

An den

Chef der Sicherheitspolizei u. des SD.

in B e r l i n SW 11
Prinz-Albrechtstr. 8

Betrifft: Jüdische Bevölkerung.

Vorgang: Dort. Erlass IV/ II 0-134/39, vom 23.10.1939

In den Städten über 20. 000 Einwohner im Dienstbereich der Einsatzgruppe z.b.V. Kattowitz sind nachstehende Bevölkerungszahlen ermittelt worden. Die Zahlen der deutschen Bevölkerung haben teilweise nur schätzungsweise angegeben werden können, da hier z. Zt. jegliche Unterlagen fehlen. Die Anzahl der Juden verringert sich ständig durch illegale Abwanderung bezw. durch die von hier durchgeführten Abtransporte.

Lfd. Nr.	Bezeichnung der Gemeinde:	Einwohnerzahl davon Volksdeutsche		Juden	Aeltestenrat eingesetzt.
1.	Kattowitz-Stadt	111.496	70.000	1.164	ja
2.	Laurahütte-Siemianowitz Stadt Kreis-Kattowitz	38.769	32.500	100	nein
3.	Schwientochlowitz-Eintrachthütte, Kreis Kattowitz	30.821	10.700	30	nein
4.	Myslowitz-Stadt Kreis Kattowitz	24.416	15.600	500	nein
5.	Schoppinitz-Gemeinde	24.679	10.000	26	nein
6.	Antonienhütte-Neudorf Kreis Kattowitz	21.000	12.500	55	nein

[. . .]

Re: Jewish population

File reference: your decree IV/II O-134/39 dated October 23, 1939

In cities with more than 20,000 inhabitants located in the operation area of Einsatzgruppe z.b.V. Kattowitz, the following population figures have been established. For the German population, some numbers could only be estimated, since no records of any kind are currently available here. The number of Jews is constantly declining as a result of illegal emigration [*Abwanderung*] or the deportations [*Abtransporte*] from here.

No.	Name of municipality	Number of inhabitants	Of these, no. of ethnic Germans	Jews	Judenrat installed
1.	City of Kattowitz	111,496	70,000	1,164	Yes
2.	City of Laurahütte-Siemianowitz [Polish: Huta Laura–Siemianowice Śląskie] Kattowitz District	38,789	32,500	100	No
3.	Schwientochlowitz [Polish: Świętochłowice]–Eintrachthütte Kattowitz District	30,821	10,780	30	No
4.	City of Myslowitz [Polish: Mysłowice] Kattowitz District	24,416	15,600	500	No
5.	Schoppinitz [Polish: Szopienice] Municipality	24,679	10,000	26	No
6.	Antoniehütte-Neudorf Kattowitz District	21,000	12,500	55	No

Document 61, a decree coming down from Himmler through the main chain of command, exemplifies his ambitious ideas of "cleansing" the annexed territory for ethnic German settlers and forcing "undesirable" local residents into the Generalgouvernement.

DOCUMENT 61: Decree by the Higher SS and Police Leader, Posen, regarding the expulsion of Jews and Poles from the Warthegau, November 12, 1939, USHMMA RG 14.041M (BAB, R 70 Polen/198), fiche 1:12–16 (translated from German).

[. . .]

1) The Reichsführer-SS and Chief of the German Police, in his capacity as Reich Commissioner for the Strengthening of Germandom, has ordered that from the formerly Polish territories now part of the Reich,

a) all Jews and

b) all those Poles who are either members of the intelligentsia or because of their Polish nationalist views can present a danger to the establishing and strengthening of German culture [*Deutschtum*] are to be deported. Criminal elements are to be treated in the same way.

The aim of the deportation is:

a) cleansing and securing of the new German territories,

b) creation of dwellings and work opportunities for the ethnic Germans immigrating.

The evacuation operation absolutely must be consistent with these aims, with no regard for other concerns of any kind.

2) On the basis of a meeting in the office of the *Generalgouverneur* in Kraków, the deportation from the Warthegau for the period November 15, 1939, to February 28, 1940, will initially include 200,000 Poles and 100,000 Jews.

3) The areas south of Warsaw and Lublin are designated as an accommodation area for the people deported from here.

4) As part of this first action, all Jews are to be expelled from the districts, in addition to at least 2,000 Poles from the smallest districts and a correspondingly larger number from the larger districts. The following independent towns [not subordinate to districts] are to make available for expulsion:

Posen:	around 35,000 Poles and all Jews
Lodsch [Polish: Łódź]:	around 30,000 Poles and
	around 30,000 Jews
Gnesen [Polish: Gniezno]:	around 2,300 Poles and all Jews
Hohensalza:	around 2,300 Poles and all Jews

In the case of the rural districts and independent towns, the quotas envisaged for deportation of Poles and Jews are to be expelled during the period stated in 2) above. Preparatory measures are to begin immediately. It must be borne in mind that the number of expellees for now is greater than the number of ethnic Germans to be resettled from the Baltic, the Generalgouvernement, and Volhynia. The cleansing and securing of the areas will be achieved only when the intellectual elite, the entire intelligentsia, and all political and criminal elements have been removed. All people with Polish nationalist sentiments are to be deported as well. In the case of the intelligentsia, evidence of political or anti-German activity need not be present. Beyond this, the aspect of creating dwellings and jobs for the immigrating Reich Germans and ethnic Germans must be taken into account in every way. [. . .]

Only small parts of these proposed plans were implemented due to the huge obstacles standing in the way, many of which would grow as World War II intensified. Yet they clearly indicate the ideological culture and political context within which German officials, not only in the Warthegau but beyond its borders, were expected to operate in the future with respect to both Jews and local populations in general.

ESTABLISHING LONG-TERM RULE

In the aftermath of the Polish campaign and as part of the transfer of occupation authority from the Wehrmacht to civilian administrators, the mobile Einsatzgruppen were gradually converted into stationary Sipo/SD offices, from which points they continued persecuting members of the Polish intelligentsia and others they perceived to be "enemies of the Reich." The evolving civilian structure was first represented by the chiefs of civil administration, who accompanied each of the five German armies on their march eastward, then, as of October 1939, by agencies installed in the areas annexed to the Reich or administered as part of the Generalgouvernement. Hitler's regional fiefs tried to integrate the Einsatzgruppen into an administrative system established to ensure economic gains for the Reich and to exert control over the civilian population. Eager to assert their new authority, they found that police colleagues keen on continuing their established practices did not always feed them reliable information.

DOCUMENT 62: **Report by the district head of Pszczyna to the Chief of Civil Administration, Katowice, regarding cooperation with the Security Police, September 19, 1939, APK, 119/1637 (translated from German).**

After the three Security Police detachments suddenly departed from the Pless [Polish: Pszczyna] District in the last week, a Security Police detachment from Rybnik appeared on Saturday at the office of the head of the district gendarmerie, demanding that the insurgents in custody in Pless be handed over to be shot. He said there was an order from the Reichsführer-SS [Himmler], directing that the insurgents be shot. Thereupon the head of the district gendarmerie contacted me, and so I called in the NSDAP representative as well. I decided that those individuals who, on the basis of clear documentary evidence, can unequivocally be characterized as insurgents should be handed over to the Security Police. What the Security Police then does with the insurgents handed over to them does not concern us; providing the assistance they request is out of the question.

The Security Police then reportedly did indeed shoot 6 insurgents near the city of Pless. The local military headquarters provided prisoners of war to dig the grave.

The head of the district gendarmerie immediately noted the incident in his next situation report. I myself am making this report only today, after learning to my astonishment that the Chief of Civil Administration is said to have no knowledge of the aforementioned order of the Reichsführer-SS.

[illegible signature]

In trying to expand his position in German-dominated Poland beyond his police and resettlement domain, Himmler claimed that all policy matters in the annexed or occupied territories were related to the strategic goals of "pacification" and "Germanization" under his charge. Forced labor thus formed part of his remit.

DOCUMENT 63: **Express letter by Reinhard Heydrich to the Einsatzgruppen, September 30, 1939, APŁ 175/10 b (translated from German).**

[. . .] There are reports from different quarters that mostly teenage Polish elements are engaging in especially provocative behavior in the occupied territories. The Reichsführer-SS and Chief of the German Police has therefore ordered that such elements be combined to form work gangs.

Under strictest supervision, they will support the work of the Reich Labor Service, which has been deployed by the Wehrmacht, and they will be used to the broadest extent for clearing rubble, etc. I am informing you of this with the request for further action. The chiefs of the Einsatzgruppen of the Security Police in the occupied territories have received the same information. [. . .]

Despite the head start given him by his police and SS units as they followed on the heels of the Wehrmacht into Poland, Himmler faced competition from other officials eager to assert themselves as the new masters in the east. On September 25, Chief Civil Administrator Arthur Greiser reported the situation in his region as satisfactory but saw no reason to replace violence with more conciliatory measures toward the civilian population.

DOCUMENT 64: **Report by the Chief of Civil Administration, Poznań, September 25, 1939, APP 289/50 (translated from German).**

[. . .] Within a week it was possible in close cooperation with the military to sift through and cleanse not only the towns but also the vast majority of the districts [*Landkreise*]. The situation today can generally be regarded as pacified. The demand that weapons be surrendered, which was coupled with the threat of the death penalty, and which in a few cases has indeed resulted in executions, has stripped all the unsafe elements of their weapons [*Gewaltmittel*]. The issuing of weapons to reliable ethnic Germans has increased general security in the countryside. The police detachments, which in the meantime have arrived in all the district towns, and the large numbers of German troops in the province ensure absolute safety. Police activities are now focused on the screening and cleansing of the Polish population. All the elements that have committed offenses against ethnic Germans, to the extent that these elements were still in the province, have been arrested and, in the most serious cases, have been summarily shot. The number of public executions, which must be viewed as highly necessary for pacification purposes, was unfortunately very small. It is thus to be expected, however, that the armed civilians, etc., large numbers of whom are still to be tried by the special court that will be used from now on, will be publicly shot as a deterrent. The focus of the police has been on the Polish upper class. All the hate-filled teachers and clerics who were present have been arrested and are being deported to concentration camps. The clergy has been forcefully warned, and in some places Catholic clerics have been shot because they were demonstrably guilty of persecuting Germans.

Greiser defined the parameters of the administrative tasks before he moved from his post as chief of civil administration in Poznań to become Hitler's vassal (*Reichsstatthalter*) in the newly annexed "Reichsgau Posen" (later renamed Reichsgau Wartheland or Warthegau) in late October 1939.

DOCUMENT 65: **"Guidelines for the Administrative Reconstruction in the Districts and Cities of the Province of Posen," September 29, 1939, BAL, B 162/Vorl. Dok. Slg. Polen 365 (translated from German).**

[. . .]

Each locality is to be given a German character as quickly and as thoroughly as possible. Initially this state of affairs will be achieved by erecting signs with German names.

Loitering Poles are absolutely not to be tolerated. They must be used for public relief work and, if necessary, combined to form forced labor gangs. In addition to their civilian labor assignments, the work gangs must be made available above all to the local military commanders and construction battalions.

Ethnic Germans who are suitable for deployment in administrative offices, or at least for assistance in such offices, are to be used in an appropriate manner.

A suitable building for later use for NSDAP purposes is to be selected and secured in advance.

Firearm-control actions are to be conducted repeatedly in concert with the military authority and jointly with the military and the police. District administrators and mayors must repeatedly make it clear that Poles who are charged [with possession of firearms] in the course of such a firearm-control action will be publicly executed. The organs of the military authorities as well as, more recently, those of the police and the SD are in a position to accommodate the political requirements of my representatives by means of quickly constituted summary courts. The directives received by the military authorities, the SD, and the Order Police make it possible to crack down much faster and far more forcefully in this area. Because the real establishment of peace in the province can be achieved only by taking uncompromising action in this regard, I am making the district administrators and mayors responsible for the use of such drastic measures.

Funds and assets of Polish organizations are to be seized and used in the interest of Germandom [*Deutschtum*] and reconstruction work. Accurate supporting documents for these seizures and accurate accounting are an ironclad necessity.

The NSV [Nationalsozialistische Volkswohlfahrt; Nazi public welfare organization] has commenced its work. Shops and stocks that have been abandoned by Polish owners can, in suitable cases, be made available to the NSV for its work. These are to be seized, and an inventory is to be made.

Lists of Polish leaders and the Polish intelligentsia (priests, teachers, large landowners, businessmen, and industrialists) are to be compiled under the strictest secrecy and forwarded to me personally through official channels, marked "Secret Reich Business" ["*Geheime Reichssache*"]. [. . .]

In conjunction with Sipo/SD presence, courts-martial formed an important element of continuity linking the first phase of German occupation with the period after the establishment of a civil administration. As proceedings became more formalized, incoming German officials recorded some of them. The unsigned report presented in document 66, filed by the state prosecutor in Leszno, describes the rapid processing of cases by Einsatzgruppe VI in the Poznań region.

DOCUMENT 66: Unsigned account of Einsatzgruppen court proceedings in Leszno, October 24, 1939, IZ doc. II/857 (translated from German).

In a consultation regarding another matter, State Prosecutor Verlohren-Lissa today made the following observations about the summary court proceedings held in the last few days:

On Saturday, October 21, 1939, a summary court ordered by the Reichsführer-SS assembled in Lissa. The court was presided over by SS-Sturmbannführer Flesch of Stapo-Einsatzkommando 14 [1/VI], and the associate judges were SS-Sturmbannführer Holz (Kripo) and an SS-Obersturmführer; the court recorder was an SS-Scharführer. There was no prosecutor. Three ethnic Germans from Lissa, including Pastor Bickerich, who is especially active there in German cultural work [*Volkstumsarbeit*], acted as interpreters and at the same time as informants regarding the political activities of the accused.

The summary court assembled at 7:00 a.m. in a room in the court building. Also present at the session were the district administrator, Dr. von Baumbach; the Selbstschutz commander, SS-Sturmbannführer Möller; Police Councilor [Polizeirat] Grund from the administrative district office; and the commander of the Lissa Stapo detachment, Wulf.

On trial were 53 people, all of whom were in Stapo custody. There was not one among them for whom a court arrest order was produced.

The accused were led into the courtroom in groups of 3 or 4 and were interrogated by the presiding judge with the aid of written notes. He read the charges to them. Only one witness was interrogated. The informants were questioned about the political bent of the defendants.

The summary court then retired to deliberate for about 20 minutes. Thereupon 33 of the accused, who were not sentenced to death, were transported back to the prison.

The remaining 20 defendants, who were brought before the court once again, were informed by the presiding judge that they had been sentenced to death, some for rabble-rousing and some for physical attacks and assaults on ethnic Germans. The sentence would be immediately carried out, they were told. The condemned men next had to put their valuables, headwear, etc., into three buckets that were provided, and then they were taken by the Order Police in two groups of 10 men each to the castle square. An Order Police detachment of 30 men under the command of a police lieutenant was standing by there. Along one wall, sandbags were stacked up to trap the bullets. The condemned had to stand with their hands raised in front of this backstop, facing the wall. Then the police squad fired. [. . .] Among those executed in Lissa were a professor (a leading member of the Westmarkenverein), a Polish lawyer (who had recently been the acting Polish mayor), and a businessman. These three were found guilty of anti-German agitation [*Hetzereien gegen das Deutschtum*]. The remaining 17 had committed acts of violence against Germans. After this, the summary court moved to Storchnest [Polish: Osieczna], where it tried 15 people, three of whom were shot. Further summary court proceedings were held, partly also on October 23, in Kosten [Polish: Kościan] (around

20 shot), Gostyn [Polish: Gostyń], and Schmiegel [Polish: Śmigiel]. The shootings took place on the market squares. [. . .]

If the new administration placed stronger emphasis on creating the preconditions for long-term German rule than its military predecessor, it made sure that violence against any form of civilian resistance and the systematic pursuit of the Reich's racial agenda remained a core element of Nazi domination. Greiser was responsible for massive crimes perpetrated in the Warthegau through the end of the war, including in the ghetto in Łódź and the extermination camp in Chełmno, the first death camp established by Nazi Germany in late 1941.[113]

With the change in the administrative structure, Einsatzgruppen leaders assumed new functions as part of a larger, more intricate system established in German-controlled Poland that included other branches of Himmler's apparatus, most notably the Order Police (organized along similar lines as the Sipo/SD) and the emerging Waffen-SS. In the Generalgouvernement, they came under the supervision of the Reichsführer's direct representative, Higher SS and Police Leader (HSSPF) Obergruppenführer Friedrich-Wilhelm Krüger, with Einsatzgruppe I chief Bruno Streckenbach as the new Commander of the Security Police and SD (BdS), who answered to Krüger as well as the RSHA in Berlin. In the Generalgouvernement's four districts, Krüger oversaw the work of SS and Police Leaders (SSPFs), who in turn supervised the regional Sipo/SD and Orpo offices (KdS and KdO, respectively) and the Selbstschutz.[114] The KdS offices were organized along the lines of the RSHA, with Division (Abteilung) I responsible for personnel and administration, Abteilung II for SD work, Abteilung III representing the Gestapo, and Abteilung IV the Criminal Police (Kripo).[115] Himmler formalized the new police structure in the Generalgouvernement in November.

---

113. Browning, *Origins*, 316–19; Catherine Epstein, *Model Nazi: Arthur Greiser and the Occupation of Western Poland* (Oxford: Oxford University Press, 2010). On Chełmno, see Patrick Montague, *Chełmno and the Holocaust: The History of Hitler's First Death Camps* (Chapel Hill: University of North Carolina Press, 2012).

114. See Andreas Mix, "Organisatoren und Praktiker der Gewalt: Die SS- und Polizeiführer im Distrikt Warschau," in *Krieg und Verbrechen: Situation und Intention: Fallbeispiele*, ed. Timm C. Richter (Munich: Meidenbauer, 2006), 123–34.

115. Decree by RSHA I V 1, January 5, 1940, USHMMA RG 14.016M (BAB, R 58/241), fiche 5:232.

DOCUMENT 67: Decree by Himmler regarding police organization in the General-gouvernement, November 1, 1939, USHMMA RG 14.016M (BAB, R 58/241), fiche 5:211–12 (translated from German).

1. The Higher SS and Police Leader East reports directly to the *Generalgouverneur* in Poland. The following report to the Higher SS and Police Leader East:

    a) the Commander of the Order Police (BdO),

    b) the Commander of the Security Police and the SD (BdS),

    c) the leaders of the SS and the Selbstschutz, with their staffs.

Directly reporting to them are the units from their areas of command that are deployed in the Generalgouvernement.

2. The four district chiefs in Warsaw, Lublin, Radom, and Kraków who report to the *Generalgouverneur* will be allocated "SS and Police Leaders," who report directly to the Higher SS and Police Leader. The SS and Police Leaders are the district chiefs' advisors on all police matters and are required to comply with the instructions of the district chiefs, unless they are in conflict with the orders of the Higher SS and Police Leader and his representatives. The following report to the SS and Police Leader:

    a) a commanding officer of the Ordnungspolizei (KdO),

    b) a commanding officer of the Security Police (KdS),

    c) a leader of the SS and of the Selbstschutz, with their staffs.

3. The provincial governors [*Landeshauptmänner*] who report to the district chiefs are in charge of the police, SS, and Selbstschutz forces attached to them.

In the annexed areas, the organization of SS and police agencies resembled that of the Reich, with the inspector of the Security Police and SD (IdS) as the highest authority for each region, represented by Tröger in Danzig–West Prussia and Damzog in the emerging Warthegau.[116] The Einsatzgruppen, which were officially dissolved on November 20, 1939, distributed their staff over the new Sipo and SD offices; where necessary, additional personnel were brought in from the Reich.[117] This first major expansion of German rule provided the precedent for occupation structures established in the further course of the war, with many of the Einsatzgruppen members originally deployed in Poland later transferred

---

116. SDHA I 11, September 8, 1939, USHMMA RG 14.016M (BAB, R 58/825), fiche 1.
117. Mallmann, Böhler, and Matthäus, *Einsatzgruppen in Polen*, 99–103.

to similar positions elsewhere in German-controlled Europe. There, they would work to uphold the German version of "pacification" and play a key role in executing the "Final Solution of the Jewish question."[118]

In the meeting held at the RSHA on September 21, Heydrich informed the Einsatzgruppen commanders about the broader parameters within which he expected them to operate in the future. The minutes of this meeting and an express letter (*Schnellbrief*) from Heydrich to the Einsatzgruppen leaders survived the war and provide important clues as to the Sipo/SD chief's line of thinking. It was certainly no coincidence that Adolf Eichmann, the RSHA's expert on "Jewish emigration," attended the meeting.

DOCUMENT 68: **Protocol of a meeting of RSHA department heads and Einsatzgruppen commanders, September 27, 1939, USHMMA RG 14.016M (BAB, R 58/825), fiche 1:14 (translated from German).**

A conference of the department heads and leaders of the Einsatzgruppen took place on September 21, 1939, led by C ["Chef"; reference to Heydrich as Chief of the Sipo/SD]. The following commanders participated:

SS-Brigadeführer Dr. Best,
SS-Oberführer Müller,
SS-Oberführer Nebe,
SS-Standartenführer Ohlendorf,
SS-Standartenführer Six,
SS-Obersturmbannführer Dr. Filbert,
SS-Sturmbannführer Rauff,
SS-Brigadeführer Beutel,
SS-Brigadeführer Streckenbach,
SS-Oberführer Naumann,
SS-Standartenführer Damzog,
SS-Obersturmbannführer Schäfer,
SS-Obersturmbannführer Fischer,
SS-Sturmbannführer Dr. Meier (Gestapa),

---

118. Among them was Dr. Hellmut Tanzmann, who in September 1941 became KdS in Lviv (German: Lemberg), where he was in charge of the murder of the East Galician Jews. See Dieter Pohl, *Nationalsozialistische Judenverfolgung in Ostgalizien 1941–1944: Organisation und Durchführung eines staatlichen Massenverbrechens* (Munich: Oldenbourg, 1996), 421; Thomas Sandkühler, *"Endlösung" in Galizien: Der Judenmord in Ostpolen und die Rettungsinitiativen von Berthold Beitz 1941–1944* (Bonn: Dietz, 1996), 438.

SS-Hauptsturmführer Eichmann (Jewish Emigration Office).

By way of introduction, C emphasized that the discussion could not be all encompassing and that only what was of highest priority for the *Einsatzgruppenleiter* was to be discussed.

[. . .] At the moment, development in the former Poland is intended to occur in such a way that the former German provinces will become German *Gaue*, and in addition a *Gau* with a non-German-speaking population will be created with Kraków as the capital. [. . .] The RFSS [Reichsführer-SS] will be appointed as settlement commissioner [*Siedlungskommissar*] for the east. The Führer has granted permission for deportation of the Jews into the non-German-speaking *Gau*, deportation across the demarcation line. Nevertheless, the entire process will be spread out over the course of a year. Solution of the Polish problem—as already explained many times—in different ways, based on the leadership class (Polish intelligentsia) and the lower-working-class Polish people. Of the political leadership, only 3% at most are still in the occupied areas. This 3% is also to be rendered harmless and is to go to concentration camps. The Einsatzgruppen must prepare lists of the prominent leaders as well as lists of the middle class: teachers, priests, nobility, legionnaires, returning officers, etc. These are also to be arrested and shifted into the remainder of the country. Catholic priests from the west are to look after the spiritual welfare of the Poles, but they are not permitted to speak Polish. The primitive Poles are to be integrated into the labor process as itinerant workers and will gradually be resettled out of the German *Gaue* into the non-German-speaking *Gau*. Jews are to be concentrated in the cities in ghettos, to permit better control and make subsequent expulsion easier. Here it is urgent that the Jew disappears as a smallholder from the countryside. This must be accomplished within the next 3 to 4 weeks. If the Jew in rural areas is a trader, we need to discuss with the Wehrmacht the extent to which these Jewish traders may remain where they are, to cover the requirements of the troops. The following comprehensive instructions were issued:

1) [Move] Jews as quickly as possible into the cities,
2) Jews out of the Reich into Poland,
3) the remaining 30,000 Gypsies also into Poland,
4) systematic removal of the Jews from the German territories, on freight trains.

The commanders of the Einsatzgruppen, in particular Schäfer for the industrial area and Damzog for the northeast, must reflect on how, on the one hand, the manpower of the primitive Poles is to be integrated into the labor process and how, on the other hand, they are to be simultaneously expelled. The goal: the Pole remains the eternal seasonal, itinerant laborer; his fixed abode must be in the Kraków area.

Shootings are to take place only in cases of self-defense or escape attempts. All other trials are to be handed over to the military courts. The military courts must be so overwhelmed with petitions that they can no longer get the work under control. C wants all military court verdicts not involving the death penalty to be submitted to him.

[. . .]

The last sentences in Heydrich's express letter reveal his goal of seemingly giving in to Wehrmacht claims to judicial prerogative while at the same time making sure that his Sipo/SD units would be perceived as upholding "law and order" vis-à-vis an "undesirable" population. Wehrmacht leaders understood. Following a meeting with Hitler on September 20 and acceptance of Himmler's authority in matters of police action, Army High Commander von Brauchitsch issued the decree to the military commanders in Poland presented in document 69. Although the specific tasks Brauchitsch was referring to remained unclear, as did what would happen if the military did not approve of police actions, the Einsatzgruppen clearly acted with the consent of the Reich's top leadership.

DOCUMENT 69: Directive by the Army High Commander regarding activities and tasks of the Einsatzgruppen, September 21, 1939, BA-MA, RH 20-14/178 (translated from German).

The police Einsatzgruppen are to perform certain ethnic-political tasks [*volkspolitische Aufgaben*] in the occupied territory on behalf of the Führer and in accordance with his instructions. To ensure consistency in command and to avoid further incidents, the following rules, which have been presented to the Führer, are effective immediately:

The Führer will inform the Army High Commander of all instructions that he gives to the Reichsführer-SS [Himmler] with regard to the occupied territory.

The Reichsführer-SS will inform the Army High Commander of all instructions issued by him in this matter to subordinated command headquarters.

The Chief of the Security Police [Heydrich] will proceed in the same manner as the Reichsführer-SS.

The commanders of the police Einsatzgruppen are to give notification of their assigned tasks to the appropriate military commander [*Oberbefehlshaber*] before carrying them out.

The Führer's tasks encompass, above all, ethnopolitical measures [*Massnahmen volkspolitischer Art*]. The details of the performance of these tasks are left to the discretion of the commanders of the Einsatzgruppen and are outside the responsibility of the military commanders. I request that the military commanders proceed in accordance with the preceding guideline and that they order the commanders of the Einsatzgruppen to bring their actions into accord with the Army's interests. The Secret Field Police [Geheime Feldpolizei] and Field Gendarmerie [Feldgendarmerie] are Army units and are not to be used for any police task of the kind mentioned above. I request that I be informed immediately by Teletype if Einsatzgruppen should be found in violation of the instructions above. I personally will keep the military commanders continuously informed of the Führer's instructions.

[signed:] v. Brauchitsch

Following Himmler's appointment in early October as Reich Commissioner for the Strengthening of Germandom (Reichskommissar für die Festigung deutschen Volkstums), his apparatus became even more heavily involved in "the elimination of all harmful influences from ethnic groups alien to Germans" and the "creation of a new German settlement area."[119] Already in late September, the stage had been set for Himmler's men to play a key role in the violent ethnic transformation of the occupied territories. "Resettlement" became the topic of sweeping grand designs and a standard feature of German policy, affecting those deemed "desirable"—such as ethnic German settlers who were to help "Germanize" the annexed Polish territories—as well as those regarded as inimical to German rule and earmarked for deportation to the Generalgouvernement.

In the new eastern provinces, the Sipo, SD, and SS Race and Settlement Main Office (Rasse- und Siedlungshauptamt) operated a system established

---

119. Hitler decree appointing Himmler Reichskommissar für die Festigung deutschen Volkstums, October 7, 1939, BAB, R 49/2. See also Robert Lewis Koehl, *RKFDV: German Resettlement and Population Policy, 1939–1945: A History of the Reich Commission for the Strengthening of Germandom* (Cambridge, MA: Harvard University Press, 1957); Phillip Rutherford, "'Absolute Organizational Deficiency': The 1. Nahplan of December 1939 (Logistics, Limitations, and Lessons)," *Central European History* 36 (2003): 235–73.

to screen local populations for their racial qualities.[120] The pattern for dealing with "undesirable" groups proved uneven. In the Łódź area, EK 2 of Einsatzgruppe III only carried out arrests until November, when the unit also began to conduct mass shootings.[121] In the province of Poznań, the Wehrmacht initially carried out most of the executions, claiming the lives of five hundred civilians.[122] In mid-September, Einsatzgruppe VI was ordered to pacify the region and in October set up summary courts-martial followed by public executions, sometimes with the help of the Order Police.[123] Estimates put the number of Poles shot in this period by the Sipo/SD in the Poznań region at several hundred.[124] Einsatzgruppe I, deployed in East Upper Silesia—a region that formed the heartland of the German-Polish struggle after World War I and the most important industrial area of Poland—acted similarly. By the beginning of October, the district head of Lubliniec near Częstochowa described what amounted to the liquidation of the Polish elite: "All Polish-minded clerics, teachers, doctors and large landowners are to be arrested and taken to a camp."[125] Those deemed more dangerous were executed.

---

120. Isabel Heinemann, *"Rasse, Siedlung, deutsches Blut": Das Rasse- und Siedlungshauptamt der SS und die rassenpolitische Neuordnung Europas* (Göttingen: Wallstein, 2003), 187–303.

121. By the end of 1939, the number executed was around 150; see Zbigniew Piechota, "Eksterminacja inteligencji oraz grup przywódczych w Łodzi i okręgu łódzkim w latach 1939–1940," *BOK* 1(1989), 17–23.

122. See Böhler, *Auftakt,* 144; Stanisław Nawrocki, *Hitlerowska okupacja Wielkopolski w okresie zarządu wojskowego: Wrzesień-październik 1939 r.* (Poznań: Instytut Zachodni, 1966), 93.

123. See IPN list for Poznań, December 15, 1975; BAL, B 162/Vorl. AR-Z 380/77, 4:546ff.; Nawrocki, *Hitlerowska okupacja,* 208.

124. See Magdalena Sierocińska, "Trzy dni terroru: Pierwsze planowe masowe egzekucje w Wielkopolsce," *BIPN* 35/36 (2003/2004): 43–48.

125. See Kazimierz Radziwończyk, *Zbrodnie generała Streckenbacha* (Warsaw: Zachodnia Agencja Prasowa, 1966), 36–37, 41.

DOCUMENT 70: **Photograph of an execution of Polish civilians conducted by a police firing squad in Sosnowiec, undated (ca. September 1939), USHMMPA WS# 72103.**

It took time and effort to create the organizational base for "spatial cleansing" (*Flurbereinigung*) as part of the Nazi plans for a new racial order in Europe.[126] In the areas earmarked as German "living space," such as the district of Kościan in western Poland, the new civilian authorities could build on what the police had started earlier.

DOCUMENT 71: **Report by the district head in Kościan to the Chief of Civil Administration, October 31, 1939, BAL, B 162/Vorl. Dok. Slg. Polen 365 r (translated from German).**

1. <u>Political Situation</u>

[. . .] The members of the Polish intelligentsia have all been identified [*restlos erfasst*] and, depending on the urgency, are being arrested by the security agencies. In connection with the settlement of the Baltic German returnees, I intend to establish an internment camp in Kosten for male members of the Polish intelligentsia. In this way, setbacks in the pacification of the district can be successfully avoided.

---

126. Browning, *Origins*, 43–72; Richard C. Lukas, *The Forgotten Holocaust: The Poles under German Occupation, 1939–1945* (Lexington: University Press of Kentucky, 1986).

2. <u>Morale of the Population</u>

The German population in the district, which makes up only about 2% of the total population, is slowly gaining confidence in the changed circumstances and is gaining backbone. However, some time will pass before the German population generally reaches the point of seeing itself as masters of the Poles. [. . .]

"Germanization" required the identification of those parts of the population Nazi officials deemed particularly suited for incorporation into the "*Volk* community." Ethnic Germans seemed obvious candidates in theory; yet in daily occupation practice, ascertaining who qualified for preferential treatment and whom to exclude remained difficult.

DOCUMENT 72: Daily report by Einsatzgruppe VI to the Chief of Civil Administration, October 3, 1939, APP 298/54 (translated from German).

[. . .] In the last reports, it was already mentioned that the various offices are issuing identity documents recognizing the bearer as an ethnic German. In addition to the uncertainty about the authority of such offices to issue such documents, objections are being raised because individual offices view the requirements for characterization as an ethnic German quite differently. Occasionally it suffices that the person concerned claims to be an ethnic German. At some times, anyone born in Posen is accepted as an ethnic German. At other offices, the presentation of a German military pass is regarded as sufficient authentication without, however, taking into consideration the fact that at the time of German rule in Posen, everyone living here had to serve in the German Army, regardless of whether he was of Polish or of German ethnicity. Other offices are satisfied when an ethnic German with any kind of identification confirms that the relevant person is an ethnic German. Almost everyone who is a member of the German Association [Deutsche Vereinigung] and the Young German Party [Jungdeutsche Partei] is recognized. To date, only one office is known to have required active membership in the Deutsche Vereinigung or the Jungdeutsche Partei as an essential prerequisite, that is, is known to have imposed a standard that could be used, if necessary, for future inclusion in the NSDAP. It seems urgently necessary to establish formal and conceptual clarity in these matters. [. . .]

Once members of the Polish population found out that they would, for the most part, have no place in the new German "Lebensraum," the level of desperation grew. Sipo/SD officers commented on what they perceived as the prevailing mood.

DOCUMENT 73: Situation report by Einsatzkommando Bromberg to IdS Danzig–West Prussia, October 14, 1939, IPNW, NTN 196/179 (translated from German).

[. . .] The dejection among the Poles in recent times has intensified still further after knowledge of the Führer's announcement that the Poles would be resettled became widespread. The speeches that Gauleiter Forster[127] gave when he visited Bromberg, speeches in which he announced that the Poles must be forced out of all locations and that within a short time West Prussia will become a blossoming, purely German province, did not fail to have the desired impression on the Poles. The Poles now are starting to realize that the authorities will very systematically drive the Poles out of every arena of life and that they will never be allowed the same rights as the Germans. [. . .] In principle, all school-age children must attend school, but the Polish children are taught separately from the German ones. The Poles can attend school through only the 7th grade. This prevents the rearing of a Polish intelligentsia, which otherwise has always proved to be at the forefront in the ethnic struggle [*Volkstumskampf*]. German is the language of instruction in all schools. [. . .]

Signs of opposition from among the Polish population took many forms, and the information compiled by the Einsatzgruppen did not offer a coherent picture. Far from being objective observers, Himmler's men focused their reports on what they expected to find and what seemed to legitimize their actions.

---

127. Albert Forster (1902–1952), Nazi Party Gauleiter for Danzig–West Prussia from October 1939 to early 1945, was sentenced to death in Warsaw in 1948 and executed in 1952.

DOCUMENT 74: Daily reports by the Chief of the Sipo/SD, September 24 and 26, 1939, USHMMA RG 15.007M (BAB, R 58/7002), reel 2, file 2:30–36, 41–45 (translated from German).

[September 24, 1939:]

[. . .]

Einsatzgruppe V:

Arrests: a total of 66 persons.

Among those arrested is Father Trzaskome. He was arrested because he told German troops that within a week they would disappear like dust. He also stated that the French have already occupied half of western Germany. Within his close circle of friends, he accused the German military of looting. Trzaskome has been handed over to the Allenstein [Polish: Olsztyn] office of the State Police for transfer to a concentration camp.

The Catholic clerics in the areas of Plöhnen [Polish: Płońsk], Góra, Dobrin, Racionz [Polish: Raciąż], and Glingjek have asked the population to keep calm and offer no resistance.

During an action in the village of Adamowo, the farmer Artur Kowalski was shot dead. Kowalski did not comply with the demand to raise his hands and instead attempted to attack the officials. Kowalski was the Polish village mayor.

[. . .]

[September 26, 1939:]

[. . .]

Einsatzgruppe VI:

[. . .] Noteworthy are the repeatedly reported statements made in circles of the Polish population that, as "servants" in a German Poland, they have better opportunities for a secure existence than they were accustomed to as "masters" in a Polish Posen. These signs of willing submission, however, cannot hide the fact that the majority of the Polish population has not yet abandoned its will to resist and persevere. Indications of this are the still unabated spreading of news from English radio broadcasts and the behavior toward ethnic Germans. For example, one ethnic German reports that on September 20, 1939, when he placed an order in German with the Polish shop owner Koszewski on the Alter Markt, he got the reply that this is a Polish shop, in which Polish is spoken. [. . .]

[. . .]

Einsatzkommando 16:

After the departure of the Führer,[128] Einsatzkommando 16 has recommenced full police security work in the area of the military commander of Danzig–West Prussia.

On September 25, 1939, in Gotenhafen [Polish: Gdynia], 2,700 people were again screened, of whom 1,200 were released while 1,500 had to be temporarily held pending further examination. [. . .]

Where Heydrich's men needed help in carrying out their mission, they could continue to rely on their Order Police colleagues—the Schutzpolizei in the cities and the Gendarmerie in rural areas—based on the administratively separate, yet practically integrated, command structure established by Himmler in the Reich and the occupied territories.

DOCUMENT 75: Instructions from Einsatzkommando 4/I to the district head of Pszczyna, September 27, 1939, APK 119/1637 (translated from German).

I request the duty stations reporting to the Gendarmerie and to the state and local police to issue instructions immediately as follows:

All matters that arise, including complaints in political police matters, are to be immediately brought forward to EK 4/I of the Security Police in Teschen: [Polish: Cieszyn], New City Hall, by the senior district administrator.

In political police matters, take independent action only in the event of imminent danger; otherwise, seek and await direction and guidance from EK 4/I.

For political reasons, in the event of imminent danger, transfer arrested persons to EK 4/I at once, with dossiers.

Political police matters include, in particular, suppression of the following: insurgents, Polish bands and associations, and all resistance by Poles in general [*Polentum*] against measures imposed by the German Reich and by authorities, establishments, and organizations concerned with execution of such measures. These matters also include intelligence policing, namely, suppression of espionage and sabotage, as well as the handling of all matters relating to the Jews.

---

128. On September 19, 1939, Hitler visited Danzig and gave a speech.

For the most part, cooperation between the Order Police and the Sipo/SD went smoothly, as the report in document 76 suggests.

DOCUMENT 76: Report by BdO Posen to Himmler, October 25, 1939, APP 298/54 (translated from German).

[. . .]

1. <u>General Situation:</u>

No changes. The observation has been repeatedly made that the Poles do not deserve mild and considerate treatment, for to some extent they are again exhibiting arrogant and impertinent behavior. [. . .]

3. <u>Operational Area and Situation Report:</u>

[. . .] Batl. 61 reports: "For 100 savagely murdered ethnic Germans, a reprisal action took place, carried out along with the SD. The following were summarily convicted and shot by the police: 183 Poles."

Josef Lemke, a resident of Wejherowo in annexed West Prussia during the war, recalled the changes in the local situation occurring toward the end of 1939 that exemplify the interactions between German agencies on the local level and the perpetuation of violence as a staple feature of Nazi rule. Absent from Lemke's account is any indication of ethnic Poles collaborating with the Germans, a widespread phenomenon at the time but one rarely addressed in Cold War–era Poland.[129]

DOCUMENT 77: Testimony by Josef Lemke on conditions in Wejherowo in late 1939, June 19, 1959, BAL, B 162/3385:45ff. (translated from German).

[. . .] The local military administration tried to work peacefully with the population, provided that these people were German. To discourage any attacks on the part of the Polish population, around 50 to 60 Polish hostages were taken as a preventive measure. After three to four days, however, this measure proved to be superfluous because no resistance was offered by the Polish population in Wejherowo. Therefore, the hostages were released. In the next few weeks, too, nothing noteworthy happened. This

---

129. See Barbara Engelking, *Jest Taki Piękny Słoneczny Dzień: Losy Żydów Szukających Ratunku na Wsi Polskiej 1942–1945* (Warsaw: Stowarzyszenie Centrum Badań nad Zagładą Żydów, 2011); Jan Grabowski, *Judenjagd: Polowanie na Żydów 1942–1945: Studium Dziejów Pewnego Powiatu* (Warsaw: Stowarzyszenie Centrum Badań nad Zagładą Żydów, 2011).

situation changed around November 1939, when NSDAP organizations had formed. Denunciation now blossomed. Overzealous Germans, wanting to demonstrate their allegiance to national socialism, denounced Polish citizens at random. The denunciations were made to the functionaries of the local groups of the newly formed NSDAP. From there, the reports were forwarded to the appropriate district leadership and then sent on to the appropriate Gestapo office. I understand that in November 1939, the Gdańsk Gestapo office was also responsible for Wejherowo. Later, the operation was conducted from Gdynia. From November 1939 on, many Poles were arrested on the basis of the reports received in the Gdańsk Gestapo office. These were predominantly members of the Polish intelligentsia. [. . .] Usually the people were taken from their homes at night and taken by truck first to the Wejherowo prison and on one of the following days from there to a nearby forest, where the executions were carried out. Several times in the last few days of November 1939, I saw prisoners being transported in trucks. Because of my work, I usually was already on the road between 5:00 and 6:00 a.m. I saw that several trucks, usually five, came from Gdańsk, loaded with prisoners. Each truck held around 30 people. Then these people were shot in the vicinity of Wejherowo. The trucks returned empty from the execution site, loaded up the people arrested during the night in Wejherowo, and then they too were shot in a forested area. Among the population, it was said at the time that as many as 300 Poles were shot every day. These shootings were repeated almost every day in November 1939. The randomness of the shootings is shown by the fact that the German builder Franz Litzbarski, too, was one of the victims. L., who was very rich, had done a great deal for his fellow German citizens during the period of Polish administration and had made personal sacrifices to maintain German culture in Wejherowo. He was, however, opposed to national socialism. The NSDAP accused him in November 1939 of reading, at some point, the anti-Nazi journal *Der Deutsche in Polen*.[130] This alone sufficed to put L. on the "Black List" and then to execute him. [. . .]

As much as German security forces saw mass executions and other forms of violence as a reliable means of deterring local populations from waging resistance, these measures raised concerns about long-term negative effects,

---

130. It was published between 1934 and 1939. See Pia Nordblom, *Für Glaube und Volkstum: Die katholische Wochenzeitung "Der Deutsche in Polen" (1934–1939) in der Auseinandersetzung mit dem Nationalsozialismus* (Paderborn: Ferdinand Schöningh, 2000).

especially for the psyche of the executioners. In late 1939, the RSHA started an investigation into killings that had taken place under the authority of SS-Sturmbannführer Alfred Hasselberg, who commanded EK 3/I, but by that time he had become KdS in Lublin. Hasselberg had organized the shooting of Polish civilians and assisted with forcing eighteen thousand Jews across the San River into Soviet-held territory. His case led to one of several internal SS investigations opened to counteract what were seen as lapses in discipline and leadership. All across German-occupied Poland, raids and executions had gone hand in hand with acts of theft and physical violence. But in Hasselberg's case, sadism and other base motives were so prevalent that they undermined his claim of just having "followed orders."[131] Document 78, a statement by one of Hasselberg's subordinates from the SS investigative record, reflects perpetrators' perspective on their deeds and the framework within which they operated in those early months of the war.

DOCUMENT 78: Interrogation of Fritz Liebl, member of Einsatzkommando 3/I, by SS and police investigators, December 1939, NARA SSO Dr. Alfred Hasselberg (translated from German).

[. . .] [SS investigator] Mylius: Criminal Detective [Kriminalkommissar] Herzberger reports that when he asked you one day why you looked depressed, you told him you had just spoken with two comrades about what would happen once you were back at home and whether you would then be able to leave behind your criminal habits. What did you mean by the term "criminal habits"?

Liebl: By the term "criminal habits," I meant partly the shootings but partly also other unwarranted brutality. Based on my actions in Einsatzkommando Hasselberg [i.e., EK 3/I], I have come to the conclusion that a human life has absolutely no value there. In the beginning, several shootings were undertaken without obtaining a verdict from the military courts [Standortgerichte]. Later the persons in question were brought before the military court, which sentenced them to death. Personally, however, I was especially disgusted by the way these executions were carried out. All those sentenced to death were executed by being shot in the back of the neck with a pistol. The condemned had to step up to the edge of a pit that had been dug beforehand, and then they were killed with a shot to the back of the neck.

---

131. Interrogation of Alfred Hasselberg, December 16, 1939, BAB BDC-SSO file Dr. Alfred Hasselberg.

Mylius: Did it happen that those sentenced were not dead yet after the first shot?

Liebl: Yes. In these cases, further shots were fired. The members of the execution squad were just not trained for these tasks. In my opinion it would have been quite possible to hand the people [those to be shot] over either to the Wehrmacht or to the Schutzpolizei for the carrying out of the death sentence. I think these people [the members of the execution squad] should at least have been shown how to perform executions so that they would not just fire haphazardly into the back of the neck without causing, as already mentioned, immediate death. I attended one execution where I shot one of the condemned men myself. At first I stood by, and after the shots had been fired and the condemned men had fallen into the pit, I noticed that one person had not been hit at all but had fallen—apparently out of fear—into the pit. I then killed that person from above, specifically with a shot to the back of the head.

In Berlin, rather than the executions themselves, the fact that Hasselberg had failed to take care of his men raised concerns. Discipline and group cohesion were threatened; more than one unit member stated that Hasselberg "deserves a bullet."[132] Although they faulted him for "improper" execution methods and uncontrolled looting after 1939 in the city of Lublin, his superiors did not at all criticize his systematic mistreatment of the Jews in the district.[133] In the eyes of his subordinates, Hasselberg's cruel abuse of a "purebred" English setter weighed more heavily than mass shootings of Jews and Poles: the former act indicated a severe character deficiency, while the latter fell under the rubric of "doing one's duty."[134] Not surprisingly, Heydrich stopped the investigation in January 1940 and agreed to Hasselberg's request to be transferred to the Wehrmacht.[135]

---

132. Interrogations of Franz Kubin and Hermann Rohlfing, December 12, 1939; Heinrich Küthe, December 9, 1939; Hans Block, December 8, 1939, BAB BDC file Dr. Alfred Hasselberg.

133. Interrogation of Alois Fischotter, December 13, 1939; Hans Block, December 8, 1939, BAB BDC file Dr. Alfred Hasselberg.

134. Interrogation of Lothar Hoffmann, December 13, 1939, BAB BDC file Dr. Alfred Hasselberg.

135. CdS to Hasselberg, January 10, 1940, BAB BDC file Dr. Alfred Hasselberg. In 1940 Bischoff also came under scrutiny for robbery, but the investigation was soon quashed. See RSHA to BdS Generalgouvernement, September 12, 1940; RSHA to KdS Warsaw, October 17, 1940, both in APW, 482 (SSPF)/105.

At the end of 1939 and beginning of 1940, some local military commanders would still object to the undisciplined way the police and SS treated the population in the absence of significant Polish resistance. Protests by army officers such as Major Langhaeuser came to nothing due to a lack of support from their superiors,[136] who were eager to differentiate between necessary ruthlessness and incriminable "excesses," as document 79, a directive from the commanding general of the 14th Army, attests.

DOCUMENT 79: **Directive by the Commander of the 14th Army, Generaloberst Wilhelm List, to subordinate commanders, October 1, 1939, BA-MA, RH 53-23/12 (translated from German).**

Because of the repeated demands of the combat troops, a special police unit was deployed to cleanse the occupied territory of bands, snipers, and looters. Under the command of SS-Obergruppenführer v. Woyrsch, these police units, which now have been withdrawn, have taken uncompromising action and have essentially completed their assignment. Wherever excesses (illegal shootings) have allegedly occurred in the process, a review is under way. The aggressive implementation of this action has become known—often in an exaggerated form—to the combat troops as well. As a result, obvious ill feeling has arisen in many places, expressed in comments by officers, noncommissioned officers, and troops about all individuals who wear the SS field uniform. It must be emphatically stated that the "Einsatzkommandos der Sicherheitspolizei," working in close cooperation with the AKs [Army corps], did not participate in any way in the measures or possible excesses carried out in the course of the above-mentioned action. The intelligence officers of the AKs and divisions have been thoroughly informed, in a conference held on September 30 at the AOK [Supreme Army Command], of the extraordinarily successful activities thus far carried out by these Einsatzkommandos in the interest of the troops and about their composition and tasks. You are asked to explain this to the subordinate units in an appropriate way. Extensive support for the Einsatzkommandos in their border policing and their state security tasks is in the interest of the troops.

Reporting on the situation after the transfer of administrative control to German civilian authorities, the regional Wehrmacht administrator in the

---

136. See document 10.

Warthegau depicted the army as the unbiased arbiter in a situation dominated by self-obsessed rival factions. In fact, however, a pattern of violence that would have been impossible without the support of the German military had long been established in Poland.

DOCUMENT 80: **Report by General Petzel, Chief Defense Region (Wehrkreiskommando) XXI, to the Commander of the Reserve Army (Befehlshaber des Ersatzheeres), November 23, 1939, BA-MA, N 104/3 (translated from German).**

The Warthegau must be regarded as pacified. Repeated rumors of uprisings have not proven to be true in any instance. The reason for this is not a change in the mood of the Polish population but the realization that an insurrection is hopeless. There is no failure to recognize that the large number of released prisoners and otherwise returned Polish soldiers presents a danger requiring constant observation, especially since countless officers have not yet been recorded. Suppression of this danger is possible only through the military occupation of the country in the current form; the offices of the civil administration are completely incapable of that with the police forces at hand.

The large rebuilding effort in all areas is not being furthered by the intervention of SS formations, which are deployed with "Special Ethnic Missions" and therefore are not under the control of the Reich plenipotentiary [*Reichsstatthalter*]. One sees here a tendency to exceed the scope of these missions and to intervene definitively in all administrative areas and create "a state within a state." This phenomenon is not without repercussions for the troops, who are indignant about the ways in which these tasks are carried out and who as a result, generally speaking, come into conflict with the [civil] administration and the Party. I will eliminate the danger of serious conflicts by issuing strict orders. It cannot be denied that this entails a real challenge to troop discipline.

In almost all the larger locations, public shootings by the aforementioned organizations have taken place. The selection [of those to be executed] in these instances was completely disparate and often incomprehensible, and the carrying out of the shootings was often dishonorable.

In some districts, all the Poles who are large landowners have been arrested and interned with their families. Arrests were almost always accompanied by lootings. In the cities, evacuations took place, with blocks of houses vacated at random and the inhabitants loaded at night onto trucks and taken to concentration camps. Here, too, lootings were constant side effects. The accommodations and food supplies in the camps were such that the army corps medical officer feared an outbreak of epidemics and thus a threat to the troops. In answer to my appeal, remedial action is being taken.

In several cities, anti-Jewish actions were carried out; they degenerated to the level of extremely serious assaults. In Turek, on October 30, 1939, three SS trucks under the command of a senior SS officer drove through the streets, and the people on the street were randomly beaten about the head with bullwhips and [other] long whips. Ethnic Germans were also among the victims. Finally, a number of Jews were driven into the synagogue, where they had to sing as they crawled through the pews while being continuously struck by the SS men with whips. Then they were forced to drop their trousers so their naked backsides could be beaten. One Jew, who defecated in his trousers out of fear, was forced to smear the excrement on the faces of the other Jews. [. . .]

The experience of German mass violence and the ever-present threat of more terror was an essential element of Polish civilians' perceptions of Nazi rule. It determined their expectations about what lay in store for them during the war and increased the pressure to comply with German demands or expectations. From their own lopsided perspective, the security police in Bydgoszcz reported a strange sense of normalcy in late October 1939 in a city heavily battered by ongoing German "actions."

DOCUMENT 81: Situation report by Einsatzkommando Bromberg to the RSHA, October 20, 1939, IPNW, NTN 196/179 (translated from German).

[. . .] The self-confident demeanor of the Poles on the Bromberg streets is striking; some of them use the Polish language uninhibitedly. A regulation from the appropriate district leader banning the Polish language on the street is being prepared. [. . .] In the last few days the first transport of 50 Congress Poles [Poles from territory administered by Russia after 1815] from the Bromberg District [*Landkreis*] to Kraków took place. These are Polish settlers from Congress Poland (known as Poniatowskis), who were settled in West Prussia by former minister of agriculture Poniatowski in his day. There are plans to implement further transports of Congress Polish settlers (Poniatowskis) in the future. (In this regard, it should be pointed out that even the Poles who have been established here for a long time must be resettled without recourse. These old-established Poles, some of whom describe themselves as Polish Prussians, do not suffer from an inferiority complex, as do the Congress Poles, but see themselves as on par with the Germans. Because these Poles are uniformly proficient in German and incredibly accomplished at assimilating, they must be considered all the more dangerous.) The Geheime Staatspolizei and the Selbstschutz have carried out operations in West Prussian cities to arrest Polish teachers and transport them to the Krone [Polish: Koronowo] prison. Liquidation of radical Polish elements is planned. In addition, in recently executed systematic actions, members of the Polish intellectual class in particular were arrested. It is to be assumed that with these recently implemented actions, the vast majority of the Polish intelligentsia has been taken into custody. Above all, a stop will have been put to the activities of the members of the Westmarken-Verband. During the conduct of the actions, however, certain difficulties arose in Bromberg, resulting from the fact that in some cases the arrests jeopardized further operation of essential businesses. In these cases, various Poles had to be released again. [. . .] In the field of religion, no essential changes have occurred. As before, the behavior of the clerics gives no cause for intervention. A large proportion of the Catholic clerics have been eliminated as a result of their known radical Polish nationalist stance, so that the remaining ones are either greatly intimidated or categorized as soft-hearted and apolitical in the first place. Likewise, the Jews in the area present no problem. As a result of deportation and other measures, their numbers are so small that they are of no consequence in an assessment of the situation. [. . .]

"Other measures" were readily at hand in case what the occupiers regarded as resistance from the civilian population broke the quiet. In Bydgoszcz, SS-Sturmbannführer Dr. Rudolf Oebsger-Röder was certain that he had the backing of Himmler in dealing with local opposition groups or those considered as such.[137]

---

137. Rudolf Oebsger-Röder (1912–1962), a Nazi Party member since 1931, had been an assistant professor at the University of Leipzig before he joined the SD in 1937. In the winter of 1939–1940, he became head of the Resettlement Office (Einwandererzentralstelle) in Łódź, followed by an appointment as department head at the RSHA. In the summer of 1940, he took over the SD office in Gdańsk. Between September 1941 and May 1942, Oebsger-Röder was assigned to Einsatzgruppe A in the Soviet Union. Beginning in May 1944, as KdS in Cluj (German: Klausenburg), he was responsible for the deportation of Hungarian Jews; he returned in August 1944 to RSHA Office VI. After the war Oebsger-Röder joined the emerging West German intelligence service. He was never charged for his crimes during World War II.

DOCUMENT 82: **Situation report by Einsatzkommando Bromberg, October 24, 1939, IPNW, NTN 196/179 (translated from German).**

[. . .] The previously announced action targeting members of the West-marken-Verband was carried out on the night of October 18. Besides the local officials, three Selbstschutz groups of 100 were on hand. Of the 260 members of the Westmarken-Verband in Bromberg, 91 people, including 21 women, were apprehended in this wave of arrests. Almost without exception, they are representatives of the Polish intelligentsia who returned after previously fleeing and believed they would be left alone. The result of this action can be viewed as extremely favorable, for the major-ity of the Westmarken-Verband members have either fled or already been shot. [. . .] The action conducted jointly with the Selbstschutz against the Polish teachers was also a complete success. In the city of Bromberg alone, 185 Polish teachers were arrested, and their treatment is based on their classification as follows:

a) Pomerelians [*Pommereller*]

b) Congress Poles

c) Germanophobes and anti-German agitators

d) Members of Polish associations, especially the Westmarken-Verband.

Personnel files, to the extent that they are still in existence, form the chief basis for the screening of these Poles; these files are supplemented by the personal knowledge of the ethnic German teachers working here. The intention is to rehire the suitable teachers placed in category a), given the teacher shortage that now exists here; to deport those in category b) to the *Reichsghetto*,[138] if there is no evidence against them; and to liquidate the radical Polish elements placed in categories c) and d). This proposed measure, as well as everything that has transpired thus far under the Stapo, has met with the full approval of the RFSS [Himmler], to whom I was permitted to make an oral report on the evening of October 20, here in the "Danziger Hof" [a hotel]. [. . .]

As in the early stage of the military campaign, measures taken by officers on the ground evolved in the context of broader plans by the Reich's top leadership for Polish civilians. In the long run, local officials saw the need to complement the threat of violence—so credibly conveyed by way of public executions and

---

138. This was most likely a reference to plans that the Generalgouvernement would serve as the "dumping ground" for "undesirable" groups among the population, including but not restricted to Jews.

mass arrests—with what they considered subtler means. Document 83 presents Oebsger-Röder's attempt to make the case for the use of propaganda as a small carrot attached to a big stick.

DOCUMENT 83: Proposal by Einsatzkommando Bromberg for propaganda aimed at Poles in Danzig–West Prussia, undated (late October 1939), IPNW, NTN 196/179 (translated from German).

[handwritten cover note:]
 District Party Head [*Kreisleiter*] Kampe, FYI
 Original via SD-Hauptamt for presentation to Reich Propaganda Ministry. It should be added that the Poles' high level of moral resistance, among other things, results from their display, in most cases, of fearless, brave conduct when "liquidation" is in progress.
 Yours,
 Röder
 [typewritten proposal:]
 According to the Führer's will, a German West Prussia is to be established immediately in Polish-controlled Pommerellen. To carry out these tasks, the following measures are called for, in the unanimous opinion of all relevant authorities:
 1. physical liquidation of all Polish elements that
  a) have in the past emerged in any way as leaders on the Polish side or
  b) can in the future be involved in a Polish resistance movement.
 2. expulsion or resettlement of all "local Poles" and "Congress Poles" to remove them from West Prussia.
 3. transplanting of racially and otherwise valuable Poles to the middle of the Old Reich, provided that they reflect lost German bloodlines and assuming that they can be smoothly absorbed into the German racial body [*Volkskörper*].
 The measures listed have been undertaken from the outset. However, the following remarks appear necessary, to substantiate the need for additional recommendations:
 Regarding 1: Liquidation can continue to be carried out for only a short time to come. Then the German administration, as well as other factors outside NSDAP control, will make direct actions impossible. In any case, in the end, despite all our toughness, only a fraction of the Poles in West Poland will be eliminated (circa 20,000).

Regarding 2: Naturally, the resettlement or expulsion will take months and years, since extensive technical and other operations must be carried out.

Regarding 3: To date, the deliberate, orderly transfer of racially valuable Poles to the Old Reich has barely begun. There will be difficulties in selecting the racially valuable Poles (an example: a Polish doctor, an internationally recognized cancer researcher, who has stated that if he really has to accept a subordinate role, then he would rather bow to the Germans than to the Jews, etc.; he would like to pursue his research in peace). The number of people to be transferred in this way will be small.

Thus the remarks regarding items 1–3 make it clear that even in the coming months and years, one must still expect a considerable number of pure and self-identified Poles. The Poles, in keeping with their mentality as proven by history, will always be inclined in the future, too, to act in a conspiratorial way, commit acts of sabotage, and devise plots. Even today, after the destruction of the Polish state, the overwhelming majority of the Polish population is convinced that a liberation and comeback through English and French assistance will occur. Whoever doubts the truth of these statements need only send a Polish-speaking informant, dressed in rags, to stand in one of the lines that form daily in front of the shops in towns in West Prussia. To frustrate the Poles' machinations, of course, it is primarily political, economic, security police, and other measures that are required. In addition, however, in our estimation the moral resistance of the Poles must be destroyed by suitable propaganda measures. Thus the following measures ought to be considered: institution of a "Polish corner" in the present ethnic German newspapers to relate official German Army communiqués and other brief news reports that weaken Polish resistance, placards and newspapers mounted on walls with lots of pictures, roughly analogous to the well-known poster: "*England Dein Werk*," etc.[139] But here it should be noted that the Poles barely have any radios left and at least to a considerable extent are not proficient in the German language. Therefore, in our estimation, discussions between the Reich Propaganda Office in Danzig–West Prussia and the Reich Propaganda Ministry must be undertaken immediately.

---

139. German propaganda booklet by Rudolf Schauff, *Der polnische Feldzug. England! Dein Werk!* (Berlin: Verlag "Die Wehrmacht," 1939).

The Sipo/SD painted a picture in its reports of constant action and vigilance in pursuit of the twin goals of "Germanization" and "pacification." Within the distorted image of daily life under occupation portrayed by German officials in the region, one can discern signs of frustration emanating from the clash between ideology-driven expectations and the reality on the ground.

DOCUMENT 84: **Situation report by Einsatzkommando Bromberg, November 1, 1939, IPNW, NTN 196/179 (translated from German).**

[. . .] Even though it cannot be said that a change in mood has occurred within the Polish population during the reporting period, there are, nevertheless, certain signs here and there that in the poorer social classes, people are beginning to breathe more freely. One can tell that the German authorities and party offices are primarily battling the intelligentsia. The whole aim of this more or less apathetic class is to gain possession of ethnic German identification papers so as to also have the benefits that lift the German citizen above the mass of the Polish element. Rumors from Polish workers' circles, which we were able to confirm on various occasions, also run along these lines, and according to these rumors, all Polish girls in the foreseeable future will be forced to marry only Germans. Everyone who possibly can is trying by all available means to get recognized as German so as to receive permission to remain in the region, by hook or by crook. [. . .] The expulsion of the Congress Polish settlers continues in full swing. To date around 1,000 Congress Poles have been deported to the east. The now vacated settlers' places are being farmed for the time being by the neighboring owners. However, it is becoming apparent that precisely the ethnic Germans often try to snatch the best tracts of land from each other and that in general their duties as trustees are not being taken seriously. In these circles, there is still a belief that one day they can acquire the farms entrusted to them. Some large landowners also express similar views and absolutely do not accept that the Polish settlers' places, which they owned before the forced parceling, will not be awarded to them again. The number of inquiries from the Old Reich about farmsteads that are becoming available is so large that they cannot even be processed at the moment. [. . .] In the city proper, too, the confiscation and expropriation of Polish possessions continues at a rapid pace. The goal is first to make the city center completely free of Poles and, provided the Poles qualify as suitable residents, to resettle them in the outlying districts. Furniture and other household goods are not allowed to be taken along [by the Poles] in this action but instead are to be seized as compensation for ethnic Germans who have been robbed. Similarly, there is no intention to provide compensation for expropriated Polish properties in the city.

Although it is impossible to establish the exact number of their victims in Poland, the Einsatzgruppen were certainly responsible for the greater part of the mass executions through the end of 1939, which took the lives of tens of thousands of civilians. Quantifying the deadliness of the Einsatzgruppen is difficult for various reasons: after the invasion, Poland suffered more than five years of German occupation, at the end of which one in seven Polish citizens had been killed. Furthermore, the Germans systematically tried to destroy traces of mass graves prior to their withdrawal. As a result, postwar Polish authorities had enormous difficulties in coming up with a reliable count. Compounding this problem, the testimonies of eyewitnesses are often not very reliable when it comes to the perpetrators' affiliation or victim figures, particularly where estimates were made under the highly traumatizing circumstances of the time. Although the Einsatzgruppen regularly reported their activities to Berlin, they were reluctant to transmit exact execution figures. On occasion, however, Sipo/SD reports like the one from Bydgoszcz in document 85 present a glimpse of the real scale of their violent actions in Poland.

DOCUMENT 85: **Situation report by Einsatzkommando Bromberg, November 10, 1939, USHMMA RG 14.041M (BAB, R 70 Polen/83), fiche 1:31–35 (translated from German).**

[. . .] The action carried out against the Polish intelligentsia is to be regarded as concluded. In the period from October 30 to November 10, the following were:

	Liquidated	Evacuated	Released
Teachers	73	68	66
Lawyers and notaries	3	2	1
Pharmacists	2	—	5
Judges	—	1	1
Tax officials	13	3	10
City administration	1	—	4
Miscellaneous professions	2	1	4

Three months after the German attack, Sipo/SD officers could look back on what they regarded as a successful campaign against those deemed a threat to German rule in the annexed territory.

DOCUMENT 86: Situation report by Einsatzkommando Bromberg, November 14, 1939, IPNW, NTN 196/179 (translated from German).

[. . .] In a large-scale roundup on November 11, 1939, at 5:00 a.m., carried out by the Gestapo in collaboration with the SD, Schutzpolizei, and Wehrmacht, a search of all houses was conducted, and all males between the ages of 18 and 65 who were not in possession of an identity document stamped by the Security Police were taken into custody. In the course of the sweep, 3,800 persons were apprehended, of whom only 1% were included in search lists or card indices. This percentage is low because the city of Bromberg has already experienced a similar action, in which a thorough job was done.

[. . .] The church-related situation in the meantime remains unchanged. Surveillance of the churches continues unabated, but the clerics' behavior thus far has given no cause for intervention. In general, it must be noted in this regard that extermination [*Ausrotten*] of the radical Polish priests has made it virtually impossible to foment any passive resistance in church-related matters; the remaining clerics are to be regarded as moderate and are proving very cautious in every respect. There is no longer a Jewish problem in Bromberg, as the city is completely free of Jews. All Jews who had not opted for escape before the cleansing action have been liquidated.

The enforced quiet was tenuous at best; with the ongoing war and the radicalization of German policy, ever more "undesirable" people became targets of execution or other violent measures. Again, the Einsatzgruppen were to play a key role in this radicalization process.

POSTSCRIPT: POLAND, 1939– SOVIET UNION, 1941
EINSATZGRUPPEN ACTIONS IN COMPARISON

"**W**E SHALL establish beyond the realm of doubt facts which, before the dark decade of the Third Reich, would have seemed incredible. The defendants were commanders and officers of special SS groups known as Einsatzgruppen—established for the specific purpose of massacring human beings because they were Jews, or because they were for some other reason regarded as inferior peoples."[1] Benjamin Ferencz, U.S. chief prosecutor at the Nuremberg Einsatzgruppen Trial, made this opening statement not coincidentally on September 29, 1947. Exactly six years earlier, on September 29, 1941, members of Sonderkommando 4a of Einsatzgruppe C had staged a two-day massacre in the ravine at Babi Yar near Kiev in which more than thirty thousand Jews—men, women, and children—were murdered.[2] Within six months—from late June to

---

1. Opening statement by Benjamin Ferencz in Case 9 (the Einsatzgruppen Trial) on September 9, 1947, in *Trials of War Criminals before the Nuernberg Military Tribunals under Control Council Law No. 10* (Buffalo, NY: William S. Hein & Co., 1997), 4:30. See also Hilary Earl, *The Nuremberg SS-Einsatzgruppen Trial, 1945–1958: Atrocity, Law, and History* (New York: Cambridge University Press, 2008); Benjamin Ferencz, "The Einsatzgruppen Trial," in *The Nuremberg Trials: International Law since 1945*, ed. Herbert R. Reginbogin and Christoph J. M. Safferling, with Walter R. Hippel (Munich: K. G. Saur, 2006), 153–63. For further reading, see Annette Weinke, *Die Nürnberger Prozesse* (Munich: C. H. Beck, 2006); Kim C. Priemel and Alexa Stiller, eds., *NMT. Die Nürnberger Militärtribunale zwischen Geschichte, Gerechtigkeit und Rechtschöpfung* (Hamburg: Hamburger Edition, 2013).

2. Ereignismeldung UdSSR No. 97, September 28, 1941, published in Klaus-Michael Mallmann et al., eds., *Die "Ereignismeldungen UdSSR" 1941. Dokumente der Einsatzgruppen in der Sowjetunion I* (Darmstadt: WBG, 2011), 589–600.

the end of 1941—the three thousand German men in the ranks of Einsatzgruppen A, B, C, and D who had marched into the Soviet Union on the heels of four German army groups had, with the help of the Wehrmacht and local collaborators, killed between five and eight hundred thousand civilians, the overwhelming majority of them Jews. Even compared to what Heydrich's units had done in Poland in 1939, this killing spree was unprecedented. Unlike in 1939, the Einsatzgruppen recorded many—though far from all—of these murders and communicated the details back to the RSHA, which compiled extensive reports on German occupation policy in the Soviet Union.[3]

How was violence on such a scale possible? Different factors converged, some new, but most already discernible in 1939. We have seen that during the Polish campaign, even those German generals highly critical of the Einsatzgruppen's violent measures at the same time endorsed the notion of "pacifying" the rear army areas. In the course of the war against Poland, the Wehrmacht's role had undergone a transformation, as historian Christopher Browning writes, "from abdication to complicity"; during Operation Barbarossa—the attack on the Soviet Union starting June 22, 1941—the German army leadership would move "to outright participation" in a genocidal campaign.[4] Again, Hitler set the broad goals that would determine how Nazi Germany waged war.[5] On March 30, 1941, just as he had on August 22, 1939, prior to the attack on Poland, he put forward his views before the assembled senior generals, but this time with even more ominous implications: Bolshevism was an "asocial crime"; Germany would "have to step back from soldierly comradeship. The communist was not and is not a comrade. This is a fight of annihilation." The war was about the "destruction of the Bolshevist commissars and the communist intelligentsia," a task that the Wehrmacht could not accomplish alone and that called for the

---

3. Mallmann et al., *Die "Ereignismeldungen UdSSR" 1941*; see also Andrej Angrick et al., eds., *Deutsche Besatzungsherrschaft in der UdSSR 1941–1945. Dokumente der Einsatzgruppen in der Sowjetunion II* (Darmstadt: WBG, 2013). For additional sets of Einsatzgruppen reports, see Peter Klein, ed., *Die Einsatzgruppen in der besetzten Sowjetunion 1941/42: Die Tätigkeits- und Lageberichte des Chefs der Sicherheitspolitizei und des SD* (Berlin: Edition Hentrich, 1997).

4. Christopher R. Browning, with contributions by Jürgen Matthäus, *The Origins of the Final Solution: The Evolution of Nazi Jewish Policy, September 1939–March 1942* (Lincoln and Jerusalem: University of Nebraska Press and Yad Vashem, 2004), 72–81.

5. See Geoffrey P. Megargee, *War of Annihilation: Combat and Genocide on the Eastern Front, 1941* (Lanham, MD: Rowman & Littlefield, 2006); also Idem., *Inside Hitler's High Command* (Lawrence: University of Kansas Press, 2000), 102–69; Johannes Hürter, *Hitlers Heerführer. Die deutschen Oberbefehlshaber im Krieg gegen die Sowjetunion 1941/42* (Munich: Oldenbourg, 2007).

assistance of Himmler's forces. The 1940 French campaign not far from his mind, Hitler harkened back to ideas about "the east" that had driven German policy in Poland since 1939: "The fight will be very different than in the west. In the east harshness today means leniency for the future. The commanders will have to overcome their doubts."[6] Few of Hitler's generals would have such doubts; already on March 27, 1941, Army High Commander von Brauchitsch, whom Hitler had promoted to field marshal half a year earlier, informed senior Wehrmacht officers that "the troops have to realize that this struggle is being waged by one race against another, and proceed with the necessary harshness."[7]

These radical notions formed the core context of Operation Barbarossa and would transform into equally radical directives in the next few weeks.[8] When in late April 1941 the Army High Command instructed field units that "special detachments" of the Sipo and SD would perform "special tasks" behind the front line,[9] the lack of specificity in outlining this assignment of Heydrich's Einsatzgruppen indicated that the Wehrmacht had given his units carte blanche. Jews played a much more central role as Germany's archenemy than they had in Poland. Despite the interlude of the Hitler-Stalin pact, right-wing circles and the Nazi elite remained wedded to a strong belief in the inseparability of Jews and Communists, the rulers of the Soviet empire.[10] Other orders sent the same message. The "decree on the exercise of military jurisdiction in the 'Barbarossa' zone and on special measures by the troops," dated May 13, 1941, went further than the directives issued by the top Wehrmacht commanders in 1939: it replaced courts-martial against civilians with a stipulation that "partisans" were

---

6. Franz Halder, *Kriegstagebuch: Tägliche Aufzeichnungen des Chefs des Generalstabes des Heeres 1939–1942*, ed. Hans-Adolf Jacobsen (Stuttgart: W. Kohlhammer Verlag, 1962), 2:336–37.

7. Quoted from Megargee, *War of Annihilation*, 33. See also Jürgen Förster, "Operation Barbarossa as a War of Conquest and Annihilation," in *Germany and the Second World War*, Vol. 4: *The Attack on the Soviet Union*, ed. Militärgeschichtliches Forschungsamt (Oxford: Clarendon, 1998), 485.

8. Megargee, *War of Annihilation*, 35–41. See also Jürgen Förster, "Verbrecherische Befehle," in *Kriegsverbrechen im 20. Jahrhundert*, ed. Wolfram Wette and Gerd R. Ueberschär (Darmstadt: Primus, 2001), 137–51; Johannes Hürter, *Hitlers Heerführer. Die deutschen Oberbefehlshaber im Krieg gegen die Sowjetunion 1941/42* (Munich: Oldenbourg, 2007), 247–65. For reproductions of key campaign documents, see *War of Extermination: The German Military in World War II, 1941–1944*, ed. Hannes Heer and Klaus Naumann (New York: Berghahn Books, 2000).

9. OKH (Brauchitsch) regarding deployment of Sipo/SD units in conjunction with the Wehrmacht, April 28, 1941, BA-MA, RH 22/155.

10. See Jeffrey Herf, *The Jewish Enemy: Nazi Propaganda during World War II and the Holocaust* (Cambridge, MA: Belknap Press of Harvard University Press, 2006), 92ff.

"to be finished off ruthlessly in battle or while attempting to escape," whereas other attacks were to be "crushed by the troops on the spot using the utmost means, until the attacker is annihilated." Due to the suffering inflicted by Bolshevism on the German people in 1918, criminal acts committed by German soldiers against the civilian population would no longer be "automatically" prosecuted.[11]

If Wehrmacht generals had moral qualms about excessive violence during the Polish campaign, their tolerance for atrocities committed by their own troops in the war against the Soviet Union was much higher, even before it began. An order dated June 6 authorized frontline troops to execute, contrary to international laws, any Red Army soldiers identified as political commissars, who were collectively deemed the "originators of barbaric Asian fighting methods." The Wehrmacht High Command's "Guidelines for the Behavior of Troops in Russia," dated May 19 and issued to all soldiers before the attack, exceeded in sharpness even Hitler's proclamation against the "Jewish-Bolshevist intelligentsia": this battle demanded "ruthless and energetic action against Bolshevik agitators, saboteurs, and Jews, and the total elimination of all active or passive resistance."[12] In conjunction with the ideologically driven perception of "the enemy," the initiative field commanders of both the Wehrmacht and the Sipo/SD were expected to take in executing these orders led to the rapid escalation of violence against civilians, first and foremost against Jews, from the first days of Operation Barbarossa.[13]

According to the agreement finalized in late April between the German military and police leadership, Einsatzgruppen units would be operating in the rear army areas, "responsible for executive measures against the civilian population." They would report to the three new Higher SS and Police Leaders appointed by Himmler (HSSPF Russland-Nord, -Mitte, and -Süd) and were to keep army commanders informed, without being subordinated to them. Unlike in Poland, executive power was now divided; Wehrmacht leaders felt relief at not being responsible for the activities of Heydrich's units. Eduard Wagner, promoted to the rank of major general and the new quartermaster general who had been Heydrich's partner in brokering the agreement, embraced the "fundamental principle" that "the implementation of the Führer's political requirements

---

11. See Felix Römer, "The Wehrmacht in the War of Ideologies: The Army and Hitler's Criminal Orders on the Eastern Front," in *Nazi Policy on the Eastern Front, 1941: Total War, Genocide, and Radicalization*, ed. Alex J. Kay, Jeff Rutherford, and David Stahel (Rochester, NY: University of Rochester Press, 2012), 73–100.

12. Megargee, *War of Annihilation*, 37–38.

13. See Browning, *Origins*, 245–67.

is not a concern for the army";[14] as "the army cannot be burdened with every task," he was pleased by the establishment of a "cooperation with the Reichsführer-SS in police [. . .] matters."[15] At the same time, Wehrmacht and police leaders smoothed over issues related to the past: on April 18, SS-Obergruppenführer Karl Wolff, chief of Himmler's personal staff, met with a Wehrmacht colonel for a discussion of "the events in Poland 1939." On May 2, Wolff reported on the resolution of "the continuing conflicts over the SS activities in Poland." Finally, on July 31, 1941, Himmler felt confident that the chapter on the Polish campaign had been closed.[16]

The initial directives Himmler and Heydrich gave to their men about how to understand and implement their "special tasks" were remarkably nondescript compared to the orders Hitler and military commanders gave to Wehrmacht troops in the run-up to Operation Barbarossa. Issued in writing in early July 1941 after he had met with unit leaders before their deployment, Heydrich's orders to his Einsatzgruppen reflected the overall operational framework with its vague yet expandable focus on eliminating "Jewish Bolshevism": communist functionaries, as well as "Jews in party and state positions," were to be shot. Having received the first reports from field units on executions, Heydrich consciously extended the spiral of violence by allowing the shooting of "other radical elements (saboteurs, propagandists, snipers, assassins, agitators, etc.)."[17] The emotionally charged phantom of "Jewish Bolshevism" massively enlarged the 1939 "intelligentsia" scarecrow and created a command climate that bred violence against civilians. Nevertheless, the transformation of this fixation into a reality that would affect millions of people living beyond the German-Soviet border depended, as during the Polish campaign, to a large degree on the situation on the ground and decisions made by local German officials.[18]

Following in the Wehrmacht's footsteps, the Einsatzgruppen not only came across people who somehow met the description of their broadly defined target groups but also encountered groups that shared the German obsession with "Jewish Bolshevism." In the Baltic states and eastern Poland, under Soviet rule since 1939–1940, locals often welcomed Germans as liberators from Stalin's

---

14. File note 16th Army/Qu. 2, May 19, 1941, BA-MA, RH 20-16/1012.

15. Discussion points for the meeting with heads of the general staff on June 4–5, 1941, BA-MA, RH 2/129.

16. Halder, *Kriegstagebuch*, 2:372, 390, 135.

17. CdS to the HSSPF in the East, July 2, 1941, USHMMA RG 14.016M (BAB, R 58/241), fiche 7:314–19.

18. See Jürgen Matthäus, "Controlled Escalation: Himmler's Men in the Summer of 1941 and the Holocaust in the Occupied Soviet Territories," *HGS* 21, no. 2 (2007): 218–42.

yoke. Numerous massacres of local prisoners committed by the NKVD, the Soviet secret service, in the last minutes before the Red Army's retreat fueled public outrage in these regions and fed the German propaganda machine.[19] The gruesome NKVD crimes in Lwów [German: Lemberg] and other cities to some extent appeared as a variation of the "Slavic baseness" theme first virulent among Germans in 1939 in Bromberg and provided a similar subterfuge for violence, this time from groups of locals—mostly Lithuanians, Latvians, Ukrainians, and Poles—in the form of pogroms against Jews.[20] For the Germans, these pogroms served as a spur to action and legitimated the projection of every real or imagined danger onto the proclaimed enemy, the Jews and the Bolsheviks. Eager to ratchet up violence, Heydrich immediately instructed the Einsatzgruppen not to hinder the "self-cleansing measures by anti-communist and anti-Jewish circles in the newly occupied territories."[21] If there was need for another pretext to further escalate the war against the civilian population, Stalin's proclamation of July 3 calling for partisan warfare behind German lines provided one. On July 16, Hitler demanded, in the presence of top Nazi leaders, that "the vast area must be pacified as quickly as possible; this will happen best by shooting anyone who even looks sideways at us." A day later he signed a decree that considerably expanded Himmler's latitude in the occupied territories.[22]

Compared to the Polish campaign, the German push toward "pacification" in the Soviet Union was framed in a more radical ideological context and also involved more men. Together with the Wehrmacht's three million soldiers, a greater number of SS and police forces—Einsatzgruppen, Order Police, and Waffen-SS units—came to be deployed. Among those additional troops was the "Kommandostab Reichsführer-SS," a special task force comprising roughly ten thousand elite Waffen-SS men that Himmler started using in late July 1941 for the purpose of "pacifying" parts of Ukraine and Belorussia. With some officers adopting for the first time a tactic they called "de-Jewification" (*Entjudung*), the Kommandostab added significantly to crossing the threshold from persecution

---

19. See Bogdan Musial, *"Konterrevolutionäre Elemente sind zu erschiessen." Die Brutalisierung des deutsch-sowjetischen Krieges im Sommer 1941* (Berlin: Propyläen, 2000).

20. For examples, see Andrej Angrick and Peter Klein, eds., *The "Final Solution" in Riga: Exploitation and Annihilation, 1941–1944* (New York: Berghahn Books, 2009), 64ff.; Jan T. Gross, *Neighbors: The Destruction of the Jewish Community in Jedwabne, Poland* (Princeton, NJ: Princeton University Press, 2001); Alexander B. Rossino, "Polish 'Neighbors' and German Invaders: Contextualizing Anti-Jewish Violence in the Białystok District during the Opening Weeks of Operation Barbarossa," *Polin* 16 (2003): 431–52.

21. Browning, *Origins*, 272.

22. Ibid., 266–67.

to annihilation.[23] Within a month, the mass murder of Jews, including women and children, had become a feature of daily life.

In addition to the almost frictionless cooperation between the Wehrmacht and the police during Operation Barbarossa, a marked difference between 1939 and 1941 involved the evolution of the radicalization process. In the Polish case, the Einsatzgruppen had escalated the violence when the Wehrmacht was phasing it out, whereas in the Soviet Union, atrocities against civilians and POWs accompanied the German attack from the start and characterized German rule until the Wehrmacht withdrew. Simultaneously, Heydrich's executive portfolio expanded far beyond keeping an eye on the advance of the Einsatzgruppen. In mid-July, he started organizing selections by his Sipo/SD units of Soviet POWs in Wehrmacht camps to pick out communists and "all Jews," adding to the staggering death toll of two million captured Red Army soldiers in the first year of the war in the east.[24] Furthermore, Heydrich assumed a key function in the history of the Holocaust when, on July 31, 1941, Göring empowered him to make "all necessary preparations [. . .] for a complete solution to the Jewish question in the German sphere of influence in Europe."[25] The German-occupied parts of the Soviet Union were the first areas in Europe in which such a "solution" was taking shape by way of physical annihilation.

From the east, the deadly dynamic started to engulf other regions; beginning in late 1941, different Nazi agencies interacted on many levels to organize the "Final Solution." More than just orders and obedience determined the path of Nazi genocide. As Christopher Browning has put it, "Hitler's words and Himmler's and Heydrich's actions at the center set in motion waves of political signals that radiated outward. Like expanding concentric circles, they encompassed more and more people who, reading these signals, became aware that something new was expected of them."[26] The activism of field officers eager to outdo one another in their degree of radicalism fueled the anti-Bolshevist crusade and racial war; nothing conveyed this message more strongly than execution figures. British intelligence interceptors at Bletchley Park who had

---

23. See Martin Cüppers, *Wegbereiter der Shoah: Die Waffen-SS, der Kommandostab Reichsführer-SS und die Judenvernichtung 1939–1945* (Darmstadt: WBG, 2005); Browning, *Origins*, 279–84; Matthäus, "Controlled Escalation," 225.

24. See Christian Streit, *Keine Kameraden: Die Wehrmacht und die sowjetischen Kriegsgefangenen 1941–1945* (Stuttgart: DVA, 1978). This definitive study on the fate of Soviet POWs in Wehrmacht custody is still not translated into English.

25. See Peter Longerich, *Holocaust: The Nazi Persecution and Murder of the Jews* (Oxford: Oxford University Press, 2010), 259–77.

26. Browning, *Origins*, 317.

managed to decipher German radio transmissions from behind the eastern front concluded with regard to the HSSPFs deployed in the occupied Soviet Union that "the leaders of the three sectors stand somewhat in competition with each other as to their 'scores.'"[27] The murder of "gypsies," hospital patients, "racially inferior subjects with Asian characteristics," and other "unwanted" people followed the logic of Nazi policies already visible in Poland in 1939 but was not a predetermined development. Contingencies mattered as much as personal decisions made by the perpetrators.

Having opened the doors to genocide beyond the German-Soviet border, top Nazi leaders only had to praise and encourage those under their command to show they were pleased with further activities of this type. When, about a week after the beginning of Operation Barbarossa, Himmler and Heydrich met with Sipo/SD officers who had just completed a "cleansing operation" in the German-Lithuanian border region that had claimed the lives of several hundred civilians, primarily Jewish men, they "completely approved."[28] And the Reichsführer-SS sent a clear message during his visit to the Ukrainian city of Mykolaiv (German: Nikolajew) on October 4 when he promoted Otto Ohlendorf, leader of Einsatzgruppe D, which was leaving a bloody trail in its wake in southern Ukraine, in front of his men.[29] The news that Hitler was personally receiving reports "about the work of the Einsatzgruppen in the east" must have had a similar effect.[30] Without many words or written directives, Himmler's men in the field understood that the mass murder they committed had approval at the highest level. There seemed little need for conferences of Einsatzgruppen leaders in Berlin, which had frequently taken place in 1939. Reports from the periphery to the center sufficed in conjunction with occasional inspections from the SS leadership to make sure radical "pacification" remained at the core of a German occupation policy that was to devastate vast regions, destroy the lives of millions in the east, and foster the evolution of the "Final Solution" on a Europe-wide scale.

---

27. Summary of German police decodes, August 21, 1941, British National Archives Kew, HW 16/6. Cf. Richard Breitman, *Official Secrets: What the Nazis Planned, What the British and Americans Knew* (New York: Hill and Wang, 1998), 91ff.; Nicholas Terry, "Conflicting Signals: British Intelligence on the 'Final Solution' through Radio Intercepts and Other Sources, 1941–1942," *YVS* 32 (2004): 351–96. See also Klaus-Michael Mallmann, "Der qualitative Sprung im Vernichtungsprozess. Das Massaker von Kamenez-Podolsk Ende August 1941," *Jahrbuch für Antisemitismus* 10 (2001): 239–64.

28. See Browning, *Origins*, 253–56.

29. Andrej Angrick, *Besatzungspolitik und Massenmord. Die Einsatzgruppe D in der südlichen Sowjetunion 1941–1943* (Hamburg: Hamburger Edition, 2003), 253; BAB, BDC-SSO file Otto Ohlendorf.

30. Browning, *Origins*, 312.

LIST OF DOCUMENTS

Directives and Initial Actions

Document 1: Agreement between the Wehrmacht and Sipo/SD regarding "Guidelines for the Foreign Deployment of the Security Police and the SD," undated (August 1939), USHMMA RG 14.016M (BAB, R 58/241), fiche 4:169–75 (translated from German).

Document 2: Interrogation of Lothar Beutel, former commander of Einsatzgruppe IV, in West Berlin, July 20, 1965, BAL, B 162/Vorl. Dok. Slg. Leitzordner Einsatzgruppen in Polen II (translated from German).

Document 3: Diary notes by SS-Hauptsturmführer Erich Ehlers, Einsatzgruppe II, for August 19 to September 1, 1939, CAW (translated from German).

Document 4: Notice by the Chief of Civil Administration of the 8th Army, September 6, 1939, APŁ, 175/10 b (translated from German).

Document 5: Diary notes by SS-Hauptsturmführer Erich Ehlers, Einsatzgruppe II, for September 1 to 5, 1939, CAW (translated from German).

Document 6: Testimony by Roman Tynczyk, 1939, inhabitant of Ślesin, June 1, 1970, BAL, B 162/Vorl. AR-Z 124/78, vol. 3:407–8 (translated from German).

Document 7: Testimony by Władysława Winiecka, 1939, inhabitant of Danzig, September 29, 1973, BAL, B 162/Vorl. AR-Z 51/75, vol. 1:112–13 (translated from German).

Document 8: Testimony by Zofia Semik on German violence in Limanowa, May 13, 1977, BAL, B 162/Vorl. AR-Z 304/77-K-:14–15 (translated from German).

Document 9: Photographs of Jews arrested by Sipo/SD in the area of Ustronie/Opatów, undated (September 1939), Bundesarchiv Bildarchiv Bild 101I-380-0069-34, 39.

Document 10: Notes for a report by Army Group South (Oberquartiermeister IV) for Oberbefehlshaber von Brauchitsch, September 17, 1939, BAL, Dok. Slg. USA 15:26a (translated from German).

Document 11: Photograph of Polish clergy and prominent citizens arrested by members of Einsatzgruppe IV, police, and German soldiers on the Bydgoszcz market square, undated (September 9–11, 1939), USHMMPA WS# 50837.

Document 12: Report by Helmuth Bischoff, leader of Einsatzkommando 1/IV, on his deployment in Bydgoszcz, September 7 and 8, 1939, undated (late 1939), IPNW, NTN 196/180 (translated from German).

Document 13: Photograph of a group of SS, police, and ethnic German auxiliaries preparing to conduct a search during the "pacification" of Bydgoszcz, undated (September–November 1939), USHMMPA WS# 15872.

Document 14: War diary of the Commander of the 580th Rear Army Area regarding the situation in Bydgoszcz on the morning of September 9, 1939, BA-MA, RH 23/167 (translated from German).

Document 15: War diary of the Commander of the 580th Rear Army Area regarding the situation in Bydgoszcz on September 10, 1939, BA-MA, RH 23/167 (translated from German).

Document 16: Daily report by the Chief of the Sipo/SD special office "Operation Tannenberg," September 9, 1939, USHMMA, RG 15.007M (BAB, R 58/7001), reel 2, file 1:23–27 (translated from German).

Document 17: Photographs of Polish hostages arrested and executed by Einsatzgruppe IV and German Order Police during the "pacification" of Bydgoszcz, September 10, 1939, USHMMPA WS# 15753, 15752.

Document 18: Interrogation of Bruno G., former member of Einsatzkommando 2/IV, regarding "reprisals" in Bydgoszcz, December 1, 1964, BAL, B 162/Vorl. AR-Z 13/63, vol. 1:128–29 (translated from German).

Document 19: Interrogation of Erich M., former member of Einsatzkommando 1/IV, regarding "reprisals" in Bydgoszcz, November 30, 1964, BAL, B 162/Vorl. AR-Z 13/63, vol. 1:117ff. (translated from German).

Document 20: Daily report by the Chief of the Sipo/SD special office "Operation Tannenberg," September 11, 1939, USHMMA RG 15.007M (BAB, R 58/7001), reel 2, file 1:46–49 (translated from German).

Document 21: Photographs of Polish prisoners executed by SS and Volksdeutscher Selbstschutz in the Tuchola Forest near Bydgoszcz, October 27, 1939, USHMMPA WS# 50093, 50097, 50840.

Document 22: Interrogation of Ewald S., former member of the Selbstschutz in Bydgoszcz, August 6, 1962, BAL, B 162/3268:478–82 (translated from German).

Document 23: Letter by Lily Jungblut, near Inowrocław, to Hermann Göring, December 6, 1939, USHMMA RG 14.021M (BAB, R 43 II/1411 a), fiche 4 (translated from German).

Document 24: Photograph of Polish men and one woman lined up for execution in the forest near Szubin, October 21, 1939, USHMMPA WS# 50096.

Expanding the Scope of Violence

Document 25: Interrogation of Max-Franz Janke, former member of Einsatzkommando 16 stationed in Gdynia, July 10, 1969, BAL, B 162/16658 (translated from German).

Document 26: Testimony by Josef Lemke about German atrocities in Wejherowo in late 1939, February 10, 1971, BAL, B 162/Vorl. AR-Z 368/67, Sonderheft vol. 2:168–69 (translated from German).

Document 27: Testimony by Franciszek Komar about German atrocities in Toruń in November 1939, June 26, 1968, BAL, B 162/3242:1107, 1109, 1111 (translated from German).

Document 28: Photograph of Poles executed by Gestapo and Selbstschutz members in the Barbarka Forest near Toruń, October 1939, USHMMPA WS# 50849.

Document 29: Testimony by Richard Otto Dey regarding German atrocities in Toruń, July 24, 1962, BAL, B 162/3240:662–63 (translated from German).

Document 30: Photograph of German police headquarters on Szucha Avenue, Warsaw, undated (November 1939), Bundesarchiv Bildarchiv 121-0286.

Document 31: Activity report by Einsatzgruppe IV in Warsaw, October 10, 1939, APŁ, 175/41 (translated from German).

Document 32: Photographs of women about to be shot by German police in the Palmiry Forest near Warsaw, undated (October–December 1939), USHMMPA WS# 50646, 50642, 50069.

Document 33: Testimony by Marianna Kazmierczak regarding German atrocities in the autumn of 1939 in Zakrzewo, October 12, 1971, BAL, B 162/Vorl. AR-Z 26/72, vol. 2:222–23 (translated from German).

Document 34: Testimony by Paula von Karlowska regarding violence in Gostyń, January 14, 1965, BAL, B 162/Vorl. AR-Z 268/67:41–42 (translated from German).

Document 35: Situation report by Einsatzkommando 1 subunit stationed in Środa Wielkopolska to Einsatzkommando 1/VI, September 22, 1939, APP 305/2 (translated from German).

Document 36: Situation report by Einsatzkommando 16 subunit stationed in Bydgoszcz, September 26, 1939, IPNW, NTN 196/179 (translated from German).

Document 37: Testimony by Stanisław Szałapieta regarding a summary trial by Einsatzkommando 2/VI held on October 20, 1939, in Środa Wielkopolska, November 14, 1972, BAL, B 162/Vorl. AR-Z 380/77, vols. 1–2:150–51 (translated from German).

Document 38: Photographs of men about to be shot by German police in Leszno, October 20, 1939, USHMMPA WS# 50273, 50290.

Document 39: Testimony by Roman Klamrowski on the arrest of inhabitants of Kostrzyn, September 17, 1973, BAL, B 162/Vorl. AR-Z 345/67, vol. 8:1186–87 (translated from German).

Document 40: Interrogation of Willy Panse regarding court proceedings in Kórnik, May 19, 1967, BAL, B 162/Vorl. AR 2654/65:84–85 (translated from German).

Document 41: Report by the district head of Lubliniec to the Chief of Civil Administration in Katowice, October 2, 1939, on the relationship with the Sipo/SD, APK, 119/1637 (translated from German).

Persecuting Jews

Document 42: Account by Berta Lichtig on the burning of the synagogue in Mielec, undated (ca. 1943), USHMMA RG 15.084M (ŻIH 301/1029) (translated from Polish).

Document 43: Photograph of an SS officer and civilian posing in front of the ruins of the Great Synagogue in Będzin destroyed by Einsatzgruppe Woyrsch on September 10, 1939, undated (1939–1940), USHMMPA WS# 18542.

Document 44: Testimony by Jakub Gąsecki on German anti-Jewish atrocities in Dynów, January 21, 1969, BAL, B 162/Vorl. AR-Z 302/67, 3:498–99 (translated from German).

Document 45: Testimony by Sacher Grünbaum on German anti-Jewish atrocities in Dynów in September 1939, June 11, 1945, USHMMA RG 15.084M (ŻIH 301/4534) (translated from Polish).

Document 46: Account of anti-Jewish violence in Przemyśl, cited from Bruno B. Shatyn, *A Private War: Surviving in Poland on False Papers, 1941–1945* (Detroit, MI: Wayne State University Press 1985), 121–22.

Document 47: Photo album pages by SS-Oberscharführer Hermann Baltruschat of Einsatzgruppe V regarding "Jewish actions" in Raciąż and Płońsk, undated (late September 1939), IPN (captions translated from German).

Document 48: Excerpts from the memorial book for Raciąż, *Gal'ed li-ḳehilat Ratsyonz'*, ed. Efrayim Tsoref (Tel Aviv: ha-Irgun shel 'ole Ratsyonz', 1964) (translated from Yiddish).

Document 49: Interrogation of Kurt G., former member of Einsatzkommando 1/IV, regarding anti-Jewish violence in Białystok, November 13, 1965, BAL, B 162/Vorl. AR-Z 13/63, vol. 4:767 (translated from German).

Document 50: Excerpt from the memorial book for Raciąż, *Gal'ed li-ḳehilat Ratsyonz'*, ed. Efrayim Tsoref (Tel Aviv: ha-Irgun shel 'ole Ratsyonz', 1964) (translated from Yiddish).

Document 51: Photograph of the public humiliation of Jewish civilians conducted by members of the German Order Police in Sosnowiec (Upper Silesia), undated (1939–1940), USHMMPA WS# 74401.

Document 52: Express letter by Reinhard Heydrich to the Einsatzgruppen on the "Jewish Question in the Occupied Territory," September 21, 1939, USHMMA RG 14.016M (BAB, R 58/954), fiche 4:181–85 (translated from German).

Document 53: Testimony by Leon (Leib) Salpeter, Kraków, on the formation of the Jewish council, undated (ca. 1945), USHMMA RG 15.084M (ŻIH 301/832) (translated from Polish).

Document 54: File note by RSHA "resettlement" expert SS-Hauptsturmführer Adolf Eichmann, October 6, 1939, YVA 0-53/93 (translated from German).

Document 55: Testimony by Helena Aussenberg about German atrocities in Radomyśl Wielki, October 15, 1945, USHMMA RG 15.084M (ŻIH 301/1145) (translated from Polish).

Document 56: Daily report by the Chief of the Sipo/SD, September 20, 1939, USHMMA RG 14.016M (BAB, R 58/7002), reel 2, file 2:5–10 (translated from German).

Document 57: Anonymous report on the murder of the Jewish journalist Lipe Kestin in October 1939 in Łuków, April 21, 1941, USHMMA RG 15.079M (ŻIH Ring. I/1019) (translated from Yiddish).

Document 58: Testimony by Moses Zwas about early anti-Jewish measures in Cisna, May 31, 1945, USHMMA RG 15.084M (ŻIH 301/280) (translated from Polish).

Document 59: Testimony by Pola Ajzensztajn regarding anti-Jewish violence in Krasnystaw and Rejowiec, September 30, 1946, USHMMA RG 15.084M (ŻIH 301/1885) (translated from Polish).

Document 60: Express letter by Einsatzgruppe z.b.V., Katowice, to the Sipo Berlin, November 8, 1939, USHMMA RG 11.001M (RGVA 500-1-431), reel 6 (translated from German).

Document 61: Decree by the Higher SS and Police Leader, Posen, regarding the expulsion of Jews and Poles from the Warthegau, November 12, 1939, USHMMA RG 14.041M (BAB, R 70 Polen/198), fiche 1:12–16 (translated from German).

Establishing Long-Term Rule

Document 62: Report by the district head of Pszczyna to the Chief of Civil Administration, Katowice, regarding cooperation with the Security Police, September 19, 1939, APK, 119/1637 (translated from German).

Document 63: Express letter by Reinhard Heydrich to the Einsatzgruppen, September 30, 1939, APŁ 175/10 b (translated from German).

Document 64: Report by the Chief of Civil Administration, Poznań, September 25, 1939, APP 289/50 (translated from German).

Document 65: "Guidelines for the Administrative Reconstruction in the Districts and Cities of the Province of Posen," September 29, 1939, BAL, B 162/Vorl. Dok. Slg. Polen 365 (translated from German).

Document 66: Unsigned account of Einsatzgruppen court proceedings in Leszno, October 24, 1939, IZ doc. II/857 (translated from German).

Document 67: Decree by Himmler regarding police organization in the General-gouvernement, November 1, 1939, USHMMA RG 14.016M (BAB, R 58/241), fiche 5:211–12 (translated from German).

Document 68: Protocol of a meeting of RSHA department heads and Einsatzgruppen commanders, September 27, 1939, USHMMA RG 14.016M (BAB, R 58/825), fiche 1:14 (translated from German).

Document 69: Directive by the Army High Commander regarding activities and tasks of the Einsatzgruppen, September 21, 1939, BA-MA, RH 20-14/178 (translated from German).

Document 70: Photograph of an execution of Polish civilians conducted by a police firing squad in Sosnowiec, undated (ca. September 1939), USHMMPA WS# 72103.

Document 71: Report by the district head in Kościan to the Chief of Civil Administration, October 31, 1939, BAL, B 162/Vorl. Dok. Slg. Polen 365 r (translated from German).

Document 72: Daily report by Einsatzgruppe VI to the Chief of Civil Administration, October 3, 1939, APP 298/54 (translated from German).

Document 73: Situation report by Einsatzkommando Bromberg to IdS Danzig–West Prussia, October 14, 1939, IPNW, NTN 196/179 (translated from German).

Document 74: Daily reports by the Chief of the Sipo/SD, September 24 and 26, 1939, USHMMA RG 15.007M (BAB, R 58/7002), reel 2, file 2:30–36, 41–45 (translated from German).

Document 75: Instructions from Einsatzkommando 4/I to the district head of Pszczyna, September 27, 1939, APK 119/1637 (translated from German).

Document 76: Report by BdO Posen to Himmler, October 25, 1939, APP 298/54 (translated from German).

Document 77: Testimony by Josef Lemke on conditions in Wejherowo in late 1939, June 19, 1959, BAL, B 162/3385:45ff. (translated from German).

Document 78: Interrogation of Fritz Liebl, member of Einsatzkommando 3/I, by SS and police investigators, December 1939, NARA SSO Dr. Alfred Hasselberg (translated from German).

Document 79: Directive by the Commander of the 14th Army, Generaloberst Wilhelm List, to subordinate commanders, October 1, 1939, BA-MA, RH 53-23/12 (translated from German).

Document 80: Report by General Petzel, Chief Defense Region (Wehrkreiskommando) XXI, to the Commander of the Reserve Army (Befehlshaber des Ersatzheeres), November 23, 1939, BA-MA, N 104/3 (translated from German).

Document 81: Situation report by Einsatzkommando Bromberg to the RSHA, October 20, 1939, IPNW, NTN 196/179 (translated from German).

Document 82: Situation report by Einsatzkommando Bromberg, October 24, 1939, IPNW, NTN 196/179 (translated from German).

Document 83: Proposal by Einsatzkommando Bromberg for propaganda aimed at Poles in Danzig–West Prussia, undated (late October 1939), IPNW, NTN 196/179 (translated from German).

Document 84: Situation report by Einsatzkommando Bromberg, November 1, 1939, IPNW, NTN 196/179 (translated from German).

Document 85: Situation report by Einsatzkommando Bromberg, November 10, 1939, USHMMA RG 14.041M (BAB, R 70 Polen/83), fiche 1:31–35 (translated from German).

Document 86: Situation report by Einsatzkommando Bromberg, November 14, 1939, IPNW, NTN 196/179 (translated from German).

Concordance of Place Names

(City names with the same spelling in German and Polish are not listed here.)

GERMAN	POLISH (OR OTHER LANGUAGE AS NOTED)
Allenstein	Olsztyn
Arys	Orzysz
Bendzin/Bendsburg	Będzin
Bialystok	Białystok
Bielitz	Bielsko-Biała
Blonie	Błonie
Breslau	Wrocław
Bromberg	Bydgoszcz
Brzozow	Brzozów
Chelm	Chełm
Danzig	Gdańsk
Dramburg	Drawsko Pomorskie
Dünhof	Dynów (Ukrainian: Dyniv)
Elbing	Elbląg
Gdingen/Gotenhafen	Gdynia
Gleiwitz	Gliwice
Gnesen	Gniezno

GERMAN	POLISH (OR OTHER LANGUAGE AS NOTED)
Görlitz	Gorlice
Gostyn	Gostyń
Grabau	Grabowek
Gross-Strehlen	Strzelin
Guhrau	Góra
Guttentag	Dobrodzień
Hohensalza	Inowrocław
Ilmenau	Limanowa
Jassel	Jasło
Kattowitz	Katowice
Königsberg	Kaliningrad (Russian)
Königshütte	Chorzów
Konskie	Końskie
Koschentin	Koszęcin
Kosten	Kościan
Kostschin	Kostrzyn
Krakau	Kraków
Krone	Koronowo
Krossen/Wislok	Krosno (Ukrainian: Korosno)
Kulmhof	Chełmno
Kurnicker Burgstadt	Kórnik
Küstrin	Kostrzyn nad Odrą
Laurahütte	Huta Laura
Lemberg	Lwów (Ukrainian: Lviv)
Leobshütz	Głubczyce
Liegnitz	Legnica
Lissa	Leszno
Litzmannstadt/Lodsch	Łódź
Lublinitz/Loben	Lubliniec
Luckau	Łuków
Lyck	Ełk
Marienwerder	Kwidzyn
Myslowitz	Mysłowice
Neu Sandez	Nowy Sącz (Hungarian: Újszandec)
Neustadt	Prudnik
Neustadt	Wejherowo
Opatow	Opatów

GERMAN	POLISH (OR OTHER LANGUAGE AS NOTED)
Oppeln	Opole
Ostenburg	Pułtusk
Petrikau	Piotrków Trybunalski
Piaschnitz	Piaśnica
Pless	Pszczyna
Plöhnen	Płońsk
Pommerellen	Pomerelia
Posen	Poznań
Praschnitz	Przasnysz
Przemysl	Przemyśl (Ukrainian: Peremyshl)
Pultusk/Ostenburg	Pułtusk
Racionz	Raciąż
Radomysl Wielki	Radomyśl Wielki
Reichshof	Rzeszów
Santomischel	Zaniemyśl
Schlüsselsee	Ślesin
Schmiegel	Śmigiel
Schoppinitz	Szopienice
Schroda	Środa Wielkopolska
Schwedenhöhe	Szwederowo
Schwersenz	Swarzędz
Schwientochlowitz	Świętochłowice
Siemianowitz	Siemianowice Śląskie
Sockelstein	Sokolniki
Sompolno	Sępolno
Sosnowitz	Sosnowiec
Storchnest	Osieczna
Tarnau/Tarnow	Tarnów
Teschen	Cieszyn
Thorn	Toruń
Trischen	Tryszczyn
Tschenstochau	Częstochowa
Tuchel	Tuchola
Wreschen	Września
Zabno	Żabno
Zichenau	Ciechanów
Znin	Żnin

SS and Army Officer Ranks

SS	GERMAN ARMY	U.S. ARMY
Reichsführer-SS (RFSS)	Generalfeldmarschall	General of the army
Oberst-Gruppenführer	Generaloberst	General
Obergruppenführer	General	Lieutenant general
Gruppenführer	Generalleutnant	Major general
Brigadeführer	Generalmajor	Brigadier general
Oberführer	—	—
Standartenführer	Oberst	Colonel
Obersturmbannführer	Oberstleutnant	Lieutenant colonel
Sturmbannführer	Major	Major
Hauptsturmführer	Hauptmann	Captain
Obersturmführer	Oberleutnant	First lieutenant
Untersturmführer	Leutnant	Second lieutenant

Bibliography

Alberti, Michael. *Die Verfolgung und Vernichtung der Juden im Reichsgau Wartheland 1939–1945.* Wiesbaden: Harrassowitz, 2006.

Aly, Götz. *"Final Solution": Nazi Population Policy and the Murder of the European Jews.* London: Arnold, 1999.

Angelow, Jürgen. "Accomplices with Reservations: German Diplomats and the Preparation of the Polish Campaign of September 1939." *Australian Journal of Politics and History* 50, no. 3 (2004): 372–84.

Bednarek, Monika. *Kraków under Nazi Occupation: 1939–1945.* Kraków: Muzeum Historyczne Miasta Krakowa, 2011.

Bergen, Doris L. "Instrumentalization of 'Volksdeutschen' in German Propaganda in 1939. Replacing/Erasing Poles, Jews, and Other Victims." *German Studies Review* 31 (2008): 447-70.

Bethell, Nicholas. *The War Hitler Won: September 1939.* London: Penguin, 1972.

Böhler, Jochen. *Auftakt zum Vernichtungskrieg. Die Wehrmacht in Polen 1939.* Frankfurt am Main: Fischer Taschenbuch Verlag, 2006.

———, ed. *"Grösste Härte . . ." Verbrechen der Wehrmacht in Polen September/Oktober 1939.* Ausstellungskatalog. Warsaw: Friedrich-Ebert-Stiftung, Historisches Forschungszentrum, 2005.

———. "Intention oder Situation? Soldaten der Wehrmacht und die Anfänge des Vernichtungskrieges in Polen." In *Krieg und Verbrechen. Situation und Intention: Fallbeispiele,* ed. Timm C. Richter, 165–72. Munich: Martin Meidenbauer, 2006.

Böhler, Jochen, and Stephan Lehnstaedt, eds. *Gewalt und Alltag im besetzten Polen 1939–1945.* Osnabrück: Fibre, 2012.

Borodziej, Włodzimierz. *Terror und Politik. Die deutsche Polizei und die polnische Widerstandsbewegung im Generalgouvernement 1939–1944.* Mainz: Philipp von Zabern, 1999.

Breitman, Richard. *The Architect of Genocide: Himmler and the Final Solution.* New York: Alfred A. Knopf, 1991.

Broszat, Martin. *Nationalsozialistische Polenpolitik 1939–1945.* Stuttgart: Fischer Bücherei, 1961.

Browder, George C. *Hitler's Enforcers: The Gestapo and the SS Security Service in the Nazi Revolution.* New York: Oxford University Press, 1996.

Browning, Christopher R. *Ordinary Men: Reserve Police Battalion 101 and the Final Solution in Poland.* New York: HarperPerennial, 1998.

———. *The Path to Genocide: Essays on Launching the Final Solution.* New York: Cambridge University Press, 1992.

Browning, Christopher R., with contributions by Jürgen Matthäus. *The Origins of the Final Solution: The Evolution of Nazi Jewish Policy, September 1939–March 1942.* Lincoln and Jerusalem: University of Nebraska Press and Yad Vashem, 2004.

Cüppers, Martin. *Wegbereiter der Shoah. Die Waffen-SS, der Kommandostab Reichsführer-SS und die Judenvernichtung 1939–1945.* Darmstadt: WBG, 2005.

Davies, Norman. *God's Playground: A History of Poland*, Vol. 2: *1795 to the Present.* New York: Columbia University Press, 1982.

Engel, David. *In the Shadow of Auschwitz: The Polish Government-in-Exile and the Jews, 1939–1942.* Chapel Hill: University of North Carolina Press, 1987.

Epstein, Catherine. *Model Nazi: Arthur Greiser and the Occupation of Western Poland.* Oxford: Oxford University Press, 2010.

Evans, Richard J. *The Third Reich at War, 1939–1945.* London: Allen Lane, 2008.

Friedlander, Henry. *The Origins of Nazi Genocide: From Euthanasia to the Final Solution.* Chapel Hill: University of North Carolina Press, 1994.

Friedländer, Saul. *Nazi Germany and the Jews*, Vol. 1: *The Years of Persecution, 1933–1939.* New York: HarperCollins, 1997.

———. *Nazi Germany and the Jews*, Vol. 2: *The Years of Extermination, 1939–1945.* New York: HarperCollins, 2007.

Friedrich, Klaus-Peter, and Bill Templer. "Did the Nazi War of Extermination in Eastern Europe Start in September 1939?" *Yad Vashem Studies* 35, no. 1 (2007): 193–204.

Furber, David. "Near as Far in the Colonies: The Nazi Occupation of Poland." *International History Review* 26, no. 3 (2004): 541–79.

Garbarini, Alexandra, with Emil Kerenji, Jan Lambertz, and Avinoam Patt. *Jewish Responses to Persecution*, Vol. 2: *1938–1940.* Lanham, MD: AltaMira Press in association with the USHMM, 2011.

Gerwarth, Robert. *Hitler's Hangman: The Life of Heydrich.* New Haven, CT: Yale University Press, 2011.

Goldenberg, Myrna, and Amy Shapiro, eds. *Different Horrors, Same Hell: Gender and the Holocaust.* Seattle: University of Washington Press, 2013.

Groscurth, Helmuth. *Tagebücher eines Abwehroffiziers 1938–1940. Mit weiteren Dokumenten zur Militäropposition gegen Hitler*, ed. Helmut Krausnick and Harold C. Deutsch. Stuttgart: Deutsche Verlags-Anstalt, 1970.

Gross, Jan T., ed. *The Holocaust in Occupied Poland: New Findings and New Interpretations.* New York: Peter Lang, 2012.

———. *Polish Society under German Occupation: The Generalgouvernement, 1939–1944.* Princeton, NJ: Princeton University Press, 1979.

Hofmann, Tom. *Benjamin Ferencz, Nuremberg Prosecutor and Peace Advocate.* Jefferson, NC: McFarland & Company, 2014.

Jansen, Christian, and Arno Weckbecker. *Der "Volksdeutsche Selbstschutz" in Polen 1939/40.* Munich: Oldenbourg, 1992.

Jastrzębski, Włodzimierz. *Der Bydgoszczer Blutsonntag. Legende und Wirklichkeit.* Poznań: Westinstitut, 1990.

Kochanski, Halik. *The Eagle Unbowed: Poland and the Poles in the Second World War.* Cambridge, MA: Harvard University Press, 2012.

Krausnick, Helmut. *Die Truppe des Weltanschauungskrieges. Die Einsatzgruppen der Sicherheitspolizei und des SD 1938–1942.* Stuttgart: Deutsche Verlags-Anstalt, 1981.

Kühne, Thomas. *Belonging and Genocide: Hitler's Community, 1918–1945.* New Haven, CT: Yale University Press, 2010.

Lehnstaedt, Stephan. *Okkupation im Osten. Besatzeralltag in Warschau und Minsk 1939–1944.* Munich: R. Oldenbourg Verlag, 2010.

Lehnstaedt, Stephan, and Jochen Böhler, eds. *Die Berichte der Einsatzgruppen aus Polen 1939.* Vollständige ed. Berlin: Metropol, 2013.

Longerich, Peter. *Heinrich Himmler.* Oxford: Oxford University Press, 2012.

———. *Holocaust: The Nazi Persecution and Murder of the Jews.* Oxford: Oxford University Press, 2010.

Löw, Andrea, and Markus Roth. *Juden in Krakau unter deutscher Besatzung 1939–1945.* Göttingen: Wallstein, 2011.

Lukas, Richard C. *The Forgotten Holocaust: The Poles under German Occupation, 1939–1944.* 2nd rev. ed. New York: Hippocrene, 1997.

Madajczyk, Czesław. *Die Okkupationspolitik Nazideutschlands in Polen 1939–1945.* Berlin: Akademie Verlag, 1987.

———. "Die Verantwortung der Wehrmacht für die Verbrechen während des Krieges mit Polen." In *Kriegsverbrechen im 20. Jahrhundert,* ed. Wolfram Wette and Gerd R. Ueberschär, 113–22. Darmstadt: Primus, 2001.

Mallmann, Klaus-Michael, Jochen Böhler, and Jürgen Matthäus. *Einsatzgruppen in Polen. Darstellung und Dokumentation.* Darmstadt: WBG, 2008.

Mallmann, Klaus-Michael, and Bogdan Musial, eds. *Genesis des Genozids. Polen 1939–1941.* Darmstadt: WBG, 2004.

Mazower, Mark. *Hitler's Empire: Nazi Rule in Occupied Europe.* London: Allen Lane, 2008.

Megargee, Geoffrey P. *Inside Hitler's High Command.* Lawrence: University of Kansas Press, 2000.

Messerschmidt, Manfred. *Die Wehrmacht im NS-Staat. Zeit der Indoktrination.* Hamburg: R. V. Decker, 1969.

Młynarczyk, Jacek Andrzej, ed. *Polen unter deutscher und sowjetischer Besatzung 1939–1945.* Osnabrück: Fibre, 2009.

Pohl, Dieter. *Nationalsozialistische Judenverfolgung in Ostgalizien 1941–1944. Organisation und Durchführung eines staatlichen Massenverbrechens.* Munich: Oldenbourg, 1996.

Richter, Timm C. *Krieg und Verbrechen. Situation und Intention: Fallbeispiele.* Munich: Meidenbauer, 2006.

Röhr, Werner. "Terror und Politik: Über die Funktionen des Terrors für die faschistische Okkupationspolitik in Polen 1939–1945." *Zeitschrift für Geschichtswissenschaft* 43, no.1 (1995): 27–54.

Rossino, Alexander B. "Destructive Impulses: German Soldiers and the Conquest of Poland." *HGS* 7 (1997): 351–65.

———. *Hitler Strikes Poland: Blitzkrieg, Ideology, and Atrocity.* Lawrence: University Press of Kansas, 2003.

———. "Nazi Anti-Jewish Policy during the Polish Campaign: The Case of Einsatzgruppe von Woyrsch." *GSR* 24, no. 1 (February 2001): 35–53.

Rössler, Mechthild, and Sabine Schleiermacher, eds. *Der "Generalplan Ost." Hauptlinien der nationalsozialistischen Planungs- und Vernichtungspolitik.* Berlin: Akademie Verlag, 1993.

Rutherford, Philip T. *Prelude to the Final Solution: The Nazi Program for Deporting Ethnic Poles, 1939–1941.* Lawrence: University Press of Kansas, 2007.

Schenk, Dieter. *Hitlers Mann in Danzig. Gauleiter Forster und die NS-Verbrechen in Danzig-Westpreussen.* Bonn: J. H. W. Dietz, 2000.

Snyder, Timothy. *Bloodlands: Europe between Hitler and Stalin.* New York: Basic Books, 2010.

Szarota, Tomasz. "Poland and Poles in German Eyes during World War II." *Polish Western Affairs* 19 (1978): 229–54.

Ueberschär, Gerd R. "Der militärische Widerstand, die antijüdischen Massnahmen, 'Polenmorde' und NS-Kriegsverbrechen in den ersten Kriegsjahren (1939–1941)." In *NS-Verbrechen und der militärische Widerstand gegen Hitler,* ed. Gerd R. Ueberschär, 31–43. Darmstadt: Primus, 2000.

Wasserstein, Bernard. *On the Eve: The Jews of Europe before the Second World War.* New York: Simon & Schuster, 2012.

Weinberg, Gerhard. *A World at Arms: A Global History of World War II.* New York: Cambridge University Press, 1994.

Weiss, Aharon. "Jewish Leadership in Occupied Poland—Postures and Attitudes." *YVS* 12 (1977): 335–65.

Westermann, Edward B. "Friend and Helper: German Uniformed Police Operations in Poland and the General Government, 1939–1941." *Journal of Military History* 58 (1994): 643–61.

———. *Hitler's Police Battalions: Enforcing Racial War in the East.* Lawrence: University Press of Kansas, 2005.

Wildt, Michael. *An Uncompromising Generation: The Nazi Leadership of the Reich Security Main Office.* Madison: University of Wisconsin Press, 2009.

Wolf, Gerhard. *Ideologie und Herrschaftsrationalität. Nationalsozialistische Germanisierungspolitik in Polen.* Hamburg: Hamburger Edition, 2012.

Index

Page numbers followed by "n" indicate footnotes. Page numbers in *italic* indicate illustrations and photographs. Polish place names are used throughout; for non-Polish alternatives for these names, see p. 169.

About the Authors

Jochen Böhler is a research fellow at the Imre Kertész Kolleg at Jena University, Germany. His most recent publications are (ed. with Jacek Andrzej Młynarczyk) *Der Judenmord in den eingegliederten polnischen Gebieten 1939–1945* (Osnabrück: Fibre, 2010); (ed. with Stephan Lehnstaedt) *Gewalt und Alltag im besetzten Polen, 1939–1945* (Osnabrück: Fibre, 2012).

Klaus-Michael Mallmann is director emeritus of the Forschungsstelle Ludwigsburg at the Universität Stuttgart, Germany. From his many publications: (ed. with Andrej Angrick, Jürgen Matthäus, and Martin Cüppers) *Deutsche Besatzungsherrschaft in der UdSSR 1941-45* (Darmstadt: Wissenschaftliche Buchgesellschaft, 2013); (with Martin Cüppers) *Nazi Palestine: The Plans for the Extermination of the Jews in Palestine* (New York: Enigma Books, 2010).

Jürgen Matthäus, historian, director of the Applied Research Division at the Center for Advanced Holocaust Studies of the United States Holocaust Memorial Museum. His most recent publications are (ed. with Martin Cüppers and Andrej Angrick) *Naziverbrechen. Täter, Taten, Bewältigungsversuche* (Darmstadt: Wissenschaftliche Buchgesellschaft, 2013); (with Emil Kerenji, Jan Lambertz, and Leah Wolfson) *Jewish Responses to Persecution, 1941-1942* (Lanham, MD: AltaMira Press in association with the USHMM, 2013).